W9-ADC-297

Marrano as Metaphor

Marrano as Metaphor
The Jewish Presence in French Writing

Elaine Marks

Columbia University Press
New York

Parts of this book have been published elsewhere: chapter 3 appeared in a slightly altered form and under a slightly different title as "'Sapho 1900': Imaginary Renée Viviens and the Rear of the Belle Époque" in The Politics of Tradition: Placing Women in French Literature, *edited by Joan DeJean and Nancy K. Miller,* Yale French Studies *75. 1988: 175–189, reprinted in* Displacements: Women, Tradition, Literatures in French, *edited by Joan De Jean and Nancy K. Miller, Johns Hopkins University Press, 1991: 211–227; a few passages in chapter 5 will appear in my essay "The Poetical and the Political: The 'Feminist' Inquiry in French Studies" in a volume edited by Domna Stanton and Abby Stewart to be published by the University of Michigan Press in 1995; chapter 6 has been published more or less in toto in the* Journal of Narrative Theory, *edited by Susan Stanford Friedman, vol. 20, no. 2, spring 1990: 210–220; chapter 8, with some modification, has appeared in* Auschwitz and After: Race, Culture, and "the Jewish Question" in France, *edited by Lawrence D. Kritzman and published by Routledge, 1994:35–46; and chapter 10, also with modification, is scheduled to appear in* Wrestling with the Angel: Jewish Identity in the Academy, *edited by Shelley Fisher Fishkin and Jeffrey Rubin-Dorsky, published by the University of Wisconsin Press.*

Columbia University Press
New York   Chichester, West Sussex
Copyright © 1996 Columbia University Press

Library of Congress Cataloging-in-Publication Data
Marks, Elaine.
    Marrano as metaphor : the Jewish presence in French writing / Elaine Marks.
        p.   cm.
    Includes bibliographical references and index.
    ISBN 0-231-10308-5
    1. Jews in literature. 2. Antisemitism in literature. 3. French literature—History and criticism. 4. French literature—Jewish authors—History and criticism. 5. Holocaust, Jewish (1939–1945)—France—Influence.   I. Title.
PQ145.7.J4M37   1996
840.9'35203924—dc20   95-9627
                                                             CIP

Casebound editions of Columbia University Press books are printed on permanent and durable acid-free paper.

Printed in the United States of America
c 10 9 8 7 6 5 4 3 2 1
p 10 9 8 7 6 5 4 3 2 1

The foreigner is within us. And when we flee from or struggle against the foreigner, we are fighting our unconscious—that "improper" facet of our impossible "own and proper." Delicately, analytically, Freud does not speak of foreigners: he teaches us how to detect foreignness in ourselves. That is perhaps the only way not to hound it outside of us. After Stoic cosmopolitanism, after religious universalist integration, Freud brings us the courage to call ourselves disintegrated in order not to integrate foreigners and even less to hunt them down, but rather to welcome them to that uncanny strangeness, which is as much theirs as it is ours. . . . To discover our disturbing otherness, for that indeed is what bursts in to confront that "demon," that threat, that apprehension generated by the projective apparition of the other at the heart of what we persist in maintaining as a proper, solid "us." By recognizing our uncanny strangeness we shall neither suffer from it nor enjoy it from the outside. The foreigner is within me, hence we are all foreigners. If I am a foreigner, there are no foreigners.

—Julia Kristeva, *Strangers to Ourselves*

Some have seen in the Marranos the "beginning of modernization in Europe." Even without going so far, however, it is clear that a person who had been educated as a Christian and who then chose to return to Judaism could not belong entirely or simply to either faith. He would of necessity be faced with enormous difficulties in reintegrating himself into the community to which he indeed belonged, but whose daily life and deepest values and symbols were not actually part of his experience. It is not hard to understand how a man who is neither a Christian nor a Jew, but who is divided between the two or who possesses memories of the one existing within the other, might be inclined to develop doubts about both, or even to question the foundations of religion altogether. As Yosef Yerushalmi has argued, the wonder is not that the return of the Marranos to Judaism gave rise to doubts and heresies, but rather that the majority should have succeeded as far as they did in reintegrating themselves into the framework of normative Judaism. In any case, Spinoza did not lack predecessors in his heresy among the Marranos—the dough of the "New Jews" seems to have contained a leavening agent that gave rise to a constant intellectual ferment from within.

—Yirmiyahu Yovel, *Spinoza and Other Heretics*

Contents

PREFACE   IX

ACKNOWLEDGMENTS   XIX

1   Theoretical Considerations   1

2   Jewish Biblical Literature in French Literature: *Les Juifves*
and Esther   21

3   "Sapho 1900": Imaginary Renée Viviens, Charles Maurras, and
the Rear of the Belle Epoque   43

4   Jewish Literature and Jewish Writing in French Literature:
Albert Cohen and the *Revue Juive*   59

5   *La France et Le Juif*: Identity and a Significant Other   70

6   Getting Away with Murd(h)er—Author's Preface and Narrator's
Text: Reading Marguerite Yourcenar's *Coup de Grâce*
"After Auschwitz"   85

7   The Corset and the Corpse: Antisemitism and the Death
of God   96

8   *Cendres Juives:* Jews Writing in French "After Auschwitz"   114

9   Marrano as Metaphor   127

10   *Juifemme*   143

NOTES   155

BIBLIOGRAPHY   163

INDEX   175

Preface

> But Bloom and Hartmann are barely deconstructionists. They
> even write against it on occasion. Though they understand Niet-
> zsche when he says "the deepest pathos is still aesthetic play,"
> they have a stake in that pathos: its persistence, its psychological
> provenance. For them the ethos of literature is not dissociable
> from its pathos, whereas for deconstructionist criticism literature
> is precisely that use of language which can purge pathos, which
> can show that it too is figurative, ironic or aesthetic.
> —Geoffrey Hartman, *Deconstruction and Criticism*

My work over the past thirty years includes research, writing, and teaching on late nineteenth- and twentieth-century French literature with a
special emphasis on women writers, on questions relating to the feminist inquiry and critical theory, on autobiographical and biographical
texts. My administrative duties with the Women's Studies Program and
the Women's Studies Research Center at the University of Wisconsin-
Madison from 1978 to 1984 brought me into contact with biological
and social scientists working on questions that overlapped with mine.
Their formulations and other changes within the intellectual scene in
the United States and Western Europe during the 1970s and 80s have
obliged me to rethink one of the central areas of debate within the
humanities: the relative weighting of discursive practices and the status
of the referent, the importance accorded on the one hand to language
and to "theory" and on the other to lived experience and to history.

A major shift in the focus of my research occurred during the summer of 1987. I was completing work on two articles, one for *A New History of French Literature*, edited by Denis Hollier, on "1927, *L'Histoire de
la littérature féminine* [The History of feminine literature] by Jean
Larnac," the other on "'Sapho 1900': Imaginary Renée Viviens and the
Rear of the *belle époque*" for an issue of *Yale French Studies* edited by
Joan DeJean and Nancy K. Miller. The books and journals I consulted
for these articles dealt with the effects of late nineteenth-century

nationalist, sexist, racist, and antisemitic discourses on women writers, on the representation of women, and on the coding, encoding, and decoding of the feminine in literature and in art. I was also engaged in a lot of "new" reading in preparation for a course I was going to teach for the first time in the fall of 1987 on "La Question Juive de l'Affaire Dreyfus à Auschwitz" (The Jewish question from the Dreyfus affair to Auschwitz),[1] a course in which Emile Zola, Marcel Proust, Louis-Ferdinand Céline, and Jean-Paul Sartre were the only four writers whom I had read and studied regularly over the years to be included. The summer of 1987 was also the summer in which the trial of Klaus Barbie, the head of the Gestapo in Lyons from November 1942 until the end of the German Occupation of France, took place; the summer of the publication of the first two issues of the journal *Annales d'Histoire révisionniste* (Annals of revisionist history), whose articles affirmed what a few French, North American, and Swiss historians had been claiming since the late 1970s, namely, that the destruction of European Jews in the Nazi death camps had not taken place; the summer in which Claude Lanzmann's film *Shoah* was shown for the first time on public television in France. I was, therefore, both looking at and being confronted with a considerable quantity of material in books, journals, weekly and biweekly magazines, newspapers, and television in which the *Jewish question* figured prominently. I was fascinated by the resemblances and the disjunction between historical accounts and fictionalized accounts of historical events, between anti-Jewish and antisemitic discourses of the late nineteenth century, the 1930s, and the late twentieth century, between the various accounts of what had happened to Jews in France during the time of the Vichy regime. I became particularly interested in exploring further the Jewish question as a constitutive element within French literature and culture.

During part of the summers of 1988, 1989, 1990, and 1991 I did research in Paris at the Centre de Documentation Juive Contemporaine (Center for Contemporary Jewish Documentation), founded clandestinely in 1943 in Grenoble by Isaac Schneerson with the assistance of Leon Poliakov and Joseph Billig. The purpose of the center was, and is, to document as thoroughly as possible the anti-Jewish persecutions. After the liberation of Paris in August of 1944, the center moved from Grenoble to Paris. The center is now located in that part of Paris that has been inhabited by Jewish communities since the sixth century and is still referred to as "the shtetl of Paris," even though, since 1962 and the end of the Algerian War of Independence, Sephardic Jews living in this district have begun to outnumber Ashkenazi Jews. Today the center has an impressive collection of archives as well as a library. It also supports a journal that appears four times a year, *Le Monde Juif* (The Jewish world), now in its forty-seventh year, and that combines in each issue documentation and analysis with an insistence on the need for remembering.[2] In the same building that houses the center there is also a permanent exhibit on "Jews in the struggle against Hitler" presented country by country. In 1956 the center and the museum became part of the Memorial to the Unknown Jewish Martyr. The memorial is composed of two elements. Outside the main building is an immense bronze basin whose form recalls that of an urn filled with ashes, on which the names of some of the major "cities of death" appear in relief: Auschwitz, Maidanek, Treblinka, Bergen-Belsen, Sobibor, the Warsaw Ghetto. Inside is the crypt and the tomb of the Unknown Jewish Martyr, a place of meditation. This ensemble is dedicated to remembering through documentation and information, research and interpretation as well as individual and collective meditation.

The Centre de Documentation Juive Contemporaine is a place in which scholarship and lived experience coincide almost daily. Among those who come to the center to consult the archives and books, there are each day one or two people who come in search of one particular book, the *Mémorial de la déportation des Juifs de France/Memorial to the Jews Deported from France 1942–1944*.[3] The *Mémorial* was published in its French edition in 1978 by the Beate Klarsfeld Foundation and edited with introductions by Serge Klarsfeld. It is based on the deportation lists consisting of name, year of birth, and country of origin prepared in quadruplicate by the Germans before each of the eighty-six convoys left the Paris region, usually from Drancy, for the extermination camps in Poland, usually Auschwitz. I frequently witnessed the reactions of men and women coming to consult the lists, looking for the name of a family member or a friend who had disappeared during the years of the German Occupation of France. Whether they found or did not find what they were looking for, those who came to consult the lists were invariably overwhelmed with grief.

At the Modern Language Association of America convention meetings in 1989, 1990, and 1991 I delivered papers that have become, with significant modification, three chapters of this book: *"Cendres Juives"* (Jewish ashes), *"La France et Le Juif"* (France and Jew), and *"Juifemme"* (I am a Jewish woman). In December of 1990 at a session of the Theory Colloquium at the University of Wisconsin-Madison, I presented a paper on "The Jewish Question in French Writing: Theoretical Considerations," which has since become, after frequent rewritings, the first chapter of this book. Indeed, the successive versions of this chapter trace the changes in the direction of my work on this project between 1988 and 1995.

One of the most significant changes was the change in the working subtitle from *The Jewish Question in French Writing* to *The Jewish Presence in French Writing*. *Question* was initially chosen both to echo Jean-Paul Sartre's famous essay *Réflexions sur la question juive* (1946), appearing in English as *Antisemite and Jew*, and to use a familiar phrase, *the Jewish question*, with a very specific and less frequent emphasis on written texts. *Presence* emerged in my description of the project for the Guggenheim Foundation:

> Although I am interested in pointing to the existence of antisemitic discourses and figures in unexpected places (and here my work may resemble Jeffrey Mehlman's in his *Legacies of Anti-Semitism*, 1983), what I am attempting to do in each chapter is to protect the reality of a Jewish presence or Jewish persecutions and suffering within the French historical experience, at the same time as I explore the complexities of writing, representation, identity, the subject, experience, mourning, and memory.

The Guggenheim Foundation used the word *presence* in its presentation of my award, and after some hesitation, I have kept it. My hesitation was based on the fear of being accused of naïveté by Derrideans and other poststructuralist scholars, and yet as I pondered the question of the title and reread what I had written, it became increasingly clear that my work relies heavily on three different if occasionally overlapping domains: history, literary theory, and psychoanalysis, and that the word *presence* can be justified both as a referent and as a trace. *Presence* also has the advantage of not focusing uniquely, as *question* tends to do, on how Jews and Judaism are perceived, spoken about, and written about by non-Jews. The *Jewish presence* then is meant to include the *Jewish question* as well as *Jewish questions*, differences between non-Jews and Jews but also among non-Jews and among Jews, and even, to continue my borrowing from Teresa de Lauretis, within individual non-Jews and individual Jews.[4]

Furthermore, I became aware of the return in my own work, as I was reading, writing, and thinking through this complex and often painful material, particularly the increasingly impressive scholarship on the *Shoah*,[5] of the themes of death, dying, and mortality. When I began to teach in the 1950s under the influence of such French existentialist (as they were called then) writers as Jean-Paul Sartre, Albert Camus, and Simone de Beauvoir, my conscious objective was to teach anguish, to provoke students into an awareness of their precarious situation in the world. In the late 1960s this direction was deflected by social movements that emphasized community: the Civil Rights movement, the Women's Liberation movement. These movements obliged many of us to confront the question of difference: how to recognize and understand and articulate differences? My reading of texts and the work I did with my students in the classroom during the late sixties and the seventies focused on questions of repression (using psychoanalytic and deconstructive theories) and oppression (using political and social theories). Since the late 1980s, both in my teaching and in my writing on the Jewish question and presence, I have been trying to accommodate the earlier universalist position with the later relativist position, teaching mortality and community, intellectual pleasure and social commitment. This return of the theme of mortality to a central place in my research came about not only because of repeated reading about the unrelieved death and dying, torture and suffering of Jews during the Second World War but also through work on the historic moment at the end of the nineteenth century in France and in Germany, when nihilism, God is dead, and antisemitism appeared together on the European scene.

The return of mortality has also contributed to my already existing sense of the severe limitations of historical research and historiography in a serious treatment of the Jewish question and presence and of antisemitism. I shall deal with this problem of disciplines, theories, and methods at some length in the first chapter on "Theoretical Considerations."

The last of the important changes that forced the title change from *question* to *presence* was a change in my understanding of the term *Jewish*. Did the term only apply to Jewish writers or to writing about and

representing Jews? It was while reading Chanan Lehrmann's book on
L'Élément juif dans la littérature française (The Jewish factor in French
literature), Denise R. Goitein's entry on "French Literature" in the
Encyclopaedia Judaica, and also rereading Robert Garnier's play *Les
Juifves* (Jewish women) and Jean Racine's play *Esther* that my conviction
grew that the rubric "Jewish Literature" might and indeed should
include major and sustained references to Jewish Holy Scriptures, references that exist, nay abound, in French literature. The significant
presence of Jewish Holy Scriptures as intertext in sixteenth- and seventeenth-century French texts, the idealizing during the Baroque period
of the Hebrew language and of the Hebrews who lived and thought and
wrote before the Christian era, is an area of research in which I am
something of a novice. This means that I have been obliged to rely on
particular books in areas where I have less learning. For example I have
relied heavily on Jonathan I. Israel's *European Jewry in the Age of Mercantilism 1550–1750*, on Yirmiyahu Yovel's *Spinoza and Other Heretics*,
and on Damon di Mauro's doctoral thesis on Robert Garnier's *Les
Juifves* in chapter 4, "Jewish Literature and Jewish Writing in French
Literature."

What I have attempted to do in this "final" version of the book is to
be inclusive without aiming at completeness, and to link literary studies and cultural studies so as to enrich the ways in which we read texts
and the world. I understand cultural studies through Roland Barthes's
definition of myth as "a chain of concepts widely accepted throughout
culture, by which its members conceptualize and understand a particular topic or part of their social experience" (*Key Concepts in Communication* 216). In this sense cultural studies analyzes the nonconscious presuppositions that organize a text. But I do not think that one can or
should stop with this ideological analysis. I tend to proceed from the
nonconscious presuppositions to the unconscious of the text, to the
analysis of the play of signifiers and of the rhetorical figures and the
ways in which they further disrupt a commonsense reading and its construction of social relations.

The chapter titles and their order within the book reflect different
aspects of my discussion of process as context. The chapters proceed,
after the first, in a chronological order determined by the date of textual events and events as texts. This preface is intended to acquaint the
reader with my ideological assumptions and preoccupations. Chapter

1, "Theoretical Considerations," stages a series of encounters between historical events, literary texts, and literary theory starting with Alain Robbe-Grillet's description and analysis of his parents' antisemitism in the first volume of his memoirs. I also contrast writers such as Jean-Paul Sartre and Marguerite Duras, who call for some discussion of the Jewish question, with other writers whose philosophical positions preclude engaging with history and/or ideology. More generally this chapter raises questions about which theories and methodologies are most useful in opening the Jewish question and questioning the Jewish presence in writing produced by a variety of disciplines and discourses.

In chapter 2, "Jewish Biblical Literature in French Literature: *Les Juifves* and Esther," I try to determine the intertextual significance of Jewish biblical writings in French literature, and to explore the possible relationship or nonrelationship between Jewish Holy Scriptures and the demography and status of Jews in France during the sixteenth and seventeenth centuries and beyond. I am also interested in mapping the fortunes of the story of Esther from Jean Racine to Marcel Proust. Toward the end of this second chapter I propose the figure of Esther as a model for both intertextuality and assimilation, for the study of both literature and culture, and introduce what will become the major metaphor for *The Jewish Presence in French Writing*, the figure of the Jew, literally and figuratively, as *marrane* (Marrano), the Jew as inevitably christianized and frenchified. Chapter 3, "'*Sapho 1900*' and the Rear of the *Belle Epoque*" examines poetic texts by Renée Vivien, texts of literary criticism by Charles Maurras and Gayle Rubin, and charts the dangers inherent in discourses that insist on categorizing texts according to differences based on religion, ethnicity, race, gender, and sexual preference.

Chapter 4, "Jewish Literature and Jewish Writing in French Literature: Albert Cohen and the *Revue Juive*," focuses on the writer Albert Cohen through a discussion of whether or not the label *Jewish Literature* is necessarily derogatory and antisemitic. I study the ways in which the label was used by Jewish as well as non-Jewish writers and critics during the twentieth century, before and after the Second World War, and I note how this label reproduces questions about assimilation and identity that have haunted Jews in France (and in most of Western Europe) since their emancipation in France in 1791. I also raise the question of whether or not the term *Jewish writing* is useful in literary studies.

In chapter 5, "*La France et le Juif*: Identity and a Significant Other" I look at passages from Drumont's *La France juive* (Jewish France; 1886), Marcel Proust's *A l'ombre des jeunes filles en fleurs/Within a Budding Grove* (1919), Louis-Ferdinand Céline's *L'Eglise* (Church; 1933), and Lucien Rebatet's *Les Décombres* (Ruins; 1942) in order to demonstrate how thematic criticism and textual criticism may produce radically different interpretations of the same texts. Chapter 6, "Getting Away with Murd(h)er—Author's Preface and Writer's Text: Reading Marguerite Yourcenar's *Coup de Grâce* 'After Auschwitz,'" analyzes how the author's intentions stated in her preface are contradicted by ideological and textual criticism; how the refusal in some narratological criticism to associate author and narrator may prevent certain kinds of questions from being raised; and how antisemitism, racism, sexism, and homophobia hold together as a discursive system. Chapter 7, "The Corset and the Corpse: Antisemitism and the Death of God," postulates a relationship between nihilism and antisemitism, discourses that developed during the 1880s but whose repeated and sometimes overwhelming presence we find in French literature of the 1930s, particularly in the writings of Maurice Blanchot, Louis-Ferdinand Céline, Drieu La Rochelle, and Paul Valéry, among others. How does antisemitism operate in the texts of writers absorbed in a meditation on death and absence? Comparisons will be made between the way in which Albert Cohen and Simone de Beauvoir navigate between the social and the ontological. I will also engage a question that is I think central to the post-Shoah world even though it is difficult to state and to discuss: How does the annihilation of the Jews figure in an understanding of a world in which all human beings are always already condemned to death?

Chapter 8, *Cendres Juives*, looks at texts written by Jews in France "after Auschwitz" in which patterns of conventional narrative and authorial belief in God create representations of the Shoah that I find less powerful than the effects produced by texts whose narrative line is fragmented and whose authorial position is atheistic. Chapter 9, "Marrano as Metaphor," focuses on the question of Jewish identity in Jewish writing, the non-Jewishness and the Jewishness of Jewish writers, using as examples texts by Albert Cohen (the most frequently cited French writer in this book) and by Nathalie Sarraute. Chapter 10, *Juifemme*, is the final chapter. The title is an affirming portmanteau word borrowed from Hélène Cixous's "Sorties" (Ways out). In this concluding chapter I make connections between *The Jewish Presence in French Writing* as a scholarly adventure and my own identity as a secular Jew, an identity that has been shaped since childhood by the figure and the work of Sigmund Freud. The book ends with a meditation on the Jewish question and presence and an attempt to redefine, in a positive mode, through the metaphor of the Marrano—perhaps best exemplified in twentieth-century French literature by Hélène Cixous and Jacques Derrida—the reviled notions of assimilation and the assimilated Jew.

Throughout the past seven years three secular non-French Jews have played an important role for me as guides and models: Baruch Spinoza, Sigmund Freud, and Hannah Arendt. I do not consider Spinoza and Freud, as does Isaac Deutscher in his essay "The Non-Jewish Jew" (originally delivered as a lecture to the World Jewish Congress in 1951), to be non-Jewish, although I do consider them, as does Deutscher, to be Jewish heretics, thinkers who went "beyond the boundaries of Jewry" (Deutscher 26). As Yirmiyahu Yovel writes in his chapter on "Spinoza and Freud" in the second part of *Spinoza and Other Heretics*: "To a certain extent both Spinoza and Freud exemplify the situation of the Jew who, abandoning his orthodox tradition without being integrated in the Christian world, develops a penetrating eye for both worlds and the ability to free himself from their conventions" (2:141–42).

The most difficult aspect of writing and lecturing and teaching about the Jewish question and presence in French writing has been my interaction with Christians and Jews for whom the words *Jew* and *Jewish* can only be rightfully applied to those who practice some form of official Judaism. If there is an ethical dimension beyond the simple plea for understanding and tolerance that underlies this book, it is the plea that we view identity historically, psychologically, and linguistically in a more complex manner. I have come to view all Jews who refer to themselves as Jews or Jewish, wherever they may be, as Marranos, crypto-Jews. The Marranos, named after pigs by anti-Jewish Christians in Spain during the fifteenth century, were converts to Christianity who performed as Christians but remained secretly Jewish and faithful to Mosaic Law. I also use the name metaphorically in order to underline the curious fidelity of nonreligious secular Jews to a sense of their Jewishness.

My metaphoric Marranos—and I am aware of the risk involved in using specific terms metaphorically and outside their historical context—are Jews who have to some degree been taken in by or assimilated to the other religious cultures in which they live (these may be Christian or Muslim) and who continue in spite of this inevitable acculturation to profess a belonging to Jewishness.

Acknowledgments

There are many people whose encouragement and assistance during the seven years I have been working on this book I would like to acknowledge. Several of my colleagues at the University of Wisconsin-Madison have encouraged me by their presence at lectures I have given on the Jewish Question and the Jewish Presence in French Writing, by articles and book suggestions they have left in my mail box, and through conversations. In particular I would like to mention Herbert Hill, Nicholas Rand, Eleanor Rodini, Robert J. Rodini. My colleagues on the steering committee of the Jewish Studies Program at the University of Wisconsin-Madison, Klaus Berghahn, Gilead Morahg, George Mosse, Kenneth Sacks, Robert Skloot, have been a reassuring presence. Colleagues and professional groups elsewhere in the United States have aided me through example and invitation and letters of recommendation: Jonathan Boyarin, Daniel Boyarin, Lawrence D. Kritzman, Nancy K. Miller, Gerald Prince, Albert Sonnenfeld, the Western Society for French History, the French twentieth-century section of the Modern Language Association of America. I thank Jennifer Crewe, publisher for the humanities, and Susan Pensak, senior manuscript editor, at Columbia University Press, for their interest in my work and the reassuring swiftness of their responses.

I am particularly grateful to the archivists and librarians at the Centre de Documentation Juive Contemporaine in Paris, Madame Sara

Halpèryn and Monsieur Vidar Jacobsen, whose interest in my work at its beginning stages was invaluable. My deepest gratitude is reserved for the John Simon Guggenheim Memorial Foundation, which awarded me a fellowship that provided one of the most precious of all gifts a scholar can receive, time to think as well as to write; and for the friendship of Yvonne Ozzello, whose own passion for the topic nourished mine and whose truly superior intelligence, *savoir*, and capacity for affection have accompanied me since 1975.

Madison, Wisconsin and Etel, France

1988–1995

I   Theoretical Considerations

> Unable to respond to the questions, to all the questions, I will ask
> myself instead *whether responding is possible* and what that would
> mean in such a situation. And I will risk in turn several questions
> *prior* to the definition of a *responsibility*. But is it not an act to
> assume in theory the concept of a responsibility? Is that not
> already to take a responsibility? One's own as well as the responsi-
> bility to which one believes one ought to summon others?"
>
> —Jacques Derrida,
> "Like the Sound of the Sea Deep Within a Shell:
> Paul de Man's War"

The writing of this book would not have been possible were it not for the role played by France, *La
France,* as an object of desire in my imaginary. For
me, at least, *La France* has never ceased to be—in spite of some decep-
tions and misunderstandings—as in any enduring love affair—a source
of intellectual excitement and interminably renewed seduction.

This problematic and profound love affair with *La France* may not
be unrelated to my being Jewish, an assimilated "godless Jew" with
Russian, Polish, and German Jewish grandparents. Historians of nine-
teenth- and twentieth-century France, Michael Marrus and Paula
Hyman among others, have written about the degree to which, for most
French Jews during the nineteenth century, the French Revolution and
the emancipation of French Jews in 1791 became the basis for consider-
ing France as *the* country par excellence for Jews to live in and to flour-
ish. The Yiddish saying *Azoi wie Gott in Frankreich* (Happy as God in
France) captures this union, a union that, as myth at least, survived the
period of the Dreyfus case, 1894–1906, and even the Shoah, the destruction of two-thirds of European Jewry and one-fourth of French Jewry
between 1939 and 1945.

The Jewish question(s), fed by an endemic if changing discourse,
from the anti-Jewish bias of Christian France and Europe that becomes
evident with the Crusades and continues through the French Revolu-

tion to the racial antisemitism of the nineteenth and twentieth centuries, can now be understood as always present—almost, one is tempted to suggest, with the force of a religious belief—and essential to the continuing construction of a French identity. It would be naive to assume that this religion of antisemitism died after the Second World War and the abundant and well-documented progressive revelations concerning the full extent of the crimes committed against Jews by the Nazis and their French collaborators. Not only has the power of antisemitism *not* been dulled by these revelations but the more evidence that is published about the centrality of antisemitism to Nazi ideology and the intention of ridding Europe once and for all of Jews, the more strident is a counter discourse attributing the documentation and revelations to a Jewish or Zionist conspiracy.

The Jewish question cannot, of course, be limited to France or to writing in French, although that is the focus of my book. I will, on occasion, refer to writings from other countries and languages, notably the United States and American English.

In France anti-Jewish and antisemitic discourses and practices since Auschwitz have taken different forms and these forms are embedded in oral and written texts of varying virulence. But we may well ask what the difference is between the obfuscation by many French men and women of what did indeed occur during the war—the role played by members of the Vichy Government and the French militia in these events—and the systematic denial by the revisionist historians, for example Robert Faurisson, of the extermination camps? What is the difference between the "ordinary antisemitism" that is reproduced in everyday language and such comments as Darquier de Pellepoix's 1978 statement quoted in *Le Monde*, "A Auschwitz on n'a gazé que des poux" (Only Lice were gassed at Auschwitz), or Jean-Marie Le Pen's comment of September 13, 1987, that the gas chambers were "un point de détail de l'histoire de la Deuxième Guerre Mondiale" (a mere detail in the history of the Second World War)?

This book, as I mentioned in the preface, has been steadily nourished by current events, the reactions of French friends to my work, my rereadings of nineteenth and twentieth-century texts, and current events and publications. A conversation with one of my oldest friends in Paris, a woman born in North Africa whose maternal grandmother was Jewish, alerted me to the tendency and the continuing need on the part of some French men and women, noted by Jean-Paul Sartre in his *Antisemite and Jew*, to silence any discussion of Jews or the Jewish question so as not to irritate certain people. As my friend warmly said, she is worried about my project and my credibility as a scholar, because the Jewish question is not a proper object of inquiry for a student of literature. It is better, she said, to be silent, to forget. Others perceive the Jewish question to be a politically incorrect object of inquiry because they feel that the Soviets did more terrible things than the Nazis, or they think that because of the present behavior of the state of Israel toward the Palestinians it is now improper to speak of Jewish suffering. More significantly, raising the Jewish question may be perceived as socially incorrect or inelegant because it violates the accepted rules of propriety and Frenchness (*la francité*) and makes people uncomfortable. My answer to such responses, and it was the response I made to my friend, is that to be silent, to forget, or to use euphemisms would be to repeat some fifty years later the gestures and the words of the exterminators.

There is a lengthy passage that I would like to quote and comment on in some detail from Alain Robbe-Grillet's autobiography, *Le Miroir qui revient* (The Mirror that returns; 1984). In this passage the narrator describes, analyzes, and unwittingly reproduces the "ordinary" antisemitism of his parents. It is one of the most comprehensive analyses of French antisemitism of the 1930s and 1940s I have encountered in my reading:

> My parents were antisemites, and they admitted it freely to anyone who cared to listen (even to our Jewish friends, if the opportunity arose). I do not want to slide over such an embarrassing point too lightly. Antisemitism still exists, pretty much everywhere, in various forms that are more or less discreet, and it constantly runs the risk of doing extensive damage here or there, like a fire that has been smoldering under the ashes to which one did not pay sufficient attention. In order to fight efficiently against such a diffuse and tenacious ideology, it is particularly important not to make of it a taboo subject.
>
> It seems to me that the antisemitism in my family was of a very banal kind: neither militant (to turn in a Jew to either German or Vichy persecution would have been unthinkable), nor religious (the god that *they* had crucified was clearly not our god), nor scornful (like Russian antisemitism), nor delirious (like in the writings of Céline), nor was it an allergy (Jews could, as well as others, be exciting to read or agreeable to frequent). Strongly irrational, however, like its more virulent varieties,

the antisemitism of my parents seems to me to have been very precisely "right-wing," because its most obvious basis was an essential concern for the maintenance of a moral order joined to a deep suspicion of any form of internationalism.

Robbe-Grillet openly confesses his parents' antisemitism, uses their antisemitism to transgress a taboo, to admit to his own embarrassment. Furthermore, he does this by comparing antisemitism not only to "a diffuse and tenacious ideology" but also, metaphorically, to "a fire that has been smoldering under the ashes to which one did not pay sufficient attention." Already in the first paragraph of the confession, antisemitism has been constructed as a natural phenomenon over which human beings may have little control.

In Robbe-Grillet's text the attempt to identify brands of antisemitism is followed by an attempt to identify and to summarize accusations made about Jews in antisemitic "right-wing" discourse: their affiliation with a conniving supernational community, their lack of authentic French roots, their control, as judeo-plutocrats, of international capitalism, their weak moral fiber, their capacity to break down familial and political order, to cause the ruin of organized society and the death of healthy nations.

And Robbe-Grillet continues:

The morbid taste for unhappiness, catastrophes, and despair that is attributed to Jews (while at the same time they are reproached with having made a fortune at the expense of the social body on whom they are becoming parasites), reminds me very exactly of what Heidegger says about anguish: it is the price one must pay for having reached at last a certain freedom of mind . . .

In their fight against the feared virus of infectious negation and metaphysical anguish (which means: of freedom), my parents were certainly far from imagining some kind of "final solution." They were perfectly content with the "reasonable" *numerus clausus* (quota system) suggested by Charles Maurras. Like many sincere men and women during the Occupation, we certainly did not know that the Nazis were undertaking something quite different. Most of the Jews who were deported did not know themselves. As for my mother, she always considered their general, organized extermination as so inconceivable that she persisted until her death in 1975 in denying the reality of the genocide. She thought it was Zionist propaganda and falsified documents: they also tried to make us believe that the Germans were responsible for the systematic massacre of Polish officers discovered in the ossuaries of Katyn.

The passage concludes, after a sentence on "the monstrous revelations about the dark horror that was the hidden face of National Socialism," with the following words, significantly in parentheses:

(Whether there were gas chambers or not, I don't see the difference, if men, women, and children died by the millions, innocent of any crime except the crime of being Jews, Gypsies, or homosexuals.) (118–22)

Robbe-Grillet's text touches on several aspects of post-Shoah discourse that I would like to examine more closely. Like Jean-Paul Sartre in *Antisemite and Jew*, Robbe-Grillet begins his analysis by insisting on the importance of breaking silences, of daring to write and to speak about antisemitism and about Jews. In the years immediately following the Second World War, there was a fear on the part of some of those Jews who had survived, and those non-Jews who were appalled at what had happened, of speaking about the Jewish question, as if to speak about it would further antisemitic reactions. For example, in the 1952 film *Nuit et Brouillard/Night and Fog* (directed by Alain Resnais with the script by Jean Cayrol), from the German *Nacht und Nebel*, the code name for the Final Solution, one of the first to use photographs and films shot by the Nazis themselves before and after gassings at extermination camps, as well as films and photographs taken by the allied armies that liberated the camps, Jews are mentioned but only as one group among a long list of victims. Nowhere is it spoken that the extermination camps were built for them. In *La Douleur*, 1985, translated into English as *War*, Marguerite Duras, narrating the return of her husband from Dachau in April of 1945, writes: "There really are huge numbers of dead. Seven million Jews have been exterminated—transported in cattle cars, then gassed in specially built gas chambers, then burnt in specially built ovens. In Paris, people don't talk about the Jews yet" (60).

Pierre Vidal-Naquet, historian of ancient Greece, in an article entitled "Le Défi de la *Shoah* à l'histoire" (The Challenge of the Shoah to history), published in *Les Temps Modernes*, 1988, proposes three reasons to explain why French historiography has shirked its obligations vis-à-vis the Shoah. The first reason, according to Vidal Naquet, is political, since any study on the extermination of the Jews must raise questions about the continuity of French history beyond Vichy. The second rea-

son involves university politics and the fact that the university has had
for a long time a timorous attitude about contemporary historical subjects. And the third reason he labels epistemological. The Annales
School of historiography chose, in general, to study "la longue durée"—
long periods of time—rather than events considered ripples, such as
the Third Reich 1933 to 1945 or Vichy 1940 to 1944. And Alain
Finkielkraut, in his essay *La Mémoire Vaine / Remembering in Vain* published in 1989, after the trial of Klaus Barbie, and dedicated to the Italian Jewish writer Primo Levi, insists on still another aspect of the
silence:

> If there was a silence on the part of the "déportés raciaux" [the racial
> deportees, as the Jews were called to distinguish them from the members
> of the French Resistance who were deported] in the years following the
> war, it is not, as a melodramatic and false cliché suggests, because they
> were unable to speak, but because no one wanted to listen to what they
> had to say. Beware of the pathos of the ineffable! The survivors of the
> final solution were not reduced to aphasia by a nameless misfortune, by
> an experience that no word could render. To the contrary, they had an
> irrepressible need to testify, if only to pay their debt to the dead. What
> was lacking was a public: "Hardly did we begin to speak," said Simone
> Veil [French magistrate and political figure who had been deported to
> Auschwitz as a child] recently, with her anger still intact, "than we were
> interrupted as if we were overly excited and talkative children by parents
> who had real problems." (39)

The intention to speak or to write about antisemitism and the Jews
is, of course, no guarantee that the speaker or the writer will not reproduce antisemitic discourse. The disbelief of Alain Robbe-Grillet's
mother with which he ends his description of the antisemitism of his
family is echoed in his own concluding statement on the problematic
existence of the gas chambers, suggesting the power of antisemitic discourse to dictate the terms in which public discourse occurs and therefore to repeat itself in spite of a particular writer's intentions.

The specificity of the Shoah, the intimate relationship between
Nazism and antisemitism, was rarely elaborated on in France during the
immediate postwar period. It is difficult to distinguish the silence that
was based on the fear of irritating or provoking the wrath of antisemites, the silence that was based on the desire to blame capitalism for
the crimes of National Socialism, the silence that was prompted by the

need to perpetuate the image of a united French Resistance, and the silence that was the result of an immediate, almost collective suppression, silence that has only quite recently, since the early 1980s and the government of François Mitterand, intermittently, but regularly, been broken. Robbe-Grillet, like Sartre before him, views antisemitism as "a diffuse and tenacious ideology," that is to say, an amalgam of nonconscious, commonsense assumptions considered evident, and natural, and therefore never subjected to critical scrutiny. The word *ideology* further suggests that antisemitism has penetrated deeply into discourses— for example discourses on religion, politics, sexuality, money—and that it lurks in these discourses and therefore does not go by its "real" name.

Robbe-Grillet's text points to the heterogeneity of antisemitisms: there is "militant" antisemitism—the Christian variety—that holds the Jews responsible for the crucifixion of Christ and that rationalizes the persecution of Jews throughout history as the justifiable and justified expiation of that original crime; there is "racist" antisemitism, the product of social Darwinism and the obsession with systems of classification and binary oppositions: male/female, white/black, superior/inferior, Aryan/Jew, etc.; there is "verbally paranoid" antisemitism, the extravagant, explosive discourse of writers like Edouard Drumont, Louis-Ferdinand Céline, and Lucien Rebatet, whose private madness seems to focus on an irrational fear of Jews and Jewish power; and there is "right-wing" banal antisemitism, which, according to Robbe-Grillet, best characterizes his parents. Accused of being communists, revolutionaries, capitalists, bankers, accused of being rootless and conspiratorial, physically grotesque and uncontrollably libidinous, contaminating the health and the order of France and of Europe, Jews are persistently denounced as foreigners and parasites who disrupt, subvert, menace, and threaten. Unlike those writers on the Jewish question who treat antisemitism chronologically, as if one variety of antisemitism were replaced or displaced by another, Robbe-Grillet's listing suggests the principle of overlapping and the contamination of one form by another. Epithets such as the *peuple élu* (the chosen people), the *peuple déicide* (the people who killed God), the *peuple aurifère* (the gold dealers, the money makers), and the *juif errant* (the wandering Jew), continue to function simultaneously.

It is interesting to note a possible connection between the *peuple déicide* and the Death of God. The Jews as Christ killers are also associated thematically and by contiguity in Robbe-Grillet's text on his parents' antisemitism with "the feared virus of infectious negation and metaphysical anguish" and with the name of Heidegger. I mentioned in the preface and will return in chapter 7 to the historical moment at which antisemitism and nihilism appear in the discourses of Western European countries, particularly France and Germany. The question that fascinates me is why those writers most preoccupied by the question of mortality, for example, the German philosopher Martin Heidegger and several (not all) of his disciples in France, are also the writers who are silent about the attempted annihilation of European Jewry. It is as if the overwhelming fact of universal mortality left no room for acknowledging differences in how death comes.

Robbe-Grillet understands his parents antisemitism as ultimately the fear of freedom and the association, in his parents' ideology, of freedom with disorder. This allows him to explain why his parents and the right-wing ideology they represent were able, in spite of their xenophobia, to come to terms with the Germans. The explanation is only partially satisfactory. Clearly something more is needed, either a more powerful theory or at least another kind of theoretical framework that might enable us to comprehend the persistence of the banal antisemitism of Robbe-Grillet's parents, and millions like them, who contributed to an ideological climate in which the persecution and the extermination of Jews was, at first, made possible and, later, deemed unmentionable or even denied.

We might look for this "something more" in the work of those theorists who have written in French, or in other languages, about the Jewish question(s) and presence in French writing. From among the possible theorists I have selected two orientations: psychoanalytic, with Rodolphe Loewenstein and Julia Kristeva, and deconstructive, with the literary analyst Jeffrey Mehlman.

In 1953 Rodolphe Loewenstein, a Freudian psychoanalyst who had been the training analyst of Jacques Lacan and who was living as a refugee in New York City, published, in French, a book entitled *Psychanalyse de l'antisémitisme/Psychoanalysis of Antisemitism*. In this book Loewenstein treats antisemitism neither as a religion, as I suggested at the beginning of this chapter, nor as a form of metaphysical anguish, as does Robbe-Grillet, but rather as a mental illness, a form of paranoia in which the figure of the circumcised Jew, the mutilated, effeminate, castrated male, plays a central role. Antisemites, according to Loewenstein, displace their castration anxiety onto the Jew, whom they treat as the scapegoat for their repressed sadistic and masochistic desires. Loewenstein is strongly indebted to *Moses and Monotheism* (1939), in which Sigmund Freud proposed a series of obvious reasons for what he refers to as "the popular hatred of Jews" as well as a series of "deeper motives." Among the "obvious" reasons Freud stresses Jewish "difference," which, he claims, because it is composed of "small differences," contributes significantly to racial intolerance. The second obvious reason, according to Freud, is that Jews "defy oppression" and persecutions do not succeed in exterminating them. "On the contrary, they show a capacity for holding their own in commercial life and, where they are admitted, they make valuable contributions to every form of cultural activity" (91). Freud attributes the "deeper motives" to the unconscious, with this caveat: "I am quite prepared to hear that what I am going to say will at first appear incredible" (91). He advances three motives: the first is that the Jewish claim to being the "chosen people, or the 'favorite' child of God" has evoked jealousy in other people, as if it were true; the second is the "uncanny impression" made on others by the rite of circumcision and its relation to castration anxiety (this is the motive developed by Loewenstein); and the third is that, according to Freud, many antisemites are relatively recent Christians, forced to convert to Christianity, and that they have remained barbarically polytheistic; their hatred for the new religion, Christianity, is projected onto the source of Christianity, i.e., Judaism. And Freud concludes: "Their hatred of Jews is at bottom a hatred for Christians, and it is not surprising that in the German National Socialist revolution this intimate relation between the two monotheistic religions finds such a clear expression in the hostile treatment of both of them" (2). We hear echoes of this in such texts of contemporary French literature as Philippe Sollers's novel *Femmes/ Women*, 1983, in which an international feminist group is considered antisemitic by the male narrator because of its persistent attacks on the Judeo-Christian tradition and on patriarchy.

The psychoanalyst and linguist Julia Kristeva, in a book published in France in 1980, *Pouvoirs de l'horreur/Powers of Horror*, develops, through a close symptomatic reading of antisemitic pamphlets written by Louis-Ferdinand Céline, a connection between the writer's verbal paranoia and repressed homosexuality. In the chapter "To jew or to die" Kristeva analyzes Céline's antisemitism in terms of "la beauté sauvage du style" (the wild beauty of the style) that refuses the Symbolic order, the Law of the Father; that refuses abstraction, reason, and Jewish monotheism; a style that reproduces elements of Dance, Music, and Rhythm associated for Céline with the world of the Aryan spirit. According to Kristeva the figure of the Jew is the condensation of three fantasms in Céline's antisemitic texts. In the first fantasm the Jew is the superior brother who is envied, for example, Youbelblat in *Bagatelles pour un massacre* (Merry songs for a massacre). The Jew has anal mastery; he possesses gold and an elusive power. This superior brother arouses in the Aryan a denied homosexual desire. In the second fantasm the Jew is in the position of the one who knows pleasure by performing anal intercourse, and the Aryan (Céline) is forced into the masochistic position of the feminine. In the third fantasm the Jew becomes the object of the father's desire, the father's woman, an abjection:

> The Jew becomes the feminine exalted to the point of mastery, the impaired master, the ambivalent, the border where exact limits between same and other, subject and object, and even beyond these, between inside and outside, and disappearing—hence an Object of fear and fascination. *Abjection* itself. He is abject: dirty, rotten. And I who identify with him, who desire to share with him a brotherly, mortal embrace in which I lose my own limits, I find myself reduced to the same abjection, a fecalized, feminized, passivated rot: "the repulsive Céline." (185)

Antisemitism, in psychoanalytic theory, is therefore linked to unconscious scenarios that can be analyzed in terms of displacement. I believe that an analysis such as Kristeva's provides exhilarating material for students of literature. However, Kristeva's exclusion of the ideological, sociological, historical, and cultural context may be viewed as condoning, trivializing, or aestheticizing antisemitism.

Jeffrey Mehlman's controversial study, *Legacies of Antisemitism in France* (1983), includes ideological and cultural analysis along with psychoanalysis and deconstructive reading strategies. His desire is to demonstrate the ubiquitousness of the Jewish question, in the form of antisemitism, in twentieth-century French literature. His introductory remarks are stunningly disturbing:

> These pages, then, are exploratory rather than accusatory. Indeed, as the analyses engage such crucial questions as the inaugural silence in Blan-

chot's sense of literature, the "style" of Lacan, the relation to Racine of Giraudoux, and the sexual politics of Gide, it will be perceived that the readings are ultimately less dependent on any category of intentionality than on the sustaining effects of a cultural *milieu* that at times seems— or seemed—anti-Jewish in its essence. As in the Jewish joke that has a German in 1942 inquire untranslatably of a young man in Paris, *"où se trouve la place de l'Etoile?"* [where is the *Etoile* Place, the place of the star], only to find his interlocutor gesturing in response to his left lapel. It is as though only the slightest displacement were necessary within the designation of the French monument to reveal therein a drama of Jewish exclusion. I have attempted, in four cases, such a displacement, aware that in the long run it is the degree of coherence of the readings proposed that will—or will not—justify the effort. (3–4)

Unlike Jacques Derrida who, in his apologetic essay "Like the Sound of the Sea Deep Within a Shell: Paul de Man's War," postulates the indeterminacy of language and uses the rhetorical device of "On the one hand . . . On the other hand" to prevent any totally accusatory or didactic reading of Paul de Man's wartime journalism, Jeffrey Mehlman, through a vast network of intertextual references, locates "marginal fragments" of antisemitic discourse throughout the French literary establishment of the 1930s. His detailed and ingenious readings suggest that before Jeffrey Mehlman, concerned readers and critics had been focusing on the obvious and the explicit—Céline, Brasillach, Rebatet, Drieu la Rochelle—whereas the larger picture that includes many more writers, and is more devastating because so pervasive, had escaped the critic's notice and understanding.

In his chapter on Maurice Blanchot, "Blanchot at *Combat*: Of Literature and Terror," Mehlman begins by making rapid connections with George Bernanos's biography in praise of Edouard Drumont, *La Grande Peur des Bien Pensants* (The Great fear of the self-righteous; 1931). He then refers back to Drumont's *La France Juive* (1886) and to the Cercle Proudhon of 1913, and forward to Thierry Maulnier, disciple of Charles Maurras at *L'Action Française* and codirector of *Combat* from 1936 to 1939, where Blanchot himself, from 1936 to 1938, was a leading writer of political articles condemning the impotence of French political life under Léon Blum and the Popular Front.

Mehlman selects extracts from Blanchot's articles in which Blanchot states that the paralysis of France under the Blum experiment can have only one solution: a renewal of the right-wing insurrection of February 6, 1934, "or, failing that, acts of terrorism" (11). Like Céline in *Bagatelles pour un massacre* (1937) and Rebatet in *Les Décombres* (1942), Blanchot views "unfettered revolutionaries and Jews," "Moscow or Israel" as foreign elements forcing young Frenchmen into war. Jeffrey Mehlman insists that Maurice Blanchot's move from political writing to literary writing involves a silencing of his political writings of the 1930s. Here is an example of one of Mehlman's most dramatic, affirmative sentences: "At the inception of a certain literary modernity . . . there is a radical falling silent" (13). It is as if Mehlman wanted to convince his readers that once an antisemite always an antisemite, and that although the events of the Second World War have eliminated antisemitism as a viable option for French intellectuals, it was nevertheless very present in their pre-World War II writings.

Jeffrey Mehlman's attack on Maurice Blanchot—and I do not think that the word *attack* is excessive—raises some disturbing questions: How should we interpret a writer's earlier and later writings that concern questions of antisemitism or racism? To what extent does Jeffrey Mehlman's reliance on Zeev Sternhell's thesis in *La Droite révolutionnaire: Les Origines françaises du fascisme, 1885–1914* (The Revolutionary right: The French origins of fascism, 1885–1914; 1978) attributing the emergence of European fascism to French thought, direct Jeffrey Mehlman's thesis and his readings? To what degree is it the silence of Martin Heidegger that prompted some of his avowed disciples and readers in France, among them Maurice Blanchot, to write about the extermination of the Jews, as if their voices compensated for his silence? What is the relationship between writing about the Shoah, or Auschwitz, as a disaster, as the "*absolute* event of history," and ignoring the more banal, less spectacular forms of antisemitism to which Robbe-Grillet refers and which seem to belong to the realm of history rather than what Maurice Blanchot in "Etre Juif" (Being Jewish) refers to as "the metaphysics of the Jewish Question."

The pleasures and the dangers of overwriting and overreading are present in both Jacques Derrida's essay on Paul de Man and in Jeffrey Mehlman's four essays on Blanchot, Lacan, Giraudoux, and Gide. I note, however, the differences between Derrida's reading of the literary in the political and Mehlman's reading of the political in the literary. How does Mehlman succeed in blackening Blanchot by making something out of almost nothing? How does Derrida succeed in putting Paul de Man and his ashes in the place of the Jewish victims by making almost nothing out of something?

It seems fitting to conclude this selective overview of theoretical considerations with an extended comment on the relationship established by some historians and literary critics in the United States between revisionism and deconstruction. Revisionism, in its post–World War II incarnation, unites those who claim that European Jews placed in concentration camps were not gassed in gas chambers, but died, in numbers far fewer than those that have been proposed, of disease and malnutrition. Among the vociferous opponents of deconstruction there are those who have established a causal relationship in which *deconstruction* in its continental philosophical origins is considered to be responsible not only for the positions taken by those who claim that the gas chambers did not exist for the purpose of killing human beings but also for the theoretical atmosphere that led to extermination in the gas chambers. Deconstruction, then, becomes responsible for the crime par excellence of the twentieth century, and for an attempt to "cover up" the crime.

There have been explicit and implicit signs of this proposed relationship in newspapers and popular magazines as well as in scholarly books and journals in the United States and Western Europe during the past fifteen or more years. I have encountered it regularly in the writing of this book. For example, in her recent book *Denying the Holocaust: The Growing Assault on Truth and Memory* (1993), Deborah Lipstadt, who holds the Dorot Chair in Modern Jewish and Holocaust Studies at Emory University, writes:

> While Holocaust denial is not a new phenomenon, it has increased in scope and intensity since the mid-1970's. It is important to understand that the deniers do not work in a vacuum. Part of their success can be traced to an intellectual climate that has made its mark in the scholarly world during the past two decades. The deniers are plying their trade at a time when much of history seems to be up for grabs and attacks on the Western rationalist tradition have become commonplace. (17)

Deborah Lipstadt is more cautious in linking denial of the Holocaust to continental (read German) philosophy and continental (read French) literary theory than many of her colleagues in the United States who have written about the context in which denial of the Holocaust occurs. But nonetheless, after a few gestures toward the importance of recognizing the role of the reader in assigning meaning to a text and the importance of recognizing "the interpretations of less powerful groups in society" (18), she completes her development on the relationship between "this approach to texts" and denial of the Holocaust with these formulations:

> At its most radical it [this approach to texts] contended that there was no bedrock thing such as experience. Experience was mediated through one's language. The scholars who supported this deconstructionist approach were neither deniers themselves nor sympathetic to the deniers' attitudes; most had no trouble in identifying Holocaust denial as disingenuous. But because deconstructionism argued that experience was relative and nothing was fixed, it created an atmosphere of permisiveness toward questioning the meaning of historical events and made it hard for its proponents to assert that there was anything off limits for this skeptical approach. (18)

Deconstructionism, in Deborah Lipstadt's version, is an essential part of the context that made historical denial possible, although she does not say directly that it bears responsibility for the notion of Holocaust denial. However, toward the end of this first chapter, "Canaries in the Mine," there is a parenthetical remark that is far more accusatory:

> I was reminded of the potency of history when, on the eve of the Louisiana gubernatorial election in 1991, one of David Duke's followers remarked in a television interview that there was all this talk about Duke's past views on Jews and blacks and his Ku Klux Klan activities. That, the follower observed, was the past; what relevance, he wondered, did it have for this election? The answer was obvious: His past had everything to do with his quest for the election; it shaped who he was and who he remained. It has never been more clearly illustrated that history matters. (Neither was it happenstance that the late Paul de Man, one of the founders of deconstructionism, also falsified his past and reworked his personal history.) (29)

Here, the word *deconstructionism* (which does not exist in the writings of those associated with deconstruction) connected to the name of one of its founders, "the late Paul de Man," appears in a new light, contaminated by its doubly metonymic relationship—causal and contiguous—with David Duke and, as a consequence of this association, deemed responsible for the destruction of European Jews.

In the subsequent ten chapters of *Denying the Holocaust* Deborah Lipstadt focuses on Holocaust deniers in France and in the United States and does not return to literary theory or to Paul de Man, nor does she ever mention Martin Heidegger. David H. Hirsch, in articles written between 1976 and 1991 and published with revisions as a book in 1991, under the title *The Deconstruction of Literature: Criticism After Auschwitz*, links the responsibility for the destruction of European Jews directly and consistently "to the exotic modes of reading that go under the rubric of 'deconstruction,' which we may now recognize for what they are: 'antihumanist'" (1). If Deborah Lipstadt, as a historian, is pointing a finger at the dangers inherent in certain reading practices, David Hirsch, professor of English and Judaic Studies, unequivocally charges literary theory with the crimes of the Shoah.

The publicity notice on the back cover of his book published by Brown University Press reads: "A relentless critique of antihumanism in deconstructionist and postmodern literary theory and its historical and ideological connections to Nazism," David Hirsch is not alone in making such explicit accusations. There were similar accusations in the popular and scholarly press following the discovery made in 1987 by Ortwin de Graef of Paul de Man's articles written in 1941 and 1942 for the Belgian newspapers *Le Soir* and *Het Vlaamsche Land* and following the publication in France, also in 1987, of Victor Farias's book on Martin Heidegger. But although I personally find these ad hominem attacks inappropriate and simplistic, I am less concerned about the reputation of Paul de Man and Martin Heidegger, whose works continue to be read and pondered, than I am about the status of literary studies in France and in the United States, where historians, philosophers, and other members of humanities disciplines and interdisciplines have joined the fray on the side of the accusers. History and philosophy, and, by association, historians and philosophers, are, by and large, taken more seriously than those who study literature. Indeed, there is no single word like *historian* or *philosopher* to account for what it is we who work in literature do. The terms *literary critic* or *literary theorist* cannot begin to compete as signifers of status in the academy, or in intellectual milieus outside the academy, with the terms *historian* and *philosopher*.

What is at stake for David Hirsch is enunciated early in his first chapter, "Derailing American Literary History," when he describes the negative influence of German philosophy and French literary theory on American cultural criticism:

> What is clear, I believe, is that American cultural criticism did not need Heidegger and the French antihumanist Heideggerians and Marxists to alert them to the evils and dangers of a postindustrial technological society and to the threat against democracy and the integrity of the individual constituted by a technocratic culture. In fact, the dominance of the cluster of ideas constituted by Marxism-Heideggerism-deconstruction imported from France constituted a serious step backward. (13)

Elsewhere in this first chapter David Hirsch rails against "poststructuralism" and "Foucauldian genealogical historicism" because of their "bitter hostility to the liberal-democratic concepts of the integrity of the individual self and the inviolability of inalienable human rights" (8).

Part 1 of *The Deconstruction of Literature* is entitled "Deconstruction in Its European Setting." The title of the chapters in part 1 introduce the names of the antagonists, the main enemies denounced by Hirsch as well as the fatal denouement (the outcome or final solution) he proposes. There is an inevitable progression from the philosophical assumptions and the pedagogical practices of deconstruction to the death camps. The titles, in order of their appearance, are: "Paul de Man and the Politics of Deconstruction," "Martin Heidegger and Pagan Gods," "Paul de Man and the Poetics of Prevarication," "French Shame and the New Theory," "Collaborators and Deconstructors," "Deconstruction and the SS Connection." What chagrins and angers me most is the repetition in Hirsch's book of the same evil persons and evildoers: Martin Heidegger, Paul de Man, the French, collaborators, the SS, and the Modern Language Association of America.

In his eagerness to establish a network of fellow culprits, David Hirsch is also guilty—as we all often are when we engage in a sustained polemic—of exaggeration and distortion of facts. In his chapter 2, "Paul de Man and the Politics of Deconstruction," he writes:

> One suspects that those same scholars who were shocked to learn about de Man's past would be equally surprised to learn about the existence of German death camps. Certainly, one would be hard pressed to acquire such knowledge by reading *PMLA* or the proliferating number of liter-

ary journals devoted exclusively to deconstruction, postmodernism, metafiction, and literary theory. Anyone who derived his or her knowledge of literature and the world only from the journals de Man and his followers would be likely to publish in and read would most likely dwell in blissful ignorance of the recent European past and would never in the least suspect that the various literary and critical "postmodernisms" may be related to the historical events of the thirties and forties. (69–70)

"One suspects," "likely," "most likely," do, of course, signal to the reader that the narrator is speculating. And this is certainly not an objectionable activity. But it is outrageous for Hirsch to state that the *PMLA* does not contain articles in which "the existence of German death camps" is referred to; see Julia Kristeva on Marguerite Duras (vol. 102, March 1987) and Nicholas Rand on Martin Heidegger (vol. 105, 1990), for example. And it is an equally blatant disregard of the evidence to conflate Paul de Man, *PMLA*, and the "journals Paul de Man and his followers would be likely to publish in," when one knows that the Committee on Research Activities of the Modern Language Association of America rejected Paul de Man's essay on literary theory written on request for the 1981 edition of *Introduction to Scholarship in the Modern Languages.*[1]

Let me further expound and expand on David Hirsch's chapter 5, "French Shame and the New Theory." At most of the major conferences I attended during 1993, France, French culture, the French language have been treated with scorn and hostility, considered inferior either to Germany, German culture, and the German language, or England, English culture, and the English language, held responsible for the cult of Martin Heidegger and the cult of Walter Benjamin, and damned for raising the question of language to a central position in the writing of philosophy, history, and literature. Among these conferences were one on "European Philosophy and the American Academy" held at the Wingspread Conference Center in Racine, Wisconsin, the National Foreign Language Council Conference held in Washington, D.C., sponsored by Richard Lambert's National Foreign Language Center, and a symposium on "The German-Jewish Dialogue: Two Centuries of a Non-Event?" sponsored by the Institute for Research in the Humanities at the University of Wisconsin-Madison.

At the Wingspread conference there were mostly philosophers critiquing and trivializing the continental philosophical tradition that

runs from Nietzsche and Heidegger to Derrida and Foucault; at the
National Foreign Language Council conference there were mostly soci-
ologists and some language methodologists critiquing and trivializing
the study of literature and culture; and at the symposium on "The German-Jewish Dialogue" the participants, mostly historians, reacted with
anger and fear to the paper of one of the speakers, which presented Jewish intellectuals at the time of the Weimar Republic—such as Gershom
Scholem and Walter Benjamin—as convinced that language was both
duplicitous and yet the only possibility of redemption. This same
speaker described the ways in which Jewish intellectuals confronted the
nihilism problematic in a post-Nietzschean world. In the discussion
that followed this paper it seemed evident to me that what was being
viewed as dangerous and antihumanist in the speaker's thesis were the
possible connections that might be made to contemporary French
philosophers Jacques Derrida or Emmanuel Lévinas, both of whom are
indebted to Heidegger in the elaboration of their own philosophical
positions. In all of these conferences the "French connection" carried a
strong negative charge that resulted in a constant ridiculing and scape-
goating of *la chose française*.

Even before the reader arrives at chapter 5 of David Hirsch's book,
we read the following sentence in his acknowledgements: "Over coffee
at Peabury's, Laurent Ditman shared with me his knowledge of French
character and the French cultural scene" (vii). To write without quali-
fiers in the early 1990s about "French character" is to suggest a belief in
national traits that is characteristic of simplified stereotypical discourse.
It does however prepare the reader for the negative affirmations about
France and the French throughout the book

The title "French Shame and the New Theory" proposes a causal
relation between the shame the French must have felt for their behavior during the years of German Occupation, the silence that until the
late 1980s surrounded those years on the part of many French intellectuals, the squelching of French Holocaust literature that appeared in
the mid to late 1940s, and the obligatory silence imposed by the "New
Theory" on the linkage between historical events and textual criticism.
"May it not be," writes David Hirsch, "that the French deconstruc-
tionists carried the self-deceptions and the moral ambiguities and
duplicities of the Nazi occupation over into the post-war period and
misled their readers by insisting that their nihilism was the result of rig-

orous philosophical deliberation instead of the residue of historical exhaustion and moral shame?" (129). As Geoffrey Galt Harpham wrote in his review of *The Deconstruction of Literature* in the *Times Literary Supplement*, August 28, 1992: "Many, including Jewish writers such as Harold Bloom and Derrida, who find themselves scorned and derided in these pages, generally in a context linking literary criticism and Nazi genocide, may well consider that Hirsch's style is a kind of Reign of Terror all by itself" (19). Harpham characterizes this "reign of terror" as an approach to reading that sees Nazism never examined as its unique frame of reference, as the guiding political and ethical grid by which all writing of a certain historical period is judged.

I do not mean to suggest that David Hirsch is alone in his condemnations of France, French intellectuals, and French developments in contemporary literary theory. He draws examples and quotations from French critics and philosophers such as Vladimir Jankelevitch, Luc Ferry, Alain Renault, and Dominique Moisi, each of whom has written about, and these are Hirsch's words, "the French poststructuralist-deconstructionist-postmodernist phenomenon in the light of what we know about Heidegger's lifelong attachment to the ideals of Nazism" (118). David Hirsch also refers to novelists writing in French about the Shoah such as Elie Wiesel and Jorge Semprun. He takes bits and pieces from their texts, and the reception of their texts, and he distorts their contextualizations with the result that the reader is usually given buzzwords instead of arguments, epithets instead of analysis. The figure of greatest evil is "deconstructionist nihilism," whose monstrousness Hirsch reduces to an absurd definition:

> One of the unfortunate, but perhaps not unintended, consequences of deconstructionist nihilism is the imposition of the dogma that all human acts must remain morally undifferentiated, since *difference* exists only in the language system, only as differences in sounds and concepts, in signifiers and signifieds, so that the only difference between a collaborator and a resister is a difference of sound images. (130)

David Hirsch considers his vision to be moral, liberal, humanist. I would argue that it is narrow, tendentious, and the result of an elaborated projection of preconceived ideas. He allows political considerations and national prejudice to dictate judgments about philosophical directions and approaches to the reading of literary texts. He conflates discourses in such a way as to make one leary about crossing boundaries recklessly, or about reading literary texts, philosophical texts, critical or interpretive texts as if there were no significant differences among them. He speaks in a unified voice, and reads other writers as if they, too, were speaking in a unified voice. He uses a scenario in which protagonist and antagonist have become stock figures, in which (French) deconstructors and (French) collaborators, as well as Martin Heidegger and Paul de Man, are paired together and eternally damned for having brought about and been complicitous in the destruction of European Jews.[2]

I have spent much time objecting to the strategy and the tactics of David Hirsch in *The Deconstruction of Literature: Criticism after Auschwitz* though I am neither an epigone of deconstruction, nor a sympathizer of those who would critique deconstruction in the name of its unholy alliance with fascism or Nazism. But I am increasingly convinced, as I noted in the preface, that the reading of French texts, literary and nonliterary, on the Jewish question(s) and presence from Edouard Drumont's *La France juive* (1886) to Jacques Derrida's *Circonfession* (1991) and from Robert Garnier's *Les Juifves* (1583) to Sarah Kofman's *Paroles suffoquées* (1985) calls for an engagement with three occasionally overlapping fields: history (social, cultural, and economic), literary theory, and psychoanalysis. Not one of these fields alone can encompass the complexities of the topic, can cope with events and their effects, events and their translation into writing, nor with the affect of individuals and the group psychology of human beings.

It is, I believe, our *responsibility*, to use Jacques Derrida's italicized word in the epigraph to this chapter, to respond to the multiple and complex questions that have been raised "after Auschwitz" by Jews and non-Jews in French and other languages by reading widely and writing as rigorously and as passionately as we can.

2

Jewish Biblical Literature in French Literature: *Les Juifves* and the Books of Esther

O mon souverain Roi!
Me voici donc tremblante et seule devant toi.
Mon père mille fois m'a dit dans mon enfance,
Qu'avec nous tu juras une sainte alliance,
Quand pour te faire un peuple agréable à tes yeux,
Il plut à ton amour de choisir nos aïeux.
Même tu leur promis de ta bouche sacrée
Une postérité d'éternelle durée.
Hélas! ce peuple ingrat a méprisé ta loi;
La nation chérie a violé sa foi;
Elle a répudié son époux et son père,
Pour rendre à d'autres dieux un honneur adultère.
Maintenant elle sert sous un maître étranger.
Mais c'est peu d'être esclave, on la veut égorger.
Nos superbes vainqueurs, insultant à nos larmes,
Imputent à leurs dieux le bonheur de leurs armes,
Et veulent aujourd'hui qu'un même coup mortel
Abolisse ton nom, ton peuple et ton autel.
Ainsi donc un perfide, après tant de miracles,
Pourrait anéantir la foi de tes oracles?
Ravirait aux mortels le plus cher de tes dons,
Le saint que tu promets et que nous attendons?
                              —Jean Racine. *Esther*, acte I, scène 4

O my sovereign King!
I am here trembling and alone before you.
My father told me a thousand times during my childhood,
That you swore a holy alliance with us,
When you wanted to give yourself a people agreable to your sight,
Your love chose our ancestors.
You promised them with your holy mouth

A posterity that would last forever.
Alas! this ungrateful people scorned your law!
The cherished nation violated its faith;
It repudiated its husband and its father,
And gave to other gods an adulterous honor.
Now this nation serves under a foreign master.
But it is not enough that this nation has become a slave, they
want to kill her.
Our proud conquerors, insulting our tears,
Attribute to their gods the good fortune of their arms,
And hope today that the same mortal blow,
Will abolish your name, your people, and your altar.
Thus a perfidious man, after so many miracles,
Could annihilate the faith of your oracles,
Could rob mortals of the most precious of your gifts,
The saint that you have promised and for whom we are waiting?

What contributed to this elusiveness, I would suggest, is that
Febvre's sixteenth century in Europe is virtually without Jews.
Dreyfusard in his youth and long friend and supporter of Berr,
Bloch, Werth, and many other "Israelites," Febvre had the characteristic attitude of patriotic republican laicity toward the Jews:
they were French citizens first and foremost, their religious practice a matter of family rather than public interest. Nothing here
encouraged him to attend to a Jewish presence in the past, even
when (as we will see in a moment) his scholarly sources might
suggest it."

—Natalie Zemon Davis.
"Rabelais Among the Censors: (1940s, 1540s)"

In his two-volume study of *L'Élément juif dans la littérature française*,
1960 and 1961, which grew out of courses given at the University of Lau-
sanne in the early 1940s, Chanan Lehrmann proposes to study works
and periods that have been neglected and to "take note of the repercus-
sions that the existence of a Jewish cultural world have had, throughout
its history, on French literature" (10). In order to accomplish this task
he establishes four categories: 1. "a passive influence," which includes
writers such as Montesquieu, Voltaire, Saint-Simon, Zola, Anatole
France, Romain Rolland, Georges Duhamel, and Jean-Paul Sartre who
became involved with religious or social aspects of the Jewish question;

2. "an active influence," which includes writers such as Pascal, Bossuet, Racine, Chateaubriand, Lamartine, Victor Hugo, and Claudel, who were inspired by Jewish Holy Scriptures, that is to say, the Jewish Bible read through Christian culture and religion; 3. "Jewish writers or writers of Jewish origin," from rabbis of the Middle Ages to contemporary poets and writers such as Edmond Fleg, Gustave Kahn, André Spire, Albert Cohen, Emmanuel Eydoux, Roger Ikor, and André Schwarz-Bart; 4. "unconscious Jews," those who barely remember their origins and appear to feel themselves to be entirely and uniquely French, writers such as Maurois, Benda, Bernstein, Tristan Bernard—writers in whose writings Lehrmann finds "reminiscences of the thought of their ancestors" (12).

I would like to comment extensively on Chanan Lehrmann's second category, "an active influence," and propose other ways of looking at the place and the function of Jewish Holy Scriptures in French literature an i culture.

It could be maintained, and indeed it will be one of my theses, that the reworking of stories and poems in French literature taken from what is known in Christian discourse as the Old Testament[1] constitutes a major and persistent intertextual presence. This presence is intimately linked to questions and theories of translation involving Hebrew, Greek, Latin, Middle and Modern French, as well as other modern European languages similarly engaged in borrowings and influences. Chanan Lehrmann reminds us that no book has been more frequently translated into French than the Bible (20). In order to make my case I will take as an example of this massive intertextual presence of "Jewish literature" in French literature, language, and culture the biblical accounts in Kings, Chronicles, and Jeremiah as well as a multitude of resonances and echoes from Genesis, Exodus, Numbers, Deuteronomy, Job, Psalms, Proverbs, Isaiah, Ezekiel, Daniel, and others used by Robert Garnier as a basis for his play *Les Juifves* (1583). I also draw on the biblical accounts from Jewish Holy Scriptures of the story of Esther from the book of Esther, used by Jean Racine for his play *Esther* (1689).[2]

I shall also refer to the "Jugements sur *Esther*" made by Madame de Sévigné, Madame de La Fayette, Robert Kemp, Charles Maurron and others, *jugements* that are included in the latest Classiques Larousse version (1975) of *Esther* presented by Jean Borie and in the Bordas edition of 1985 presented by Gabriel Spillebout. These editions, still widely used today in French *lycées*, will allow me to speculate further on the relation between Jewish literature and Jews in more or less official French literary discourse as it is presented through the educational system. In another, more interpretive mode, I shall refer to Marcel Proust's multiple allusions to and quotations from the Old Testament and from Racine's *Esther* in *Remembrance of Things Past*. These allusions and quotations occur particularly in *Combray*, where the narrator describes the two tapestries representing the coronation of Queen Esther in the church at Combray, and in *Sodom and Gomorrah*. Proust's Esther is thus associated with the Guermantes, the narrator's mother, and, later, Albertine and homosexuality. For my comments on the biblical Esther and Racine's *Esther* in Proust, I am indebted to both Eve Sedgwick, *Epistemology of the Closet*, and Antoine Compagnon, *Proust: Between Two Centuries*. Their provocative analyses have led me to conclusions that are different from theirs but that I would probably not have reached without them.

It is not difficult to support the thesis reiterated by Robert Alter and Frank Kermode in their general introduction to *The Literary Guide to the Bible* (1987) "that the Bible is probably the most important single source of all our literature" (2). Nor is it difficult to demonstrate the causal relationship established by Christian church fathers and generations of Christian readers between Jewish Holy Scriptures and the New Testament, which the Old Testament repeatedly foreshadows and by which it is historically and spiritually replaced. The Old Testament, according to this Christian version, is seen as containing the first articulation of a holy alliance between "God" and "men," a holy alliance that culminates in the New Testament. But it is difficult to analyze what the relationship might be in the minds of Christians between the Jewish Holy Scriptures as the major cultural text of Judaism *and* Jews, the relationship, within a predominantly Christian culture such as that of France, between the Book and the people of the book. Do Christians who accept some aspects of the Old Testament view it mainly as prolepsis? Does it retain any Jewish specificity? Does it confirm or subvert whatever anti-Jewish or antisemitic discourses may be prevalent during a particular period of time? These are some of the questions that have guided me and intrigued me during my readings of Garnier's *Les Juifves* and Racine's *Esther*. I would like to note, here, in the body of my text, how deeply indebted I am in my work on Robert Garnier's *Les Juifves* to Damon Di Mauro's very thorough and erudite work written in French, "Entre l'ombre et la réalité: Etude sur *Les Juifves* de Robert Garnier" (Between the shadow and reality: A study of *Les Juifves* of Robert Garnier], a 1991 doctoral dissertation at the University of Wisconsin-Madison. Although Professor Di Mauro's intentions and religious convictions are very different from my own, his interest in "the theme of divine vengeance inflicted on the chosen people" coincides with my interest in the overlapping elaboration from the Renaissance to the present of anti-Jewish and antisemitic discourses.

In *Les Juifves*, as in other Renaissance plays and poems whose sources include the Old Testament, the Jewish Bible is used to prefigure and to announce Christian dogma, that is to say, the accounts of the life, death, passion, and resurrection of Jesus Christ. According to Jewish Holy Scriptures, successive punishments are inflicted by God on the Jews because of their idolatry, their abandoning of the true God, and their refusal to heed the warnings of God's prophets. In texts written during the Renaissance this theme of punishment is reinforced by the New Testament accounts of the Jews killing Christ and the inference that they would pay forever and ever for this crime. Also frequently in Renaissance texts this punishment suggests the pitiful condition of France embroiled in bloody and devastating civil and religious wars.

Les Juifves is based on the story of King Zedekiah (the name in Jewish Holy Scriptures according to the Masoretic text). It is important to note the canonical order of the table of contents in the Hebrew Bible, established at the beginning of the Christian era. This order has a tripartite division: Law, Prophets, and Writings. The story of King Zedekiah, as told in Second Chronicles 36, is at the very end of Writings in the Jewish Bible. On the other hand, in the Catholic and Protestant Bibles, Chronicles is found toward the end of the first division, Legislation and History. The Catholic Bible, based on the Greek translation of the Old Testament, the Septuagint, ends with the Prophets, and their prophesies of the coming of the Messiah. The Jewish Bible, and the difference is essential, ends with the proclamation of Cyrus, king of Persia, concerning the rebuilding of Jerusalem and the return of the Jews to Jerusalem. The last three paragraphs of the Holy Scriptures according to the the Masoretic text make it clear how changes in the ordering of the biblical text affect interpretation and the perpetuation of certain ideological assumptions. These assumptions include the centrality of the figure of Jesus Christ and the fundamental conflict between the two tropes used to refer to Jews: the chosen people and Christ killers. I reproduce the last three paragraphs of the Masoretic text because they underline the discrepancy between the Hebrew and the Greek texts, the Jewish and the Christian versions of the relationship between God and "man," and because they relate specifically to the understanding of Garnier's play:

> Zedekiah was twenty and one years old when he began to reign; and he reigned eleven years in Jerusalem; and he did that which was evil in the sight of the LORD his God; he humbled not himself before Jeremiah the prophet speaking from the mouth of the LORD. And he so rebelled against king Nebuchadnezzar, who had made him swear by God; but he stiffened his neck, and hardened his heart from turning unto the LORD, the God of Israel. Moreover all the chiefs of the priests, and the people, transgressed very greatly after all the abominations of the nations; and they polluted the house of the LORD which He had hallowed in Jerusalem. And the LORD, the God of their fathers, sent to them by His messengers, sending betimes and often; because He had compassion on His people, and on His dwelling-place; but they mocked the messengers of God, and despised His words, and scoffed at His prophets, until the wrath of the Lord arose against His people, till there was no remedy.
>
> Therefore He brought upon them the king of the Chaldeans, who slew their young men with the sword in the house of their sanctuary, and had no compassion upon young man or maiden, old man or hoary-headed; He gave them all into his hand. And all the vessels of the house of God, great and small, and the treasures of the house of the LORD, and the treasures of the king, and of his princes; all these he brought to Babylon. And they burnt the house of God, and broke down the wall of Jerusalem, and burnt all the palaces thereof with fire, and destroyed all the goodly vessels thereof. And them that had escaped from the sword carried he away to Babylon; and they were servants to him and his sons until the reign of the kingdom of Persia; to fulfil the word of the LORD by the mouth of Jeremiah, until the land had been paid her sabbaths; for as long as she lay desolate she kept sabbath, to fulfil threescore and ten years.
>
> Now in the first year of Cyrus king of Persia, that the word of the LORD by the mouth of Jeremiah might be accomplished, the LORD stirred up the spirit of Cyrus king of Persia, that he made a proclamation throughout his kingdom, and put it also in writing, saying: "Thus saith Cyrus king of Persia: All the kingdoms of the earth hath the LORD, the

God of heaven, given me; and He hath charged me to build Him a house
in Jerusalem, which is in Judah. Whosoever there is among you of all His
people—the LORD his God be with him—let him go up." (*The Holy
Scriptures* 1269–70)

The Old Testament, in the revised standard version, 1952, and in the
Jerusalem Bible, 1955, ends with the Book of Malachi. These are the last
words of the Lord to Israel by the prophet Malachi: "Behold, I will send
you Elijah the prophet before the great and terrible day of the LORD
comes. And he will turn the hearts of fathers to their children and the
hearts of children to their fathers, lest I come and smite the land with a
curse" (*The Holy Bible* 750).

Whereas the Hebrew and Jewish version ends with a promise of a
historical return of Jews to Jerusalem, the Greek and Christian version
ends with a double vision of what the prophet Elijah will do and of
God's menacing curse. But let us not forget that the Old Testament
does not end the Christian Bible; Malachi is followed by the four
gospels of the New Testament.

Garnier's play, like Racine's *Esther*, deals with the biblical story and
history of the Jews after the fall of Jerusalem in 586 B.C., the period of
exile known as the Babylonian captivity. The captivity is one of the
most tragic moments in the collective history and memory of the Jewish people, and one of the most fertile in poetic and prophetic literature. Indeed it might be suggested that the events represented and
alluded to in *Les Juifves* form a microcosm for the representation of the
Jewish historical experience in French Christian culture from the end of
the sixteenth century to the end of the twentieth. These events include
the revolt of Zedekiah against God and Nebuchadnezzar, the capture
of Zedekiah and his family, the fall of Jerusalem, the slaughter of
Zedekiah's children before his eyes, and the blinding of Zedekiah,
accompanied by the lamentations of Jewish women echoing Jeremiah's
lamentations in Holy Scriptures, and, somewhere in the course of these
events, frequently at the end as in *Les Juifves*, a prophetic voice
announces the coming of the Messiah. But equally important, and
always implied, is that the Jews will forever be punished first for having
refused and then for having killed Jesus Christ. Whatever happens to
the Jews is a just punishment for disobeying Yahvé and not recognizing
Christ. If the text of *Les Juifves* is Hebraic and Jewish, the message is
Christian. The Jews must pay for their sins with exile, torture, and

death. As Damon Di Mauro writes in his comments on Psalm 137, Super flumina Babylonis: "Car le chant de l'exilé n'est autre que le chant de l'homme déchu" (229; Because the song of the exiled man is none other than the song of the fallen man). And later in his thesis: "The unhappiness that gnaws Garnier's *Juifves* is metaphysical. They are in Babylon like damned souls" (234).[3] This would seem to be one of the major elements of both anti-Jewish and antisemitic discourse.

Racine's *Esther* might appear less harsh in its condemnation of Jews to eternal suffering and less christological in its interpretation of the Old Testament. The first of Jean Racine's biblical tragedies, *Esther* was performed at Saint-Cyr in 1689, by the female students at the school established by the Marquise de Maintenon, Françoise d'Aubigné, daughter of the Protestant poet Agrippa d'Aubigné, and morganatic wife of Louis XIV. In 1651 Louis XIV, unlike his predecessor, had placed the Jews of France under his protection. Jews had been expelled from France by royal decree in 1394 under Charles VI and again in 1615 during the regency of Marie de Medicis. Béatrice Philippe, in her impressive study *Etre juif dans la société française du moyen âge jusqu'à nos jours* (To be Jewish in French society from the Middle Ages to the present; 1979), notes that during the sixteenth and seventeeth centuries in France there existed an "antisémitisme sans juifs" (antisemitism without Jews), and that many French men and women who were preoccupied by demonology viewed Jews as emissaries of the devil. This resulted in an obsessive tendency to see Jews everywhere. In fact, at the time of the first performance of *Esther*, and four years after the Revocation of the Edict of Nantes, there were about 25 to 30,000 Jews in France out of a general population of 18,800,000, and most of these Jews lived in Alsace, which, incidentally, had only become French in 1678. We may wonder whether or not Jean Racine knew any of them, or, as I asked in a similar vein earlier, what possible connection might have existed in Racine's mind, or in the minds of those who saw his play performed, between the Jews of Holy Scriptures and the real Jews of late seventeenth-century France?

In his preface to *Esther* Racine is or pretends to be surprised by the success of his play beyond Saint-Cyr, surprised by the success of a play whose story is "full of important examples of the love of God and of being uninfluenced by the world in the world" (812). But it is the end of his preface that may seem surprising today. Racine answers the critiques of those who found the last chorus a bit long in the following manner:

> But what would one have said of these young Israelites who had made so many vows to God for their deliverance from the horrible peril in which they were, if this peril having passed, their thanking was half-hearted? They would have sinned directly against the praiseworthy habit of their nation, in which every grace received from God was answered immediately by long hymns, for example those of Mary the sister of Moses, of Deborah, and of Judith, and of so many others with which Holy Scriptures are full. It is said that even today Jews celebrate with abundant gratitude the day that their ancestors were liberated by Esther from the cruelty of Haman. (813–14)

Clearly, Racine is more familiar with Jewish religious practices related in the Old Testament than he is with the religious practices of Jews who are his contemporaries. The "on dit que" (it is said) might even suggest that Racine was astonished that Jews did indeed still exist and that they would still celebrate their memories of deliverance and give thanks to God. The preface proposes that for Racine Jewish literature is sacred literature, and that Jews have little or no existence beyond the Old Testament. Jean Giraudoux, in his book *Racine* (1930), makes a similar evaluation: "Never did Racine come closer to the ancient, biblical truth than in the description of the magnanimity and the realism of the Jews of whom he had perhaps never known a living example" (10).

Racine's reaction is echoed by that of a colleague of mine at the University of Wisconsin-Madison, Yvonne Ozzello, who remembers studying *Esther* in her *lycée* at Versailles just after the Second World War. I asked Yvonne Ozzello whether any comments were made by the professor (or by students) to connect the plight of the Jews in France and Europe during those years with the plight of the Jews during the Babylonian captivity. She answered with a strong "No!" and explained that for her, and she thought for her classmates, the dramatis personae in *Esther* were not considered as Jews but as seventeenth-century figures in a play by a seventeenth-century writer, and that the sonority of the alexandrine lines is what captivated the students. Yvonne Ozzello's remarks are confirmed by the critical apparatus and the *judgments* included in the Classiques Larousse edition of *Esther* (1986).

Within the Jewish Bible the story of Esther is placed among Writings, and comes after Ecclesiastes and before Daniel. The Hebrew version, which is the version used by Jews today, is considerably briefer than the Greek version, written for the Jews of the diaspora between 250 and 130 B.C. (the version of the Septuagint), used by Catholics and some Protestants. In the Catholic Jerusalem Bible the story of Esther is placed after Toby and Judith and before Maccabees, and, like the Septuagint, it begins with Mordecai's dream, which is absent from the Jewish Holy Scriptures. Also absent from the Jewish version is the name of God, which occurs fifty times in the Greek text, and Esther's prayer to God before her first unauthorized meeting with Ahasuerus, which Racine follows very closely from the Greek version. The Greek version emphasizes God's "miraculous and saving acts" (Freedman, *The Anchor Bible Dictionary* 2:631) whereas the Hebrew version focuses on the establishment of Purim. Clearly Racine used the Greek version adopted by Saint Jerome in the Vulgate, which, since the Council of Trent between 1545 and 1563 and during the Counter-Reformation, has been the official Bible of the Catholic Church.

Even if the origins of the name Esther and of the festival of Purim are other than what we read in the stories that have come down to us in Hebrew and in Greek, Esther remains one of the major female figures in Jewish culture. Her story has become one of the most frequently retold and one of the most frequently subject to criticism and to praise. Among the detractors of the Book of Esther are Martin Luther, who wrote: "I am so hostile to this book [2 Maccabees] and Esther that I could wish that they did not exist at all; for they judaize too greatly and have much pagan impropriety" (*Weimar Ausgabe* 3:302 quoted in Freedman, *The Anchor Bible Dictionary* 2:635).

Although the twelfth-century Jewish scholar Maimonides ranked the Book of Esther as second only to the five books of Moses, some twentieth-century Jewish scholars such as S. Ben-Chorin have advocated that Jews abandon the book and its holiday. But, in general, the Book of Esther has enjoyed considerable popularity among Jews in spite of questions regarding its historical authenticity, its canonicity, its "vengeful, blood-thirsty, and chauvinistic spirit" (Freedman, *The Anchor Bible Dictionary*, 2:637), and its possible relation to pagan rites.

For many Jews the story of Esther relates the origin of a national liberation festival, the most joyous of all Jewish festivals. Doomed to total extermination through the machinations of Haman, the evil counselor of the Persian king Ahasuerus, the Jews are saved by the actions and courage of Mordecai and his niece Esther. Esther is the wife of the king and a *closet* Jew, the very epitome of a Marrano. Those elements of the story that are most important for our purposes, and for Racine's play, include Haman's visceral and long-standing hatred of Jews, and his virulent anti-Jewish discourse, Esther's hiding of her Jewish origins and her behavior as an assimilated Jew, and Esther's reiteration in the first part of her prayer to God, which I have used as an epigraph to this chapter, of the major tenets of Judaism as understood by a believing Christian: the sacred alliance between God and his chosen people, the Jews, Jewish idolatry, Jewish fear, and a realistic fear, of total extermination, the belief in the Messiah, the belief that God can and will intervene miraculously in human affairs and determine the outcome, frequently by massacring the enemies of the Jews.

For my purposes the biblical versions of Esther in French and Racine's play of the same name are equally important as examples of a significant Jewish biblical presence in French writing. In both the Bible in French (whatever the version) and in Racine's play, the story is set in a Manichaean universe in which Haman is evil, Mordecai and Esther are good, and the king Ahasuerus is easily swayed by his counselors and by his passion first for Vashti and then for Esther. The major difference between Racine's text and the biblical versions is that Racine's play is in verse with a chorus of young women that recites and sings accompanied by music. Because the play is written in twelve-syllable lines and in rhyming couplets, the repetition of certain key words assumes greater prominence than it would in prose. For example, the word *secret* or *secrets* is repeated four times in the first scene of act 1, thereby emphasizing the importance of Esther's being Jewish but not being known as a Jew by either the king or Haman. There are also in Racine's play numerous borrowings from other texts of the Old Testament such as Proverbs, Lamentations, Jeremiah, Psalms, and Deuteronomy. For those readers familiar with the texts of the Bible, there are recognizeable echoes. These echoes receive precise confirmation from notes written on a version of the original manuscript of the play now in the Library at Toulouse. It had been thought that these notes were written by Racine, but more recent scholarship proposes that these notes were written by one of Racine's daughters.[4]

There are three significant differences between the biblical versions and Racine's play upon which I would like to dwell. The first is the reac-

tion of the king when he is told by Esther, during her second unauthorized visit and in the presence of Haman, that she is Jewish. The second
is Esther's response to the king's reaction. The third is the aftermath of
the king's decision to kill Haman and to allow the Jews to slaughter
their enemies.

In Racine's play Esther announces her Jewishness to the king in the following line: "Esther, Seigneur, eut un Juif pour son père" (Esther, my
Lord, had a Jew as a father), and the king responds:

> "Ah! de quel coup me percez-vous le coeur?
> Vous la fille d'un Juif? Hé quoi? tout ce que j'aime
> Cette Esther, l'innocence et la sagesse même,
> Que je croyais du ciel les plus chères amours,
> Dans cette source impure avait puisé ses jours?
> Malheureux!" (*Oeuvres complètes* 1:853)

> Ah! with what a blow do you stab my heart?
> You the daughter of a Jew? You, all that I love
> This Esther, all innocence and wisdom,
> Whom I thought a loving gift from heaven,
> You owe your birth to this impure source?
> Woe is me!

The biblical versions do not insist on the paternal line. Jewishness
according to Jewish law is conferred by the mother. But in this play, in
which it is the relationship between Mordecai and Esther that is important, one can justify the emphasis on the paternal line, since Mordecai
is, depending on the biblical version, either Esther's father's brother or
his nephew, either her uncle or her cousin. A more important difference
between the play and the Bible is Ahasuerus's reaction in the former to
the unveiling of Esther's secret. In the play Ahasuerus reveals his dislike,
even his disgust for Jews, and uses a conventional anti-Jewish metaphor,
"source impure" (impure source), which has the added irony of playing
on the opposition pure/impure so central to Jewish law. Furthermore,
in the play, in contrast to the biblical versions, Esther then asks the king
for the right to explain the situation of the Jews by giving a brief history
of the Jews and their relationship to their omnipotent God. It could
therefore be said that Racine's version of the story of Esther does not
attribute anti-Jewish discourse to only the evil characters while at the

same time his *Esther* is more didactically religious than the Greek version on which he relies so heavily.

In all the biblical versions the story of Esther ends with descriptions of scenes of "massacre" and "extermination" by the Jews of their enemies and the rehabilitation and elevation of Mordecai. The numbers and names of the dead are given, and Esther keeps asking the king for the right to order still more carnage. In Racine's play the massacre of the enemies is less massive and less fierce. Racine's *Esther* ends with the chorus thanking God, praising great kings, recognizing Esther's courageous love for her God and her triumph, and celebrating the liberation of the Jews. The ending of Racine's play proposes to the reader familiar with the Bible comparisons with the stories of Joseph and Moses in the Torah. Like Moses's, Esther's religious identity is kept a secret, like Moses she must appear more than once before the ruler who holds her people captive, like the Egyptians, the Persians (in the biblical versions), are massacred in great numbers, and, like Passover, Purim is instituted as a way of commemorating the events. The major difference, of course, is that Esther is a woman, and that between Esther and God there are important male intermediaries like Mordecai and Ahasuerus.[5]

Racine's play was a great success. The courtiers rushed to see a play and to be seen seeing a play that had been commissioned by Madame de Maintenon and that was presided over by the king himself during the performances at Saint-Cyr. In her letter of February 21, 1689, Madame de Sévigné writes to her daughter, Madame de Grignan, about the performance of *Esther* she attended. She comments ecstatically about her appreciation of the poetry, the music, the songs, the acting of the young women, the adaptations of biblical passages, the fidelity to "l'histoire sainte," and she narrates her brief exchange with the king:

Le Roi vint vers nos places, et après avoir tourné, il s'adressa à moi, et me dit: "Madame, je suis assuré que vous avez été contente." Moi, sans m'étonner, je répondis: "Sire, je suis charmée, ce que je sens est au-dessus des paroles." Le Roi me dit: "Racine a bien de l'esprit." Je lui dis: "Sire, il en a beaucoup; mais en vérité ces jeunes personnes en ont beaucoup aussi: elles entrent dans le sujet comme si elles n'avaient jamais fait autre chose." Il me dit: "Ah! pour cela, il est vrai." Et puis sa Majesté s'en alla, et me laissa l'objet de l'envie; comme il n'y avait quasi que moi de nouvelle venue, il eut quelque plaisir de voir mes sincères admirations sans bruit et sans éclat. M. le Prince, Mme la Princesse me vinrent dire un mot. Mme de Maintenon, un éclair; elle s'en allait avec le Roi; je répondis à tout, car j'étais en fortune." (*Lettres choisies* 133–34)

> The king came toward us, and, after having walked around, he spoke to me and said, "Madame, I have the certainty that you were pleased." Without appearing astonished, I answered, "Sire, I am charmed; what I feel is beyond words." The king said, "Racine is very intelligent." I said, "Sire, he is indeed, but in truth so are the young women: they play their roles as if they had never done anything else." He said, "Ah! that is true." And then His Majesty moved on, and I became an object of envy; since I was the only new spectator present, there was some pleasure in seeing my sincere admiration without noise and without fuss. The prince and the princess came and said a word to me. Madame de Maintenon passed quickly; she left with the king; I acknowledged everyone, because it was my lucky day.

It is worth noting that Madame de Sévigné does not hide her pleasure at being spoken to by the king while others watched, nor does she hide from the king her admiration for the young women who performed all roles in the play. This manner of relating what others do not put into words is particularly striking and relevant for my interests. About four months later, on June 26, 1689, Madame de Sévigné writes to her daughter and comments on her daughter's description of a visit to Avignon, particularly the Jewish quarter:

> Mais vous triomphez en parlant des juifs; je sens de la pitié et de l'horreur pour eux, et je prie Dieu avec l'Eglise qu'il leur ôte le voile qui les empêche de voir que Jésus-Christ est venu. . . . Cette haine qu'on a pour eux est une chose extraordinaire. *Esther* nous a pourtant donné une jolie idée des jeunes juives; nos chrétiens n'auraient point eu d'horreur pour elles. (*Correspondance* 3:625–26)

> But you are at your best when you speak of the Jews: I feel pity and horror for them, and I pray to God that with the Church he will remove the veil that prevents them from seeing that Jesus Christ has come. . . . This hatred that one has for them is an extraordinary thing. *Esther* gave us a pleasant image of young Jewish women; our Christian gentlemen would not have felt repulsion for them.

Madame de Sévigné seems to be one of the rare spectators to have made a connection—a written recorded connection—between what she saw in the play *Esther*, based on the trials and tribulations of the

Jews of the Old Testament, and the conditions of real Jews, of real Jewish women. The "jolie idée" to which Madame de Sévigné refers may appear superficial and to concern merely the physical aspect of the young actresses, the daughters of impoverished noblemen, none of whom would have been, in fact, Jewish. But more is involved here than the physical attributes of Jewish women and their possible attractiveness for Christian men. Madame de Sévigné begins by questioning the hostile attitude toward Jews, and suggests that it is excessive. Although she repeats the Church's official position on the conversion of the Jews, this is one of the rare instances in which a connection is made between represented Jews and real Jews. And what is even rarer is that from this connection emerges a questioning of the doxa. This questioning takes place in the apparent contradiction between her own feelings of "pity" and "horror" for Jews based on her daughter's letter and her comment that Christian men would not feel horror for Racine's representation of the "young Jewish women." I am not prepared to generalize any further than to note the particular qualities of Madame de Sévigné's style and the originality of her analysis.

The first of Madame de Sévigné's letters that comments on a performance of *Esther* she attended is one of the "Judgments on *Esther*" in the Classiques Larousse edition of Racine's play. Whatever differences may exist in the evaluation of the structure of the play or its fidelity to the Bible, all the *judgments* written before the end of the Second World War note the beauty of the "diction," that is to say the order of the words and the words themselves. And all the judgments that consider the question of sources and interpretation agree that *Esther* is, in the words of K. Loukovitch, "a Christian tragedy," and that Racine, like his contemporaries, particularly Bossuet, read the Bible through Christian eyes. However, in the Bordas edition of *Esther* (1985) there is, under the rubric "A Study of *Esther*" a category called "*Esther* and politics." And here we find a quotation from the critic Robert Kemp, written in *Le Temps*, January 31, 1938, after a performance of *Esther* at the Comédie-Française. Robert Kemp makes a connection between *Esther* and Western Europe in the late 1930s:

> There is no spectator today who, more easily than a spectator in 1689, would not see in *Esther* the tragedy of antisemitism. . . . Racine's genius completes and illuminates the Bible. The Bible gives childish reasons for Haman's hatred, reasons that Voltaire mocks. . . . *Esther* reveals the racial

antagonism between the Persians and the Israelites. . . . Haman reasons like Hitler. (124)[6]

Even the judgments written after the Second World War and included in the Classiques Larousse do not, with one exception, make any connection between the persecution of the Jews in *Esther* and the persecution of the Jews in the contemporary world. If the religious question is raised, it is only in terms of Racine's religious beliefs and whether or not the Jews might be a camouflage for either the Jansenists of Port-Royal or the persecution of the Protestants. Of those critics cited in the judgments, only Charles Mauron, but without making any direct allusion to anti-Jewish or antisemitic sentiment, proposes a level of analysis different from the discourse that emphasizes Biblical sources and public events of the seventeenth century.

As I suggested in my first chapter on "Theoretical Considerations," historical analysis is rarely sufficient to construct an adequate argument about the Jewish question or presence. Although it might seem excessive to suggest that the late arrival of psychoanalytic theory on the French intellectual scene may to some degree be related to Freud's Jewishness, I will discuss this possibility in chapter 4. Here I would only insist that Charles Mauron in his search for evidence of the writer's unconscious in the text makes an equation between Esther's secret that she is Jewish and Racine's secret that he is a Jansenist. This focus on secrets that are hidden opens the text. "Esther's crime is her race—a familial flaw, a new form of original sin" (143). The need to hide one's origins, one's familial belonging, connects the Jewish presence and absence within Racine's play, points to the guiding metaphor of the Marrano, and, in unexpected ways, helps me to sort out the complex relationship between Jewish biblical literature and French literature. Nowhere is this complexity more marked than in the writing of Marcel Proust.

> Proust was himself (on his mother's side) half-Jewish; and for all his Parisian sophistication, there remains in him much of the capacity for apocalyptic moral indignation of the classical Jewish prophet. That tone of lamentation and complaint which resounds through his whole book, which, indeed, he scarcely ever drops save for the animated humor of the social scenes, themselves in their implication so bitter, is really very un-French and rather akin to Jewish literature." (Edmund Wilson, *Axel's Castle* 144)

Many French writers have been passionate and rigorous readers of Racine, but relatively few of these passionate and rigorous readers have payed as much attention to *Esther* in their fictional work as has Marcel Proust. In *Remembrance of Things Past* as well as in *Contre Sainte-Beuve* (Against Sainte-Beuve), Racine's *Esther* figures as an important intertext that we can analyze both for its multiple functions in Proust's texts and for the way in which the presence of *Esther* provides the occasion to open theoretical discussion on the relationship between intertextuality and the vexed question of social and cultural assimilation.

In the section of *Contre Sainte-Beuve* entitled "Conversations avec Maman," published in 1954 but written before *Remembrance of Things Past* between 1908 and 1910 and in a simpler, more directly autobiographical style, the strong ties between mother and sickly son are represented through a comparison with the couple Esther and Ahasuerus. The mother is a discreet, obedient Esther and the son, the narrator, is a despotic, tyrannical Ahasuerus. The comparison is further enriched and deepened by the narrator's reference to his mother's face, "the beautiful lines of her Jewish face marked by a Christian sweetness and Jansenist courage" (128). This portrait of a Jewish *and* a Christian Esther in both Racine's version and in Proust's nevertheless constitutes an exceptional moment in Proust's text. For here, and not ever in *Remembrance of Things Past*, the narrator's mother is referred to as Jewish, or at least as having a "Jewish face." This unveiling is accompanied by the memory of Reynaldo Hahn's singing the songs he composed for the chorus of young girls in *Esther*. It is important to note that the mother's "coming out" as Jewish is placed in the same paragraph as the narrator's "coming out" in relation both to his Jewish mother and to his intimate friend, the composer Reynaldo Hahn. The narrator's own ethnic and sexual identity, so carefully protected in *Remembrance of Things Past*, is obliquely disclosed in this earlier text in relation to Racine's play. It is also not without importance that the narrator reports on his mother's preference for *Esther*: "this *Esther* that she preferred above all others" (127). Esther, too, hides her Jewish identity from Ahasuerus until she is obliged by Mordecai to reveal it in order to save the Jews from annihilation.

In *Remembrance of Things Past* Esther's first appearance is as a figure in a tapestry in the church at Combray. The narrator describes the tapestry as representing the crowning of Esther and comments on the local tradition that sees in Ahasuerus a resemblance with a French king and in Esther a resemblance with a woman of the Guermantes family with whom the king was in love. In the Combray church then, and toward the beginning of Proust's long novel, the Hebrew biblical Esther is already assimilated into a Christian setting. The narrator's comments on the Esther tapestry are preceded by the mention of stained glass windows and of Saint-Louis and followed by references to Saint Eloi, Dagobert, and the son of Louis le Germanique. The Hebrew Esther is immediately situated in an amorous setting as the object of the king's affection. She is also associated from the beginning of *Swann's Way* with the theme of art and with the Guermantes family, particularly the Duchesse de Guermantes, with whom the narrator will fall in love. The Esther who appears in *Combray* is not yet Racinian. She will become so in *Within a Budding Grove* when the themes of social snobbery and of homosexual passion and hidden identity become the obsessive focus of the narrator's discourse.

There is in *Within a Budding Grove* a curious doubling of Esther. Esther—the biblical Esther of Racine's play—will be joined by Esther Lévy, sometimes mentioned by name but more usually referred to anonymously as one of Bloch's cousins, a young woman, like the young women in the chorus of Racine's play, and a lesbian, perhaps one of Albertine's intimate friends. Esther Lévy, certainly a minor character in the novel, nonetheless bears an unusual burden. Like her uncle Nissim Bernard, she is one of the rare characters who is both Jewish and homosexual, belonging to the two "races maudites" (damned races). But what are we to make of her name *Esther*, or, rather, how are we to read Esther Lévy in relation to that other biblical Esther of the tribe of Benjamin and Jean Racine's play? Perhaps we can find a path toward a still more complex interpretation in the conversation between the narrator and the Baron de Charlus that takes place during a matinee at the home of Mme de Villeparisis. Charlus is interested in the narrator's friend, Bloch, whom he has just seen, but he hides his interest with a series of antisemitic verbal attacks, suggesting that Bloch is not French because he is Jewish in the same way that Dreyfus was not French because he was Jewish and therefore could not have betrayed France. Charlus's more conventional antisemitic discourse is followed by a series of sadistic scenarios addressed to the narrator, asking him to act as intermediary:

Perhaps you could ask your friend to allow me to be present at some
great festival in the Temple, at a circumcision, with Jewish chants. He
might perhaps take a hall, and give me some biblical entertainment, as
the young ladies of Saint-Cyr performed scenes taken from the Psalms
by Racine, to amuse Louis XIV. You might even arrange parties to give
us a good laugh. For instance a battle between your friend and his father,
in which he would smite him as David smote Goliath. That would make
quite an amusing farce. He might even, when he was about it, deal some
stout blows at his hag (or, as my old nurse would say, his "haggart") of a
mother. That would be an excellent show, and would not be unpleasing
to us, eh, my young friend, since we like exotic spectacles, and to thrash
that non-European creature would be giving a well-earned punishment
to an old camel. (*The Guermantes Way* 1:922)

Charlus's sadomasochistic sexual fantasies seem to take extra
nourishment from Bloch's Jewishness. The suggestion is that Jewish
biblical texts recounting the laws governing circumcision and the stories of violence involving David and Goliath and others are like a
pornographic source book. Esther Lévy's presence may be a sign of how
the narrator reads the biblical and Racinian Esthers. At the same time
Charlus compares himself to Louix XIV, taking his pleasure where and
when he sees fit because it is his due. The ultimate in repressed fantasy,
and not only because it is the last in a series, is the whipping of the
mother's old body. This seems less to recall an episode in the Jewish
Bible than to contain a prophecy of things to come, both in the text in
which Charlus will be whipped in a male brothel and in French and
European history during the Second World War, when old women and
men, Jewish and non-Jewish, were whipped to death.

Still later in the text, and again in relation to Bloch, Charlus resumes
his anti-Jewish discourse with examples of Jewish sadism:

When they perform in Holy Week those indecent spectacles that are
called "the Passion," half the audience are Jews, exulting in the thought
that they are going to hang Christ a second time on the Cross, at least in
effigy. At one of the Lamoureux concerts, I had a wealthy Jewish banker
sitting next to me. They played *The Boyhood of Christ* by Berlioz, he was
quite shocked. But he soon recovered his habitually blissful expression
when he heard the Good Friday music. (*Cities of the Plain* 2:359)

Accusations of Jewish sadism have spread through the text from the
rite of circumcision, which is the sign of Abraham's covenant with God,

to Bloch fighting with his father and whipping his mother, to kosher butchers on the rue des Rosiers, to the Jews as the killers of Jesus Christ. This last accusation is the central narrative in Christian anti-Jewish discourse, and it resonates very differently from the sadomasochistic scenarios that seem to emanate from Charlus's personal pathology.

Deicide and the blood libel are accusations with a long and cruel history, and they affect all Jews, although in general they are aimed at men rather than women. Deicide is not an event in Jewish Holy Scriptures, but it is a Christian cultural narrative. And if Esther, like the prophets Jeremiah and Isaiah, accuses the Jews who are her contemporaries of worshipping false gods and turning away from the true God, this can easily be read in Christian terms as a sign of the Jews' infidelity, as a prolepsis for the greater sin to follow. When Charlus comes to the end of his tirade against the Jews, prompted by his repressed desire for Bloch and undoubtedly for the narrator too, and after Charlus has insisted that a people capable of producing Spinoza cannot be condemned in toto, the narrator makes the following comment: "This speech, anti-Jew or pro-Hebrew—according as one regards the outward meaning of its phrases or the intentions that they concealed—had been comically interrupted for me by a remark which Morel whispered to me, to the fury of M. de Charlus" (*Cities of the Plain* 2:361). Here, again, the biblical, the Jewish, the antisemitic, and the erotic are so tightly intertwined that although one can identify the disparate strands one cannot separate them, and certainly one cannot easily determine relations of cause and effect.

Yet the presence of this knot, which is impossible to untie in Proust's text, points to the difficulty of making moral or political judgments in relation to a literary text about the anti-Jewish or antisemitic intentions, on the one hand, and the effects produced, on the other, by the words of the writer, the narrator, or other protagonists. Charlus, like Esther, is a fictional character, and also like her he carries with him, when his name appears on the pages of Proust's book, a wealth of references, themes, and figures. Like Esther, he does not, he cannot stand alone. Like Esther, that which he tries to hide is revealed. But, unlike Esther, there is nothing Jewish about Charlus, and he exists neither in the pages of Jewish Holy Scriptures nor in the pages of a play by Jean Racine. But the fact that he is there with all the Esthers in Proust's novel demonstrates the inevitability in literary texts of intertextuality and assimilation. From the moment that the language is French and not Hebrew, from the moment that there are literary references from a variety of periods in time and places in space, there can be no Jewish literature in French literature that is not contaminated by Christian culture and the French language. But this contamination is not a negative condition. There can be no pure Esther, no Esther who is not already a combination of Hebrew text, Greek text, the Vulgate, and all the translations and editions in so many of the languages of the world.

It is also interesting to note, based on the *Souvenirs* of Mme de Caylus, a niece of Mme de Maintenon, the ironic discrepancy between Mme de Maintenon's intentions in asking Racine to write a play for the young women of Saint-Cyr and the effects produced by this play on Marcel Proust two hundred years later. According to Mme de Caylus, the young women of Saint-Cyr had interpreted Racine's *Andromaque* with such passion that Mme de Maintenon begged Racine "to write for her in his moments of leisure, some kind of moral or historical poem from which love could be completely banished. . . . *Esther* was staged a year later" (Caylus 596) If these were indeed the intentions of Mme de Maintenon, and if Racine tried to follow her directions, clearly he could not, nor could she, control the effects produced by the play on spectators and readers whether they be contemporaries or members of succeeding generations. For Marcel Proust, affected by the accounts of the original performances at Saint-Cyr in which young women played male and female roles, affected also by the constraints and tensions between Esther and Ahasuerus as well as by the presence of a single-sex chorus, Racine's *Esther* is an erotically charged play.

To conclude this chapter I will return to the question of the degree to which the Jewish text of Esther is displaced, contaminated, deflected by the Christian text and the dominant Christian culture. In his study *Autour de l'Esther Racinienne* (Concerning Racine's *Esther*; 1985) René Jasinski reviews the different arguments that have been advanced to explain Racine's choice of the story of Esther and his desire to comply with Mme de Maintenon's request for a play. Jasinski refutes the notion that Racine acted as a courtier uniquely interested in reinstating himself in the good graces of the king and his morganatic wife. He also refutes the notion that *Esther* is a plea for clemency either for the Protestants or for the Jansenists of Port-Royal. Instead, Jasinski adopts the argument of Jean Orcibal in his work, *La Genèse d'Esther et d'Athalie*

(The Genesis of *Esther* and *Athalie*; 1950): "On the other hand, more or less comparable to the persecution feared by the Jews, under the reign of Ahasuerus, there was the persecution carried out against the Daughters of Childhood" (11).

"The Daughters of Childhood" (Les Filles de L'Enfance) was a congregation of young women founded in 1662 in Toulouse by Mme de Mondoville. The congregation prospered and branches were created in other French cities. Verbally attacked by the Jesuits, the congregation was finally obliged to disband. The young women were dispersed and Mme de Mondoville was exiled and imprisoned in 1686. In 1687 Antoine Arnauld, theologian and defender of the Jansenists, wrote and published a polemical piece on the oppression of innocence through calumny, on the violence and inhumanity inflicted on the young women. Orcibal proposes, and Jasinski concurs, that Racine read Arnauld's text, and that this was the genesis of *Esther*. Further, Orcibal is convinced and Jasinski accepts that Mme de Maintenon was to play the role of Esther, and that she would explain to the king the allusions in the play to the disturbing real events that had taken place. What I find significant is that both Orcibal and Jasinski are looking for analogies within the France of the late seventeenth century for the plight of the Jews at the time of Ahasuerus, and that it is the theme of unjust persecution that directs their discourse "concerning Racine's *Esther*."

3

"Sapho 1900": Imaginary Renée Viviens, Charles Maurras, and the Rear of the Belle Epoque

> Indeed, I intend to show that the intellectual assumptions which underlay the turn of the century's cultural war on women, also permitted the implementation of the genocidal race theories of Nazi Germany.
>
> —Bram Dijkstra, *Idols of Perversity*

In this chapter I try to show what the proponents of a French national and antisemitic literature, the proponents of a French women's literature, and the proponents of an international (Western) Lesbian literature have in common; how their grounds for inclusion or exclusion in a representative body of work depend on the critics' adherence to certain principles of representation and narration, or on their views of the writer's sexual identity and origins.

Renée Vivien, the pseudonym for Pauline Tarn, 1877–1909, was born in London of an English father and an American mother; she spent much of her childhood in Paris. Her father died in 1886, and she began to write verses in French in 1887 at the age of ten. The published stories of her life, those that have been written by others than herself, focus on women whom she desired successively and, in some cases, simultaneously—Violette Shillito, Natalie Clifford Barney, Eveline Palmer, Hélène de Zuylen de Nyevelt, Kérimé Turkyan-Pacha, Jeanne de Bellune, Emilienne d'Alençon, Madeleine Rouveirollis—and older men who were her mentors and friends—Amédée Moullé, Charles-Brun, Eugène Vallée. Her female relationships usually involved geographical displacements: as a child between London and Paris and, later, trips to the United States (Bar Harbor and Bryn Mawr), to Mytilene on the island of Lesbos, and to the Middle East. They also involved Renée

Vivien's identification with and worship of the Greek Lesbian poet Sappho, whose fragments she translated into French.

At her death in 1909—she was thirty-two—Renée Vivien had written approximately twenty separate volumes composed mainly of poems but also of short stories, a novel, and a biography of Anne Boleyn. She had written a multitude of letters and an unpublished diary, part of a collection belonging to Salomon Reinach and deposited at the Bibliothèque Nationale, to be made available to scholars and other readers in the year 2000. Until the Second World War her life and her work received regular if discreet attention by critics interested in "littérature féminine," in the Sapphic tradition in verse and in mores, and in deathbed conversions to Catholicism. André Billy, in his *L'Époque 1900* (1951), coined the phrase "Sapho 1900, Sapho cent pour cent" (Sappho 1900, Sappho 100 percent; 227), implying that Renée Vivien was *the* exclusively Lesbian poet of the belle epoque, and rekindled a mild interest in her biography and in her poetry. The feminist and gay liberation movements of the late 1960s and the 1970s primarily in the United States but also in France, focusing on sociocultural contexts and subversive discourses capable of disrupting patriarchal and/or heterosexual constructions, represented Renée Vivien either as a decadent writer, an imitator of Baudelaire, politically unaware and therefore dangerous as a model, or as a conscious Lesbian feminist living within a Lesbian community in Paris at the turn of century, one of the first women writers to rewrite Western myths from an enlightened Lesbian feminist perspective. Since her early death, variously attributed to some excessive combination of alcohol, drugs, anorexia nervosa, and the desire to die, Renée Vivien has become a cult figure for a group of French male admirers, biographers, and critics such as Charles-Brun (1911), Salomon Reinach (1918), Le Dantec (1930), Paul Lorenz (1977), and Jean-Paul Goujon (1986). Complete editions of her poetry were published in Paris by Lemerre in 1923–1924 and in 1934. In 1986 Régine Desforges published a new biography of Renée Vivien by Jean-Paul Goujon, *Tes Blessures sont plus douces que leurs caresses* (Wounds from you are softer than their caresses), and, in a single volume, the *Oeuvre poétique complète de Renée Vivien* (The Complete poetwry of Renée Vivien), an edition with an introduction and notes by Jean-Paul Goujon.

Her writings in prose are not easily available in French. Her one novel, *Une Femme m'apparut / A Woman Appeared to Me*, originally published in 1904 and revised in 1905, has had no other French edition. The 1904 version is available in English in a translation by Jeannette H. Foster, published in 1976 by the Naiad Press with an introduction by Gayle Rubin. *La Dame à la louve*, a collection of short stories also published originally in French in 1904, was translated into English as *The Woman and the Wolf and Other Stories* by Karla Jay and Yvonne M. Klein and published by Gay Presses of New York in 1983. Renée Vivien's biography of Anne Boleyn was published for the first time in French in 1982 by A L'Ecart.

Renée Vivien has been placed within a variety of traditions, French and comparative, including a Baudelairean tradition, a Lesbian tradition, a tradition of significant women writers "haunted" by "the person and the poetics of Sappho,"[1] and a tradition of turn-of-the-century minor French women poets. Her critics and biographers have, almost without exception, relied on a certain concept of the belle epoque as the context within which her texts were written and her life, before it was written, was lived. These stereotypical, standardized discourses on the belle epoque describe a period in which nature, love, and women were glorified, including the figure of the Lesbian, a period of artistic innovation and feminist activity with Paris as the cultural center of the Western world. But there are other discourses *of* the belle epoque, discourses that tell of and react to the "Death of God," discourses that explicitly or implicitly often use the clichés of social Darwinism to construct antisemitic, nationalist, racist, and sexist theories, thereby strengthening and solidifying the binary categories superior/inferior, white/black, Aryan/Jew, male/female, order/anarchy. These other discourses, from the underside of the belle epoque, are still prevalent today. Therefore, the appropriate intertexts for Renée Vivien, writer and woman, include not only Sappho, Colette, Natalie Clifford Barney, and *l'art nouveau* but also Nietzsche, Freud, and Charles Maurras.

In 1905, a year before the rehabilitation of (Captain) Alfred Dreyfus, Charles Maurras, 1868–1952, one of the leaders of the movement Action Française and the principal pedagogue of monarchist, right-wing ideology in France between the 1890s and 1944, published in the same volume as his *L'Avenir de l'intelligence* (The Future of intelligence) an essay called "Renée Vivien" as part of his *Le Romantisme féminin* (Feminine romanticism).[2] In 1976 the Naiad Press published Jeannette H. Foster's translation of Renée Vivien's *A Woman Appeared to Me* with a preface by Gayle Rubin that in many ways, but not in all, is diametrically opposed to the text by Charles Maurras. I would like to confront the discourse of the nationalist, monarchist, and antisemite with the discourse of the

Lesbian feminist, cultural, and social analyst, and to raise through this confrontation a series of questions that relate to the placing of women writers in French literature. I will attempt to show how both Maurras and Rubin, in brilliant and provocative essays, use the available biographical and textual data to create an imaginary Renée Vivien, to pursue a genealogical illusion, a utopian vision of unity that reinforces a coherent ideological discourse from which metaphysical anguish and the enigma of sexual identity, the thematic core of Renée Vivien's poetry and prose, have been banished. I will also argue that because of the anomalous status of women writers in relation to the traditions of French literature and because of the assumptions about women that inform discourses on women writers at different historical moments, many critics seem unable to resist the power of their own ideological whims in the interpretation of women's texts.

By placing *Le Romantisme féminin* in the same volume as his *L'Avenir de l'intelligence* Charles Maurras informs his readers that the question of women writers and the question of gender cannot be viewed in isolation. His essay on Renée Vivien is embedded in his desire to return to another France, the France of the ancien régime, the France of grace, of charm, and of lightness. Renée Vivien and the three other women writers he discusses—Madame de Régnier, Madame Lucie Delarue-Mardrus, and the Comtesse de Noailles—are presented individually as important, original poets and collectively as a dangerous phenomenon. The very title of the collection of four essays condemns these women writers within Maurras's system: they are either not French by birth or not French in spirit, that is to say, they are "romantic," foreign, through their adherence to a Germanic or Anglo-Saxon literary tradition; they are not working within the French classical tradition, therefore they are marginal; they are not men and therefore they are or should be feminine: resigned, sweet, and patient. What is important in this scheme is that the male/female difference cannot be separated from the French/foreign binary opposition or from the classical/romantic opposition. These four women writers are, in essence, sexually different and racially impure. Moreover, if they manifest any sign of the "risque lesbien" (Lesbian danger), they are a menace to the nation. Let us look more closely at *L'Avenir de l'intelligence* and *Auguste Comte*. These texts will assist us in placing Charles Maurras, as he places "Renée Vivien," in French letters.

But, for those Catholics who have left the faith, this form of nostalgia can become so absorbing that the apologists of their religion have developed an extremely cogent argument. Human life, they say, has only one axis without which it breaks apart and drifts. Without divine unity and its consequences, which are discipline and dogma, mental unity, moral unity, and political unity disappear at the same time; they only come together again if the first unity is reestablished. Without God, there is no longer either true or false, no more rules, no more law. Without God, a rigorous logic equates the worst folly with the most perfect reason. Without God, killing, stealing are perfectly innocent acts; there is no crime that does not become unimportant, no revolution that is not legitimate; because, without God, only the principle of free examination exists, a principle that can exclude everything but that can establish nothing. The Catholic clergy gives us the choice between its dogma, with the extreme degree of organization that accompanies it, and this absolute absence of measure and regulation that annuls or wastes activity. God or nothing is the alternative proposal to those tempted by doubt. (*Auguste Comte* 105)

In 1905 Charles Maurras was nostalgically in search of an order that would resurrect what he imagined to have been the golden age, the garden of Eden of the ancien régime, the period before the French Revolution, a period in which the adjectives *French, Catholic,* and *classical* were synonymous. *L'Avenir de l'intelligence* calls for a counterrevolution, an alliance of intelligence with the old religious and philosophical traditions against those who, like Emile Zola and the "new intellectuals," were threatening civilization. Writing toward the end of the Dreyfus affair, Maurras brings together, in the camp of his enemies, Rousseau, romanticism, foreign influences, the Protestant critical spirit, and the inability of Jewish intellectuals and critics to understand "nos humanités." Charles Maurras was not a believer. He was, like Auguste Comte, one of the "Catholics who have left the faith," one of the Catholics "without God." His attempt to hold onto certain moral and aesthetic values in spite of the "Death of God" explains his interest in Auguste Comte's positivism and his initial attraction to the poetry of women writers who seem to announce a return to simplicity and sincerity of feeling in their poems. Maurras's quest for unity and order refuses contradictions, banishes anarchy and hermeticism, and posits a harmony between "lettres françaises," "l'intelligence," and "le sens national." Maurras is blatantly nationalistic. France, in his texts, has

already replaced the kingdom of God, and if he supports the Catholic
Church as the only institution capable of encouraging adherence to the
old values, it is because he views the Catholic Church as a French institution. Moreover, Frenchness, for Maurras, cannot be acquired:

> People say that culture is moving from right to left and that a new world
> is being formed. That may be. But those who have been newly promoted
> are also newcomers, unless they are their clients or their valets, and these
> foreigners, recently enriched, are terribly lacking either in seriousness
> and reflexion, in spite of their weighty appearance, or in lightness and
> grace, in spite of their false Parisian polish. I find their brutish minds
> superficial! They are so practical, so pliant that they lose the heart and
> soul of everything. How could these people have a genuine taste for our
> humanities? What can they understand about them? Understanding of
> that kind cannot be learned at the university. All the diplomas in the
> world will not make this Jewish critic who is erudite and profound
> appreciate that in *Bérénice* "charming places where my heart adored you"
> is a manner of speaking that is not banal, but simple, moving, and very
> beautiful. (*L'Avenir de l'intelligence* 12)

It would appear then that Renée Vivien, Anglo-American and
Protestant, is ipso facto, and in the company of "this Jewish critic,"
excluded from participating in Frenchness. But because she is a woman
other standards apply. Maurras does not expect Renée Vivien to have
"true philosophical ideas," but he does expect her to have "appropriate
emotions" ("Renée Vivien" 165). Because her texts cannot be judged by
the same criteria as those by which the texts of Baudelaire, for example,
are judged, Maurras does not immediately dismiss her work. His double standard implies that women writers may be placed both in relation
to "lettres françaises" and in relation to other women writers. Although
Maurras seems convinced in his essentialism, convinced that Frenchness cannot be learned if one is not born into it, he is nevertheless surprised by the quality of Renée Vivien's French and by her knowledge of
Latin and Greek as well as English literature:

> Her use of the French language, whether in prose or in verse, is remark-
> ably fluid. There is neither impropriety in the choice of words nor a false
> note in the harmony of sounds. She knows that the mute *e* is responsi-
> ble for the charm of our language. She plays with the eleven-syllable line
> of verse that Verlaine considered the most accomplished of all: "Douceur
> de mes chants, allons vers Mitylène" [Sweetness of my songs, let us sail
> toward Mitylène]. ("Renée Vivien" 148)

Not only is Renée Vivien the faithful disciple of Baudelaire and of Verlaine, but she is often, according to Maurras, their rival.

Indeed, what is most striking about Maurras's essay on Renée Vivien is the serious attention he gives to her poetry and, at the same time, the ironic and indulgent manner in which he treats women, and particularly young women, as thinkers. His text abounds in contradictions. He focuses on two texts by Renée Vivien, "La Genèse profane"/"The Profane Genesis)," in *Brumes de Fjord* (Mists of the Fjord; 1902), and "Prophéties" (Prophecies), in *Cendres et Poussières* (Ashes and Dust; 1903). In both cases he compares Renée Vivien's words to those of Charles Baudelaire, and in both cases he insists on Renée Vivien's superiority and her difference—her superiority because she is a young woman and therefore more natural and more sensual, particularly in relation to the sense of touch, and her difference because she is a woman. It is this tautological concept of absolute difference, accepted by Maurras as clear and evident, as an unquestioned assumption, that his essay does not and cannot justify.

"La Genèse profane," which Maurras compares favorably to Baudelaire's "Blasphèmes," is a prose poem in twenty-one stanzas that narrates a "profane" version of Genesis. Jehovah, who incarnates strength, creates the sky, man, the heterosexual embrace, and the poet Homer. Satan, who incarnates cunning, creates night, woman, the caress, and the poet Sappho, the Lesbian. And while Homer told of the life and the death of warriors, Sappho sang of:

> The fugitive forms of love, the pallor, and the ecstasy, the magnificent unfolding of hair, the troubling perfume of roses, the rainbow of Aphrodite, the bitterness and the sweetness of Eros, the sacred dances of the women of Crete around the altar illuminated by stars, the solitary sleep while the moon and the seven sisters disappear into the night, the immortal pride that scorns pain and smiles at death, and the charm of feminine kisses rhythmically marked by the muffled beat of the sea expiring under the voluptuous walls of Mytilene.

Maurras uses this poem as an example of the "general spirit" that pervades Renée Vivien's poetry and that informs the reader about Renée Vivien's views on religion, ethics, history, and literature. He finds this poem more Baudelairean than Baudelaire's own poetry, more forceful and more blasphemous. But he also finds the poem "a bit overwritten." Maurras recognizes that Renée Vivien has created her own imaginary

Psappha, a Psappha Baudelaireanized, Christianized, and romanticized. What is interesting is not that praise and criticism alternate, but that there is so little precision in Maurras's comments when he is not engaged in classifying. If one recalls his emphasis in *Auguste Comte* on what is implied in a concept of a world without God, it is curious to note that when a similar theme occurs in the texts of a woman writer, he does not recognize it. Seventy-one years later Gayle Rubin treats this same theme in an apparently very different manner:

> Renée Vivien read widely in myth, legend and ancient literature. She rewrote many of western culture's most cherished myths, replacing their male and heterosexual biases with female and lesbian ones. In these excerpts from "The Profane Genesis" Vivien changes the biblical story into the creation myth of lesbian poetry. (x–xi)

Maurras's essay is moving toward a particular definition of feminine difference, and Rubin's is primarily concerned with discovering ancestors for contemporary Lesbian feminism. Neither Maurras nor Rubin is prepared to read in Vivien's prose poem a Nietzschean rewriting of religious and metaphysical texts. Maurras will allow a woman poet to imitate Baudelaire but not to propose other directions. Rubin will only read a Lesbian poet in terms of post-1968 Lesbian feminist consciousness.

Toward the end of his essay, Maurras reveals the theory of feminine difference on which the belle epoque relied for many of its representations of women:

> Nature has arranged things so that women are bound to conceive of almost everything that touches them strictly in connection with vague ideas of happiness, luck, fatality, and destiny. The future is for them an innate obsession. In vain does the wise Horace warn them that things of the future are not precisely fixed. Women think of themselves as the protectors of being. All women listen to the magnificent resonance in their very entrails of the slightest conjecture about the relationship between what is or was with what will be. A maternal instinct constructs their universe in the form of a cradle, everything must work together to receive their fruit. A superstition, without a doubt. The superstition is complete. A woman without superstition is a monster. One notes, not without pleasure, that in spite of all her devilishness, Renée Vivien did not think of making herself into a thinker. A holy man murmurs: That is what will save her. . . . That is, at any rate, the most natural element of her profoundly feminine art. ("Renée Vivien" 166)

Maurras judges Renée Vivien's "art" on the basis of its conformity to a particular theory of the feminine. This theory depends on the absolute program laid down by nature and on a particular relationship to the future determined by a "maternal instinct." Maurras's presentation emphasizes the notion that what is natural is both inevitable and inferior. But there is no escape. Either a woman is natural and inferior, that is to say, feminine and superstitious, or she is a monster, a thinker, someone who breaks the natural order. The feminine, according to Maurras, is both a constraint and an obligation. The feminine defines limits that must not be transgressed. Within these limits women poets are judged on the degree to which male critics "frissonnent" (shiver) and "frémissent" (tremble) in contact with their poems, the degree to which poems by women produce effects which are sensuous and powerful. As an example of this power Maurras extracts from the poem "Prophéties" the line "One day, you will wilt, ah! my lily!" which he reads as superior to lines on the fear of aging in the poetry of Charles Baudelaire. The difference, for Maurras, is that Baudelaire's "trembling appears to be a rhetorical exercise," whereas Renée Vivien achieves her effects "par la magie du chant" (by the magic of her song; 167). Renée Vivien, the accomplished versifier of the opening pages of the essay, has been transformed by the end into a feminine magician, qualified by the adjective *diabolique* and replaced by the noun *perversité*. The monster is emerging.

Maurras's praise of the feminine disappears from the last chapter of *Le Romantisme féminin*, "Leur principe common" (Their common principle), in which he discusses what Renée Vivien and "Mmes de Noailles, de Régnier et Mardrus" have in common. As in the essay on Renée Vivien, there is in "their common principle" a significant difference between the beginning and the end of the chapter. Maurras begins by placing the four women poets in the tradition associated with the names of Rousseau, Chateaubriand, and Hugo. "We can no longer study Romanticism without referring to Mlle Renée Vivien, Madame de Noailles, Madame de Régnier, and Madame de Mardrus: by resuscitating and enlarging the scope of Romanticism, they illuminate it" (207). The rest of the chapter is subdivided into eight parts: "L'Origine étrangère" (Foreign origin), "D'Étrangetés en perversions" (From strangenesses to perversions), "L'Indépendance du mot" (The Independence of the word), "L'Anarchie" (Anarchy), Le Génie féminin" (Fem-

inine genius), "Le Prestige d'être bien soi" (The Prestige of being oneself), "La Profanation" (Profanation), and "Le Dessèchement" (The
Drying out). As the titles suggest, Maurras raises questions that are not
considered in the essay on Renée Vivien, questions about the dangers
of romanticism, the dangers of women forming a community of
women writers, a secret little world (here, too, the resemblance with
antisemitic rhetoric of the period is striking), and, finally, the greatest
danger of all, perhaps the very definition of monster, the "risque lesbien."

Maurras's text represents romanticism in terms of the feminine and,
through a series of metaphors, concludes that these four women writers are dangerous to the human race. The first and most negative aspect
of romanticism is that the authors who practice it and the ideas that
have influenced them are foreign. The term *métèques indisciplinées*,[3]
which Maurras borrows from a young nationalist writer, M. Duchot, is
used to identify the four women writers who benefit from the advantages of a French culture but who cannot accept "la discipline nationale." It is also used by Maurras to remind his readers that Rousseau,
Mme de Staël, and George Sand were not French:

> The lack of discipline of our young *métèques* only continues a tradition
> that, although it was introduced in France, has nonetheless remained
> separate from the true tradition of French literature. One must under-
> stand the heterogeneity of Sand, of Staël, and of Rousseau or desist from
> censuring their heirs; for the latter are but a wave, the last wave, of that
> gothic invasion for which Geneva and Coppet opened the way. (208)

The opposition now in place is that between France, inheritor of the
classical Greek spirit and Germany, guilty of having infected, over the
past one hundred and fifty years, Greece, Spain, and Italy with its medi-
ocrity. Maurras is not at all troubled by the facts: for example, not one
of the four women writers he discusses is of German descent. It is sufficient for him "that their blood was not from a very pure French vein"
(210). From this moment on the text takes off, as do polemical texts
based on irrational premises, in a series of fanciful accusations that
recall such outrageous and popular antisemitic texts of the belle epoque
as Edouard Drumont's *La France Juive*. The pure and the impure des-
ignate French and non-French; the Romantic tradition, for Maurras, is,
by definition, impure. Maurras reads the same "perversité sensuelle" in

Baudelaire's *Fleurs du Mal/Flowers of Evil* and in Renée Vivien's poems.
He accuses the "mallarmistes" of being feminine in their worship of the
word, and, except for their refusal of obscurity, he finds the same glori-
fication of the word in the writing of the four women. It is important
for our purposes to note that for Charles Maurras, particularly during
the middle years of the 1930s, Germans and Jews are equally despised
and frequently conflated.

But even more dangerous for Maurras than this verbal materialism is
the importance given to the ego, an importance he interprets as a sign
of revolt. Renée Vivien is accused of wallowing in eccentricity, in evil,
in images of death, decrepitude, and illness. The same sensibility that
was praised earlier in *Le Romantisme féminin* as direct and natural is
now condemned; the expression of feeling has become unhealthy. But,
in an unexpected shift, Maurras insists that romanticism has always
been feminine and that the male poets associated with the romantic
movement were subjected to a change of gender; they were feminized.
Suddenly, it is as if Hugo, Chateaubriand, Lamartine, Michelet, Baudelaire, and Verlaine had been contaminated by the feminine, a feminine
that had installed itself perniciously in the very core of romanticism.

The remainder of the essay is a diatribe against woman. In support
of his passion, Maurras quotes an anonymous woman philosopher,
who, writing for several Parisian newspapers under the pseudonym
Foemina, contends that women are more subject than men to bodily
discomforts, that women are governed by the maxim "I suffer, therefore
I am." The insistence on egoism as the feminine trait par excellence
seems to be a satisfactory explanation for Maurras as to why women
were the original discoverers of the aesthetic of harmony. From
"métèques" to "criminelles" to "bacchantes" and "ménades," women
writers constitute, according to Maurras, not only a danger for French
letters but for the entire human race. Again, the parallel with antisemitic rhetoric is obvious:

> Today, more than one woman of distinction repeats an old paradox
> reformulated as a syllogism and propagated as if it were a religious or
> moral doctrine. Woman, they say, is uniquely capable of understanding
> and of receiving, of giving and returning the essence of love that her
> heart desires: "men are hard," "lovers are brutal." . . . These women are
> being listened to. We must not exaggerate the malignancy of the symp-
> tom furnished by our cafes or our women's clubs and certain other char-

acteristics of American or British customs. As far as this topic is concerned, the philosopher has to trust nature, which tells him not to lack
confidence in life. It is nonetheless true that a society of women is in the
act of being organized, a secret little world in which man only appears
as an intruder and a monster, a lecherous and comic toy, in which it is a
disaster, a scandal for a young girl to become engaged, in which a marriage is announced as if it were a burial, a tie between a woman and a
man as the most degrading misalliance. Under the pale grey female
Apollo who illumines this world, girls and women suffice unto themselves and arrange between themselves all affairs of the heart. (229–30)

The question on which Maurras ends his *Le Romantisme féminin* is
whether or not the "cité de femmes" (city of women), the "secret petit
monde" (secret little world), and the "risque lesbien" it implies, is a danger to or a preserver of the naturally feminine. He presents the arguments of those to whom he refers as "superficial observers" as if they
were direct quotations. He avoids giving the source of the quotations,
and it is likely that these arguments are Maurras's own version of what
a positive reading of these women as preservers of femininity might be.
Maurras proposes two major points as counterargument. The first is
that one should not exaggerate the "risque lesbien" because women are
naturally fortified against Lesbianism. The second is that these young
women should be applauded rather than censured. Because their goal is
to become ever more feminine, they do not participate in the movement
of other women who are attempting to become like men and to take the
place of men. These young women are, therefore, protectors of femininity; they are benefactors. Maurras's response to his confected objec-
tions is categorical. He sees the risque lesbien as a powerful, disruptive
force, and although he persistently opposes what is natural to what is
acquired, he senses that a construction of reality which is projected,
repeated, and studied can take on a life of its own or become a second
nature. He is aware that words produce their own reality. The bacchantes who repeat "I, I, I" must inevitably be disloyal to civilization. They
do not become more feminine but rather join with the others in the goal
of imitating men, of pretending to be like men. Even more than the
female doctor or lawyer, they become like an "être insexué," they
become dry. And to be dry implies being without "charme."

What emerges from Maurras's conclusion is that women who think
about their sexuality are most apt to do so in groups, and that these

groups are likely to be inclined toward Lesbianism. The formula, then, is: it is not feminine to think *or* a woman who thinks is ipso facto a Lesbian. Reading the poetry of Renée Vivien, Maurras does not recognize the marks of a thinking woman but rather the marks of a feeling woman. Examining the women writers one by one, examining the text of their lives, Maurras is struck by a Lesbian presence that he can only attribute to a narcissistic concentration on the self. The real danger, then, of "romantisme féminin," is not only that it feminizes men, that it impedes clear communication, and that it relies on foreign, non-French, impure values, but that it changes the natural sexual orientation of women. The effects produced by the texts of "romantisme féminin" are powerful enough to create a second nature. Maurras, in *Le Romantisme féminin*, implicitly equates the menace of Lesbianism with the menace of foreigners, Protestants, and Jews.

The key word in *Le Romantisme féminin* is the word *charme*, the same word that directs Barbey d'Aurevilly's discourse on women in his prefatory dedication of *Les Bas-bleus* (The Blue stockings; 1878).[4] This undefinable charme can only be identified by men of exquisite feeling, thereby eliminating Jews and foreigners. It is the ability of women to seduce men. It is unrelated to literature, art, or science, and it is essential to the maintenance of a social and an aesthetic harmony. Without this charme that emanates from women, men's pleasure, and consequently the meaning of men's lives, evaporates. The risque lesbien, viewed as threatening to this charme, must be diagnosed and the monster eradicated. The two domains, according to Maurras, capable of eroding this charme are metaphysical anguish and the investigation of sexuality. "Sapho 1900," to the dismay of her critics,[5] was concerned with both.

What is for Charles Maurras in 1905 a dangerous "secret petit monde" is for Gayle Rubin in 1976 a "lesbian renaissance." Renée Vivien is no longer a contradictory, menacing figure but the producer of "one of the most remarkable lesbian oeuvres extant" (iv). Charles Maurras was defending his version of Frenchness and maleness against contamination by impure texts and persons. Gayle Rubin celebrates her version of Lesbian feminism by extolling texts and persons who represent "forerunners of the contemporary gay women's movement" (vii). For Maurras as for Rubin, Renée Vivien's texts and life are subversive. In one case the subversion in villainous; in the other it is heroic.

"Sapho 1900" is an ideal textual figure for those critics who maintain a Manichaean, theological view of the world and for whom good and evil, as well as absolute presence, can be located in specific texts. Gayle Rubin welcomes narratives that attack and challenge heterosexual privilege and male bias and that can be read both as fictions and as historical documents. She writes with equal passion about Renée Vivien's texts and Renée Vivien's life. She is primarily interested in the fact that Renée Vivien was a Lesbian and that Lesbian history, difficult to research, is even more difficult to transmit.

Rubin reads the 1904 version of *A Woman Appeared to Me* as a "novel [that] is also a historical document, part of the archival remains of one of the most critical periods in Lesbian history" (iv). In presenting historical and biographical contexts for the novel, Rubin insists on the changes in the concept of homosexuality that occurred toward the end of the nineteenth century, particularly the change from an understanding of homosexuality as a form of behavior to an understanding of homosexuality as an identity or a fixed character. She does not connect this change to the development of racial theories. To be Jewish, for example, during this same period became a question of racial as well as religious difference, a question of character. And this character, for both homosexuals and Jews, depended on theories of strict biological determinism. Rubin does not make the connections that are implicit in Maurras's text between the representation of Lesbians and Jews. Her texts, with its emphasis on the "specialized homosexual communities" in "nineteenth century cities" (v), seems to glorify any evidence of Lesbian society without concern for the ideological premises on which it was constructed. When Rubin writes: "The variety of lesbian society in Paris before 1910 has been charmingly described by Colette" (v), the adverb *charmingly* warns us that in spite of apparent differences there may be a significant resemblance between Maurras's fear of Lesbianism and Rubin's welcoming of it.

But contemporary investigations, such as Bram Dijkstra's in *Idols of Perversity* (1986), into the connections between discourses and representations of women, Lesbians, Blacks, and Jews during the belle epoque must make us suspicious of any discourse that conflates difference and identity and any community that depends on this conflation for its existence. And so it is incumbent upon readers of Gayle Rubin's text to question the unqualified praise she lavishes on Renée Vivien and

Natalie Clifford Barney in such phrases and sentences as "their shared vision of a society in which women would be free and homosexuality honored" . . . or "searching for their own roots, they discovered Sappho and Hellenism. They endeavored to recreate a Sapphic tradition" . . . or "the two women declared themselves pagans, spiritual descendants of the Greeks" (ix). The search for roots and origins betrays the theoretical and ideological presence of social Darwinism and its intersection with religious discourse. We have noted Maurras's insistence on the Greek connection as the basis of the French, male, classical tradition. How curious, then, to find a Greek connection, albeit a "Sapphic tradition," honored by Rubin because it was honored by Renée Vivien and Natalie Clifford Barney. History does not necessarily imply roots, but roots always imply an origin, a source from which one traces an identity that excludes all forms of difference. There is a tendency in the first part of Rubin's essay to uphold the notion of a Lesbian community based on a fundamental, "racial" difference that would be as exclusive as Maurras's French, male, Catholic community.

In the second part of her introduction, Gayle Rubin looks more closely at the text of *A Woman Appeared to Me* and the changes made by Renée Vivien in her retelling of myths and legends. Rubin is at her best in pointing out the play in the text between heterosexual and Lesbian and male and female biases and the ambiguities this play creates for the reader confronted with familiar figures and symbols—such as Saint John, or snakes, or a prostitute—that no longer adhere to their usual sexual interpretation. Like Maurras, in the first part of his essay on Renée Vivien's poetry, Rubin supplies the reader with intertexts and temporarily forgets or abandons ideological rhetoric in favor of precise examples from the texts and relevant anecdotes from Renée Vivien's life.[6] She shows convincingly Renée Vivien's interest in stories that deal with independent women, rebels who refuse men and male desire. Until the last sentence of the introductory essay, there is no sustained attempt, as there is in the beginning of the essay, to make of Renée Vivien's texts or her life and loves a paradigm for a Lesbian tradition. The examples from *A Woman Appeared to Me* and from stories such as "The Veil of Vashti" or "The Eternal Slave" are quoted in their uniqueness or related, when appropriate, to other texts in nineteenth-century French literature. The same is true of Rubin's account of the amorous relations between Barney and Vivien. They are not presented as exemplary. The last sentence is, therefore, disappointing: "At the time of Barney's death, she, Renée Vivien, and the other women linked to them were already being rediscovered by a new generation of Lesbian feminists searching for their ancestry" (xxix).

It would be as serious an error to consider Renée Vivien's Lesbianism a danger to the human race, as Maurras ultimately does, as it would be to treat Renée Vivien as an "ancestor" for a new generation of Lesbian feminists. If she is an "ancestor," then Lesbianism is a family affair, and a family, unlike a freely chosen community of associates, is a closed, imposed biological group. Lilian Faderman, in *Surpassing the Love of Men*, censures Renée Vivien for imitating "French decadent literature," for imitating nineteenth-century male writers who wrote about and who represented Lesbians in their poetry and their fiction. Faderman's condemnation depends on the notion that there is an authentic Lesbian experience, one that has been understood and transmitted by United States Lesbian feminists since the 1970s. Neither Rubin's Lesbian family nor Faderman's authentic and inauthentic Lesbian "experience" is a satisfactory reading or placing of Renée Vivien. If it is unpardonable to proscribe her because she and her texts are dangerous to humanity, it is equally unpardonable to prescribe or proscribe her because she either is or is not part of an imaginary Lesbian feminist family.

It is not Renée Vivien's place in French or in Lesbian literature that it is important to determine but the multiple discursive contexts of the belle epoque that traverse her texts. This cannot be accomplished by critics eager to establish their own arbitrary categories of classification. For it is, in the long run, the desire to classify that links Maurras and Rubin and that makes it difficult for them to approach Renée Vivien's texts. There is not one of Renée Vivien's critics who has acknowledged her preoccupation with metaphysical anguish and with sexual identity. Blinded by their own rhetoric and discourse, her critics have tended to classify "Sapho 1900" in terms of a real Lesbian identity rather than as a symbolic epithet. The result has been the creation of a succession of imaginary "Renée Viviens."

Reading Renée Vivien through Charles Maurras is also to read the "rear" of the belle epoque, the under and often hidden side of an exciting and creative period in which were developing discourses and practices that would permit the acting out in the public domain of unparalleled violence against "this Jewish critic."[7]

4 Jewish Literature and Jewish Writing in French Literature: Albert Cohen and the *Revue Juive*

There is such a thing as Jewish writing.
—Eric Gould, *The Sin of the Book: Edmund Jabès*

On the January 24, 1914, less than a year after he had rejected Marcel Proust's novel *Swann's Way* for publication by the *Nouvelle Revue Française*, André Gide wrote in his *Journal*:

It is absurd, it is even dangerous to attempt to deny the good points of Jewish literature; but it is important to recognize that there is today in France a Jewish literature that is not French literature, that has its own virtues, its own meanings, and its own tendencies. What a wonderful job could be done and what a service could be rendered both to the Jews and to the French by anyone who would write a history of Jewish literature—a history that would not have to go back far in time, moreover, and with which I can see no disadvantage to fusing the history of Jewish literature of other countries, for it is always one and the same thing. This would clarify our ideas somewhat and would perhaps check certain hatreds that result from false classifications.

There is still much to be said on the subject. One would have to explain why, how, and as a result of what economic and social reasons the Jews have been silent until the present. Why Jewish literature hardly goes back more than twenty years, or at most fifty. Why during these last fifty years its development has followed a triumphant progress. Had they suddenly become more intelligent? No, before that they did not have the right to speak; perhaps they did not even have the desire to, for it is worth noting that of all those [Jews] who now speak, there is not one who does so through an imperious need to speak—I mean whose eventual aim is the word and the work, and not *the effect* of that word, its material or moral result. They speak with greater ease than we because they have fewer scruples. They speak louder than we because they have not our reasons for speaking often in an undertone, for respecting certain things. (175–76)

For André Gide, as for Charles Maurras in the preceding chapter, Jewish writers can never make the grade in French. They are loud and uncouth and the best they can hope for as writers is to play a part that can never be theirs. André Gide moves in these opening pages of his *Journal* for 1914 from the shortcomings and some virtues of "the Jewish race" to what is for him the more serious question of "Jewish literature."

We find the same reluctance to consider the Jewish Bible as Jewish literature, the same desire to separate Jewish literature from French literature, to mark the radical distinction between them, and to praise the intellectual and stylistic superiority of the French in Paul de Man's brief article on "Les Juifs dans la littérature actuelle" (Jews in literature today), which appeared in the Belgian newspaper *Le Soir* on March 4, 1941. Paul de Man is eager to diminish the Jewish presence in European post-World-War-I literature, particularly in French literature, and he does so by considerably reducing the list of French Jewish authors, and by excluding Marcel Proust. This makes it easier for Paul de Man to label all French Jewish writers as second rank, to postulate the absolute separation between cultural life—in which the Jews have played too large a role—and the evolution of the novel, in which their participation has been minimal, and to propose, by way of a conclusion, that creating a Jewish colony isolated from Europe would solve the Jewish problem and "would not result in deplorable consequences for the literary life of the West" (*Wartime Journalism, 1939–1943*).

Alain Robbe-Grillet, in his autobiography *Le Miroir qui revient*, notes that the novels he and his mother relished during the 1930s were referred to as "Jewish literature" by his "antisemitic" parents. These were novels in which the characters wallowed in unhappiness and daily despair:

> I enumerate at random some of the novels whose titles we gaily included under this rubric, even though the authors may have no Jewish origin: *Dusty Answer* by Rosamund Lehmann, *Tessa*, by Margaret Kennedy, *For-*

tune Carée by Kessel, *Jude the Obscure* by Thomas Hardy, and also the lengthy trilogy by Jakob Wassermann (*The Mauritzius Affair, Etzel Andergast, Joseph Kerkhoven*), or *Rebecca* by Daphne du Maurier. Louis-Ferdinand Céline had, I think, the good fortune of being officially recognized as right-wing and antisemitic, otherwise *Journey to the End of the Night* and *Death on the Installment Plan*, which I consider to be his two outstanding books, would have been placed in a similar category, which would not have been a reason not to reread them with pleasure—on the contrary. (121)

"Jewish literature," according to Alain Robbe-Grillet's scenario, is recognizable by the powerful effects it produces on certain readers, an echo of André Gide's emphasis on the material and moral results of the word and work in "Jewish literature." Whereas Paul de Man's effort is directed at diminishing the Jewish presence in literature, Robbe-Grillet and his parents augment this presence by attributing the label "Jewish" to British novelists such as Margaret Kennedy, Thomas Hardy, and Daphne du Maurier who, as far as I have been able to discover, were not Jewish. The Robbe-Grillet passage emphasizes contradictory positions, whereas the Paul de Man article both simplifies drastically the literary situation in France and Western Europe and banishes to the margins mediocre writers and Jews. And yet I will propose that the literary judgments of Gide and Robbe-Grillet may well be closer to the "vulgar antisemitism" that Paul de Man rejects at the beginning of his article, because their arguments reproduce the cliché that Jews control literature and the arts. What all three writers share is their own or their milieu's conviction that Jews are religiously and racially essentially different from the French and the Europeans. For both André Gide and Paul de Man, it is imperative to prevent confusion between the two and contamination of French literature by Jews.

But this category of Jewish literature is also promoted by Jewish writers in the aftermath of the Dreyfus affair during the first half of the twentieth century: Albert Cohen in the first issue of the *Revue Juive*, January 1925, Josué Jehouda in the first issue of the *Revue Juive de Genève*, October 1932, and André Fleg in his *Anthologie juive* (1923) emphasize explicitly and deliberately the Jewish difference and insist on such essentialist expressions of identity as "race juive," "esprit juif," "pensée juive." Michael Marrus's *The Politics of Assimilation* points the finger at "assimilation," the refusal to acknowledge one's Jewish identity and Jewish culture as primary, as bearing some responsibility for the fate of the Jews at the end of the nineteenth and throughout the twentieth century. And Marrus is not alone in this accusation. Many North American historians of French Jewry, notably Paula Hyman and Jay R. Berkovitz, sound the same note in their historical writings. After the Shoah the notion of Jewish literature and Jewish culture is augmented by the notion of Jewish writing. It seems important, therefore, to examine the discourses of non-Jewish writers in relation to the discourses of Jewish writers on this question of literary specificity in order to determine the rhetorical and political ramifications of the category and to avoid affixing the label *antisemitic* indiscriminately. I will do this by juxtaposing to André Gide, Alain Robbe-Grillet, and Paul de Man a French Jewish writer who persists in using the terms *Jewish literature, Jewish culture,* or *Jewish writing* both as defining terms and as a rallying cry: Albert Cohen.

Albert Cohen (1895–1981) is one of the major French writers of the twentieth century who is Jewish by birth and whose narrators are never not conscious of their own Jewishness and the Jewishness, or relation to Jewishness, of most of the important characters in their fictional world. Albert Cohen is therefore of interest to this study as a writer of novels and autobiographical fiction and also as the editor in chief of the *Revue Juive* which had four issues during the year 1925. Because the publication of the journal antedates the publication of his fiction, I shall begin by presenting the *Revue Juive* as an example of a Jewish awareness, a willingness and a need among a group of prominent Jewish writers to declare publicly their shared identity.

The first issue of the *Revue Juive*, January 1925, includes on the cover the list of names of those who are part of the "Comité," Georges Brandès, Albert Einstein, Sigmund Freud, Charles Gide, Chaïm Weizmann, Léon Zadoc-Kahnin, and the name of the "Directeur," Albert Cohen. Albert Einstein, Sigmund Freud, and Chaïm Weizmann, the chemist and first president of the State of Israel, need no introduction. Their names guarantee the international character of the journal and underline the intention of Cohen and his collaborators to feature the most prominent Jews of the time. The only non-Jewish name included in the comité is that of Charles Gide, the paternal uncle of André Gide, a noted Protestant economist and a supporter of liberal causes. Although the *Revue Juive* was published by the Librairie Gallimard,

André Gide, one of the major figures on the editorial board of the *Nouvelle Revue Française*, also published by Gallimard, is not a member of the comité.

The first issue opens with Albert Cohen's "Déclaration," written in the first-person plural, the editorial *we* more common in official French prose than in English. "Déclaration" is a manifesto of intentions and hopes, both literary and political, with abundant use of the future tense and the "task to accomplish." It announces the journal's support for Zionism and Zionists. Zionism is considered a means of diminishing antisemitism in Europe and, interestingly, as a means of getting rid of "unassimilable elements" (9–10). It also anounces the journal's support for the Jews of the diaspora who wish to remain where they are.

The *Revue Juive* heralds the opening, to take place on the first of April 1925, of the University of Jerusalem. The optimistic and forward-looking tone is set by the epigraph from the prophet Ezekiel: "And the spirit entered into them, and they lived again, and they stood on their feet" (5). Ezekiel, narrator and prophet in the Hebrew Bible, is a captive and a watchman who sees and hears visions of God and the voice of God. The "Déclaration" of Albert Cohen, like the book of Ezekiel, moves from the problems that face "the children of Israel" to a vision of better things that will come through the power of words: "The Jewish world is in a state of decadence and resurrection. We will make distinctions in this journal between what is worth encouraging to live and what we should, quietly, encourage to die" (9). Albert Cohen, like Ezekiel, is also a captive and a watchman, a narrator and a prophet. The major differences between the two narrators is that Ezekiel takes all his cues and lines from God whereas Albert Cohen uses the Bible as intertext. And whereas Albert Cohen praises the treasures of "the Occident that [are] adorable . . . reasonable, harmonious, and formative" (7), at the same time that he calls on Jews to recognize their Jewishness and to support Zionism, Ezekiel, a captive in Babylon, who has just lost Jerusalem and the land of Israel, never ceases to rail against the enemy, Egypt, and against corrupt and decadent Jews. Ezekiel blames Egypt's betrayal and the Jews' infidelity to God for the present disastrous situation.

What Ezekiel and Albert Cohen have in common, and this in spite of the radical differences in time, place, system of belief, and status of the text (although if we were to add Albert Cohen's novels to the "Déclaration" we would have an even stronger basis for comparison), is the importance given by both to the notion of the Jews' fidelity: fidelity to God (for Ezekiel) and fidelity to being Jewish (for Albert Cohen). Fidelity in both cases is the sine qua non of a renaissance. I would propose that the epigraph from Ezekiel underlines the dangerous situation in which Jews find themselves, both in relation to God (if they are believers) and in relation to themselves, if they completely renounce their Jewishness. Already in 1925 the signs of a political and cultural climate hostile to Jews was becoming evident in Germany, Austria, and France. But at the same time the epigraph contains a positive message and indicates the possibility of standing upright if and when the word enters, if and when the prophecy is heard and taken seriously. And finally the obvious must be emphasized: the presence of a Jewish prophet announces a state of misery and suffering for the Jewish people, a misery and suffering associated with captivity and dispersion, with past disobedience (to God) and present decadence. Here the prophet's railing against the disobedient and decadent Jews can be heard, and with what irony, as resembling the voice of the French anti-semitic prophets—Drumont or Maurras or Céline—denouncing the Jewish presence as responsible for a decadent France. For the Jewish prophet, Ezekiel or Albert Cohen, a change in Jewish mentality and behavior might bring about a Jewish renaissance; for the antisemitic prophet the expulsion or extermination of the Jews would bring about a French or European renaissance. In both cases prophets explore past and present suffering and its causes in order to predict an ideal utopian future.[1]

Albert Cohen, in his "Déclaration," is not closing any doors. The *Revue Juive*, he affirms, will be open to diverse questions that touch Jews, and will attempt to educate Jews and non-Jews about "a people for a long time unrecognized." Although Albert Cohen repeats in his "Déclaration" that the journal is a literary journal, what we read in this opening message concerns the positions that the journal will take rather than a discourse on literature or the relationship between being Jewish and literature. And although Albert Cohen insists that because the Jews are a race there *is* such a thing as a Jewish aesthetic, there is no further argument given to support this claim. The "Déclaration" ends with a statement on the importance of this journal for French Jews who unlike the Jews of other nations do not have a journal that represents them and with a statement on Israel as "one of the most reliable points of articulation with Europe."[2] The good news, writes Albert Cohen, evoking the New Testament, is that "Israel is returning to Israel." The problem that Albert Cohen faces in writing this manifesto is also mine in writing this chapter and indeed this book; how to take note of a Jewish presence without establishing a rigid Jewish difference. This double view colors the rhetoric used in the "Déclaration" as well as in the "Message" written by Albert Einstein that follows as the second piece in this first issue. Einstein focuses on the danger of nationalism at the same time that he defends "the mystique of Zionism." Or, in other words, how to reap the benefits of nationalism, the sense of pride and legitimacy that Zionism gives to some Jews, without constructing exclusionary practices and an essentialist ethnicity?

Similar problems arise in the opening text, "A nos lecteurs" (To Our Readers), of the first issue of the *Revue Juive de Genève* published in October of 1932. Written by the "directeur" of the journal, Josué Jehouda, this manifesto repeats some of the same themes we found in Albert Cohen's "Déclaration," but with a difference. The difference is, in large part, a consequence of the date. Between 1925 and 1932 antisemitism in Western Europe had developed into a discourse with a political agenda and a practice. Minor differences include the word *awakening* in "To Our Readers" rather than *renaissance*, the importance of the *Revue Juive de Genève* being situated in Geneva, the home of the League of Nations, and the insistence on printing texts written in French alongside texts translated into French from Hebrew and from other languages in which Jews have written. Like "Déclaration," "To Our Readers" equates "the spirit of Israel" and "Jewish thought," and hopes to become the organ of Jewish unity with a focus on "French Judaism." But, at the same time, "To Our Readers" insists that the *Revue Juive de Genève* will take part in the "struggle" against antisemitism and the moral exclusion of Israel and will become a center of Jewish action.

The main theme of "To Our Readers" is that the *Revue Juive de Genève* will be "at the same time Jewish and universal" (8). This is possible for the two reasons to which the opening manifesto refers repeatedly but that it does not develop: the journal will be universal (antisemitic discourse would say "cosmopolitan") and Jewish because Jewish communities exist in so many different countries, and this will be made possible because of the universality of the French language. Being Jewish and the French language traverse national boundaries and borders, making possible the further assumption that what is French and what is Jewish are at the vanguard of the Western world. The ruling equation in this manifesto is that the "esprit juif" and the "esprit humain" are or will become one and the same.

In the third and fourth issues of the *Revue Juive de Genève* the French Jewish writer Armand Lunel contributed an essay on the "Jewish Renaissance in France During the Twentieth Century." This essay allows me to make an appropriate transition between these two journals and the literary production of Albert Cohen.

For Armand Lunel Jewish literature is literature written by Jews. He notes and dismisses Racine's *Esther* and *Athalie*, and those poems by the romantic poets who use biblical themes, as part of Jewish literature and he pays no attention to the presence of Hebrew and Jewish literature in the writings of other sixteenth- or seventeenth-century writers. He even dismisses nineteenth-century Jewish writers because they were, according to his standards, too assimilated, too far removed from Judaism and Jewishness. He attributes the "awakening of Jewish consciousness" to the Dreyfus affair, and he pays homage to Charles Péguy because of Péguy's interest in "la mystique juive," which is transmitted to his journal, the *Cahiers de la Quinzaine*. But Lunel is mainly interested in two events that sustained this "awakening" in the aftermath of the First World War: the "great Zionist dream" and the publication in 1923 of the first edition of Edmond Fleg's *Anthologie juive*. Armand Lunel's focus is on Jewish writers responsible for this "mode juive" and who transmit "what their soul and their blood dictated" (165). "Jewishness," according to this definition, can only exist in the blood and the soul of real Jews. His list of Jewish writings includes the journals *Revue Juive, Palestine*, and *Revue Juive de Genève*. The list of Jewish writers includes Jean-Richard Bloch, Edmond Fleg, Marcel Proust, André Spire, Josué Jehouda, and, most important, Albert Cohen. Lunel's enthusiasm, which does not exclude some criticism, is reserved for Cohen's novel, *Solal*, published in 1930:

> And aside from *And Company* of Bloch, it would perhaps be impossible to find in all of contemporary Jewish literature a novel as dense, as rich, and as eventful as *Solal* by Albert Cohen. But it must be said that there is in this big volume as much good as bad and even as much that is excellent as that is awful, magnificent gifts and little mastery, a poetry of the

everyday, observation royally nourished by the five senses, a protean irony, a lyricism related to the best biblical sources, exquisite childishness, an irresistible goodness, but also many errors of taste, a psychology that is often improbable or rudimentary, a disconcerting megalomania. Thus *Solal* may in turn please or displease infinitely. In any case, a work in which such a personality asserts itself cannot pass unseen or leave readers indifferent. The dynamism, the originality, the audacity of this novel are indisputable, and it seems to me too that everyone will agree to join me in thanking Cohen for having revealed to us these extraordinary Jews of the Ionian islands with their picturesqueness, their maliciousness, and, also, their heart. (*Revue Juive de Genève,* (1933), 1(4): 167–68)

Lunel's early admiration for and analysis of the qualities of Albert Cohen's first novel are more judicious and perceptive than his analysis of antisemitism in France. He notes, in the closing paragraph of his article, that antisemitism had never been deep or long-lasting in France and that the accusations made against Jews in antisemitic discourse—their mercantilism, their anguish, their restless nomadic spirit, and their spirit of domination—could be counterbalanced in the minds of Jews and non-Jews alike by the new "more objective" Jewish literature. It is as if Armand Lunel were proposing that a writer like Albert Cohen might play an important role in the "progressive liquidation of the storehouse of dangerous formulae and vulgar clichés" (169).

As a writer of novels and memoirs, Albert Cohen and his fictional work present the reader with at least two major themes that we find also in the writings of Marcel Proust: an obsession with the figure of the mother and with mortality. To these obsessions I would add, for Albert Cohen, a passion for the writings of Marcel Proust. But the differences between the two writers are equally important. Albert Cohen, unlike Proust, represents two explicitly Jewish families at the center of his writing: the Solals, Greek Jews originally from France, are the family of his fiction in *Solal, Mangeclous,* and *Belle du Seigneur*; and the Cohens, Jews from Corfou who settle in France at the beginning of the twentieth century, are the family of his memoirs in *Le Livre de ma mère* (My mother's book) and *O Vous, frères humains* (O, you, brother humans). The reader notes the filiation between author, narrator, and character in Albert Cohen's novels, a filiation that is deliberately obfuscated in Marcel Proust's *Jean Santeuil* and *Remembrance of Things Past.*

But it is Albert Cohen's difference from most other Jewish and non-Jewish writers of the twentieth century that I would like to emphasize. Although his characters are explicitly identified by the text as Jewish, and although they are situated in specifically Jewish milieus—even ghettos—Albert Cohen's baroque and picaresque style makes his Jews very different from the more traditional representations of Ashkenazic Jews—sensitive, brilliant, persecuted, sorrowful—to which novels and stories written between the Dreyfus case and the aftermath of the Shoah have accustomed us. Characters created by Albert Cohen such as Solal, Mangeclous, the other "valiants" are grotesque, rambunctious, ribald figures closer to the characters of François Rabelais than to those of Marcel Proust or André Schwarz-Bart. They are Jewish, with a difference, because they cannot be reduced to active stereotypes.

In the conclusion of her book *Le Juif dans le roman français 1933–1948* (The Jew in the French novel, 1933–1948) Charlotte Wardi writes: "In novels published between 1933 and 1948 the Jew is hardly ever portrayed as an individual but rather as the representative of a race. Through a single Israelite, the writer claims to describe all of Jewishness and Judaism" (263). Using the example of Albert Cohen's character Mangeclous in the novel of the same name, Wardi shows what she considers to be the difference between the Jew as seen by others and the Jew as seen by himself. She notes that Mangeclous is "an incorrigible braggart," but that Cohen's novel never suggests that excessive bragging characterizes Jews or that bragging can be explained as part of a Jewish tradition. Mangeclous is Jewish and he is a terrible braggart. Wardi is convinced that a non-Jewish novelist who is suspicious of Jews in general would inevitably see Mangeclous's boasting as part of *the* Jewish personality and that, on the other hand, a philosemitic novelist (and Cohen is once again an exception) would tend to avoid portraying Jews who had unpleasant traits.

But is *Belle du Seigneur* a Jewish novel and is Albert Cohen a Jewish writer? At the conclusion of his review of *Belle du Seigneur* in *Les Nouvelles Littéraires*, September 12, 1968, the critic François Nourissier wrote:

> I persist in thinking that there exists, for looking at the world, a Jewish look, and for writing about the world, a Jewish voice: when a great talent that is destructive, naive, and violent joins in, one is likely to find oneself, as in this case, full of gratitude and somewhat shaken, at the heart of a beautiful and slightly barbaric book. (1006)

In conclusion, then, I cannot agree (I do not want to agree) either with François Nourissier or with Edmond Jabès that there is such a thing as "Jewish writing." I would agree that sources and themes may indeed be marked as "Jewish"—for example, within Jewish Holy Scriptures the rhetoric of the prophets, the narratives of Esther and of Ruth, as well as certain forms of ritual and of persecution and of suffering. But these available discourses can be studied and echoed, imitated and assimilated by non-Jews or by Jews. Writing and style, I would maintain, are marked by historical moments and individual temperament, positioning, and variations, not by race, ethnicity, class, or gender. There are Jews who write in French, but their writing is not Jewish; it is French not by virtue of a national belonging but by virtue of language and literary tradition. Jewish literature does not belong to Jews and is not an absolute category. It is a rubric that has been used by Jews and non-Jews alike both to exalt and to denigrate, to view being Jewish as a privilege or as a stigma. It is important to examine the instances of the use of this rubric by Robbe-Grillet, Paul de Man, or Albert Cohen and to understand it as a political gesture within a particular context rather than as a serious contribution to literary studies.

5 | *La France et le Juif*: Identity and a Significant Other

> By establishing antisemitism as a system of universal explication,
> Drumont made of the Jew the negative pole of nationalist move-
> ments; it is in relation to the Jew, it is against the Jew that the
> nationalists will define their French or German identity, and
> their pride in belonging to a community, thus recognizing
> clearly the adversary who threatens the unity and the life of this
> community.   —Michel Winock, *Edouard Drumont et Cie*

B etween March 1942 and July 1944, approximately 80,000 of the 350,000 Jews living in France, includ- ing 45 percent of those Jews from Central, Eastern, and Western Europe who had sought refuge in France after 1933 and 20 percent of the French Jews born in France, were pursued, hunted down, arrested, and rounded up by the French *milice* and the German Gestapo, and sent, for the most part, first to the detention center at Drancy, outside Paris, and then shipped on seventy-six convoys, care- fully registered and noted by the German bureaucracy, to Auschwitz. Of these 80,000 about 2,500 survived.[1]

In her book, *The War Against the Jews*, Lucy Dawidowicz provides us with comparative tables concerning the estimated Jewish population in the countries of Europe controlled by the Third Reich before and after the Shoah. Ninety percent of the 3,300,000 Polish Jews were extermi- nated; 90 percent of the Jews living in the Baltic countries, in Germany, and in Austria were exterminated; 83 percent of the Jews in Slovakia were exterminated; 77 percent of the Jews in Greece were exterminated; 75 percent of the Jews in the Netherlands were exterminated; 70 per- cent of the Jews in Hungary were exterminated; 65 percent of the Jews in White Russia were exterminated; 60 percent of the Jews in Ukraine, Belgium, and Yugoslavia were exterminated; 50 percent of the Jews in Romania and Norway were exterminated; 26 percent of the Jews in

France were exterminated; 20 percent of the Jews in Bulgaria, Italy, and Luxembourg were exterminated; 0 percent of the Jews in Denmark and Finland were exterminated. I cite these figures not to place France in a favorable light by comparison to what happened to the Jewish population in other European countries, not to minimize the complicity of the Vichy government and the French police, not to forget the thirty-one concentration camps in the southern zone of France in which Jews lived and died, not to overlook a longstanding and deep antisemitism in many segments of the French population, but to remind us that there were in France, during this period, particularly in the preponderantly Protestant regions of the Cévennes mountains, French men and women who risked their lives and the lives of their families to save Jews and who succeeded in saving them. Remembering the Shoah involves remembering the Jews who were annihilated and those who were responsible for their annihilation. It also involves remembering those Jews and non-Jews who helped Jews resist, escape, and survive.[2]

In preparation for the writing of this book, I have read and seen many of the documents—articles, books, memoirs, films—that have appeared in French and in English, including translations of books that have appeared in German and in Italian dealing with what has been variously called the "Holocaust,"[3] the "Final Solution," a "genocide," the "Shoah," the "destruction of European Jews." I am not a historian, and my purpose in writing this book has not been to seek out new information about the Shoah in France, what really happened or even how it has been remembered since the end of the Second World War. But I am interested in making connections between the horrors of the Shoah and the antisemitic discourses that flourished in France, on the Left as part of a progressive ideology and on the Right as part of a conservative ideology, from the middle of the nineteenth century and throughout the Second World War. These discourses all claim to have found the cause of the ruin, shame, decline of France in "the reign of the Jew," first Rothschild, the Jewish financier, then Dreyfus the Jewish traitor, and later Léon Blum, Jewish prime minister in the Socialist Popular Front government. Antisemitic discourse does not hesitate to speak of Jews in general, but it also tends to focus on the figure of one or more prominent Jews. This is true in the major antisemitic texts of the nineteenth and twentieth centuries such as Alphonse Toussenel's *Les Juifs rois de l'époque* (The Jews, kings of the era; 1845), Edouard Drumont's best-seller *La France Juive* (1886), the French edition of *Protocoles des Sages de Sion* (*Protocols of the Elders of Zion*; 1920–1921), the French edition of Adolf Hitler's *Mein Kampf* (1925), Louis-Ferdinand Céline's *Bagatelles pour un massacre* (1937), Lucien Rebatet's best-seller during the Occupation, *Les Décombres* (1942), as well as in such antisemitic newspapers as Drumont's *La Libre Parole* (Free Speech; 1892), Maurras's *Action Française* (1899–1944), Brasillach and Rebatet's *Je Suis Partout* (I am everywhere; 1930–1944).

In the France of the early 1990s Jews seem to be most recognizable through their names. I have had the experience, more than once in the past few years, of watching a film with French friends who react to the names that appear when the credits are given with a sentence such as "Look at all the names that are not French." The names that were not French were invariably Jewish, sometimes Arab. What fascinates me is the French preoccupation with what it means to be French, and the manner in which Frenchness is defined in relation to what is not French. What is not French in France is frequently Jewish. What's in a name? In France, a monolithic, unchangeable identity perceived as otherness is thought by some to be revealed in names. In the absence of distinctive clothing and conformity to a physical stereotype (for the stereotype today might include many of the approximately three million Arabs in France) and except for the relatively small number of Orthodox Jews who can be easily identified by their dress on certain Parisian streets, and in the immediate vicinity of the synagogue in other French cities in which Jews live, to be Jewish is to have a Jewish name. The making and reading of lists of names has become, in France, a significant activity carried out both by antisemites eager to announce an overpowering Jewish presence and by Jews and others who attempt to fight against silence and to encourage remembering.

Those of us who were in France during the summer of 1987 during the trial of Klaus Barbie for crimes against humanity, and who followed the trial in newspaper accounts or on television, will remember the testimony of Serge Klarsfeld, the French Jewish lawyer who, with his wife Beate Klarsfeld, was largely responsible for bringing Klaus Barbie to trial. On June 17, 1987, before the tribunal in Lyon, Serge Klarsfeld read the list of names of the Jewish children who were in hiding as refugees not far from Lyon, at an orphanage in Izieu, and whose deportation to the death camps Klaus Barbie had ordered. The children were deported

first to Drancy, near Paris, and then sent directly to the ramp at Birke-
nau-Auschwitz. Klarsfeld read the family name and the first name of
each of the children; he gave the date and the place of their birth; he
indicated what had happened to their parents, and for each child he
repeated as a litany: "This child did not come back" (Il/Elle n'est pas
revenu[e]). There were other memorable moments during the trial, particularly the testimony of older women, either Jewish or members of
the Resistance or both, who were tortured by Barbie during endless
interrogations, who were or were not deported, but who had survived.
But nothing, I think, affected the members of the jury, those who
attended the trial, and the French men and women who followed the
trial on television or in the newspapers, as much as the reading of the
proper names of the forty-three children of Izieu.

But there are other lists of names compiled for very different reasons.
During the summer of 1987, in a neofascist bookstore in Paris called, significantly. *La Librairie Française*, I picked up a volume published in
1985, whose title is *Les Juifs dans la France d'aujourd'hui* (The Jews in
today's France). The author refers to himself as Gygès, clearly a pseudonym, the name of the seventh-century B.C. King of Lydia, purported in
myths to have a magical ring that made him invisible, and the publisher's name is *Documents et Témoignages* (Documents and testimonies).
The names of the author and of the publisher play with the notion of
visibility and invisibility; the author is invisible, or at least hidden, but
the publisher is in the business of uncovering hidden documents and
presenting otherwise concealed evidence. In many of the antisemitic
books sold publicly in France since the end of the Algerian War of Inde-
pendance, there is a preface, like the "Avant-Propos" to *Les Juifs dans la
France d'aujourd'hui*, disavowing any serious intention of antisemitism
and insisting on the need to be fair about the Jewish question, to say
both the good and the bad. This kind of preface also claims that it is
important to write about the Jews because their numbers are growing in
France and because Jews are becoming increasingly numerous in important places. The exaggeration of numbers in a pseudodemographic discourse is also typical of such prefaces. The reader is forewarned.

The purpose of *Les Juifs dans la France d'aujourd'hui* is to help readers identify Jews living and working in France. It lists Jewish writers,
Jews in the liberal professions, government, the film industry, journalism, and theater. It lists Jewish organizations, synagogues, cultural

groups and it gives the reader instructions on how to recognize modified Jewish names. When these categories and groups are exhausted, there are lists of names—Jewish names—in alphabetical order, just family names. It is an illuminating exercise to juxtapose the list of names of the children of Izieu, or the much longer lists of the names we find in Serge Klarsfeld's *Memorial to the Jews Deported from France*, with the lists of names in *Les Juifs dans la France d'aujourd'hui*. Of course, many of the names are the same. The quotation that follows is a brief but exemplary illustration of the tone and the intention of Gygès:

> In order to have an idea of the importance of Israelites in the French capital, all you have to do is to open the telephone book at the letter L, to look at Lévi or Lévy and to count the number of subscribers listed in the phone book who have one or another of these surnames. You will discover that there are hundreds upon hundreds of them, four times more of them than there are Duponts. (86)

This preoccupation with names that are recognizably Jewish, which I had noticed as I watched films with French friends, extends to blatantly antisemitic publications. It is both "banal," to use Robbe-Grillet's word about his parents' antisemitism,[4] and points to a revealing connection between banal everyday antisemitism and the events of the Shoah. It also points to an obsession with otherness in language and onomastics.

When I examine what is being written in the United States in modern foreign language and literature departments, as well as in Anglo-American language and literature departments in the early 1990s, I discern two major directions, each of which involves a concept or a definition of the "other." On the one hand, the "other" as defined by Simone de Beauvoir in *The Second Sex* (1949): "She is defined and differentiated with reference to man and not he with reference to her; she is the incidental, the inessential as opposed to the essential. He is the subject, he is the Absolute—she is the Other" (xix). This is the other who is oppressed by patriarchy, colonialism, exacerbated nationalism, or racism, the other whose authorship does not count, the other who is designated by the feminist and neomarxist insistence on including race, class, gender, sexual preference in all analyses because all analyses, at some level, are organized through relations of power and through ideology. This is, then, the other of cultural studies as it is frequently practiced in the United States.

On the other hand, there are the two other others as articulated by Jacques Lacan: the *Other* (capital O) as the domain, the place of law and language, the symbolic father, and the unconscious, the *other* (small o), the m/other, father, nurturer, with whom the child at the time of the mirror stage enters into an imaginary relation. It is interesting to note that Lacan's essay "The Mirror Stage as Formative of the Function of the I as Revealed in Psychoanalytic Experience" was delivered at the Sixteenth International Congress of Psychoanalysis in Zurich, Switzerland, on July 17, 1949, the same year as the publication of *The Second Sex*.

Those who follow the paths suggested by Simone de Beauvoir have tended to work with texts and cultural questions about the role and function of woman as other, or the black, or the Jew, or the working-class poor as other, investigating how and where in texts and institutions othering and exclusion have taken place, "the way in which class, gender, race, and other inequalities are naturalized and represented in forms which sever (as far as possible) the connection between these and economic and political inequalities" (O'Sullivan 60). Those who work in these directions have also tended to view culture as

> the terrain on which *hegemony* is struggled for and established, and hence it is the site of "cultural struggles," of resistance and oppositional discourses. Cultural studies thus conceived seeks to account for cultural differences and practices by reference to the overall map of social relations and asks the question "in whose interests." (60)

This notion of otherness and how it is constructed is neomarxist in orientation and involves working with and through such concepts as class, ideology, hegemony, but also language and subjectivity.

Those who follow the paths proposed by Jacques Lacan have tended to focus in their analyses on the unconscious of texts rather than on nonconscious presuppositions, to focus on the place of the other and desire, on the play of language, on tropes and signifiers more than on power and the making of meaningful social divisions. In these analyses language as the repressed other plays the leading role.

I would like to propose a reading of a passage from Proust that deals with *La France* and *Le Juif*, the question of identity and of a significant other in relation to whom French culture defines itself, the other of ideology, but also the Other of Jacques Lacan as the unconscious of the text, the Other as and in language. I think it would be helpful for my readers if I were to note some of the pedagogical adventures and research avenues that have entered into the Proust commentary.

The title of this chapter, "*La France et Le Juif*: Identity and a Significant Other," emerged from a French course I have taught twice at the University of Wisconsin-Madison—"La Question Juive de l'Affaire Dreyfus à Auschwitz," (The Jewish question from the Dreyfus affair to Auschwitz)—and the work I had done previously, and continue to do, on women writers and the construction and representation of woman, female sexuality, and the feminine. I was fascinated by the resemblances between the representation of the Jew in antisemitic literature in France and the representation of woman and the feminine in misogynist literature in France from the end of the nineteenth century until the end of the Second World War and by the intersections between questions of national and sexual identity in writings of the same period.

As I began to study the French authors I was interested in citing and reading together during the course—Edouard Drumont, Marcel Proust, Louis-Ferdinand Céline—writings by historians concerned with the life and death of Jews in Germany and in France (particularly since their emancipation in France in 1791), and cartoons and caricatures in the antisemitic press, another representation of *La France* and *Le Juif* began to take shape. *La France* was no longer the figure constructed solely by gentile and antisemitic nationalists of the Left and the Right. *Le Juif* was no longer the assimilated native French Jew deliberately misrepresented by the xenophobic, Catholic French. Particularly in the caricatures of Alfred Dreyfus and Emile Zola at the time of the Dreyfus case, and the caricatures in which, at the time of the Popular Front government, Leon Blum, the Jewish, Socialist prime minister, is re-presented as the wandering Jewess, the biblical Judith, or other female or feminized famous figures, I discerned a new configuration. In this new configuration *La France* and *la francité* is often masculine as well as feminine, *Le Juif* and the other is feminine as well as masculine and, perhaps most important, the primary referent for *Le Juif* is the unassimilated Eastern European immigrant Jew, wearing a caftan and speaking Yiddish, who arrived in Germany and in France in the early 1880s following a series of pogroms in Czarist Russia and whose presence in texts from the belle epoque to the Shoah is in explicit contrast to the supposedly virile, often aristocratic, ideal Aryan Frenchman.

I acknowledge my debt and my gratitude to those historians, French and North American, whose work has allowed me to read literary and nonliterary texts in other ways. I would name, in particular, Steven Aschheim, Pierre Birnbaum, Jean-Louis Bredin, Paula Hyman, Michael Marrus, George Mosse, Robert Paxton, Henry Rousso, Pierre Vidal-Naquet, Eugen Weber, Michel Winock. But written accounts of historical events by historians do not necessarily provide satisfactory explanations or interpretive arguments for literary scholars. As I suggested in chapter 1, what better place to look for missing parts than psychoanalysis, and what better place to seek help in understanding couples and coupling than deconstruction?

Sigmund Freud in *Moses and Monotheism* (1939), Rodolphe Loewenstein in *Psychanalyse de l'antisémitisme* (1952), Julia Kristeva in *Powers of Horror* (1980), and Sarah Kofman in *L'Énigme de la femme* (*The Enigma of Woman;* 1980) suggest ways of beginning to think about the relationship between *La France* and *Le Juif* that do not replace the work of the historians, but supplement and displace it through such concepts as transference, castration anxiety, father and son rivalry, sibling rivalry, repressed homosexuality and repressed femininity. And deconstructive strategies propose that the first term in a binary couple, for example *La France*, is more dependent on, implicated in the second term, for example *Le Juif*, for its own existence and sense of unique identity than most nondeconstructionists could ever admit. At the end of the nineteenth century, without *Le Juif*, without the "significant other"—an essential relationship that is not legally recognized, and without which the first term would not be—*La France* could not assert itself and its values in the same imperious hegemonic way.

Here are four passages, in my English translation, by writers whose works are central to any discussion of the Jewish question in France during the period that interests us: Edouard Drumont's *La France Juive*, a veritable source book for French antisemitism and a best-seller during the last decade of the nineteenth century and the first decade of the twentieth, Marcel Proust's *Within a Budding Grove* (1919), Louis-Ferdinand Céline's play *L'Eglise* (1933, published in 1952), and Lucien Rebatet's *Les Décombres* (1942), a best-seller in France during the German Occupation. After discussing resemblances between the four passages, I will propose a reading of the passage from *Within a Budding Grove* that focuses both on nonconscious presuppositions and on signifiers.

In volume I of Drumont's *La France Juive* there is a physical portrait of the Jew many of whose details are frequently repeated in antisemitic texts and cartoons:

> The main signs by which one can recognize the Jew are: the famous curved nose, the blinking eyes, the clenched teeth, the protuberant ears, the square rather than almond-shaped finger nails, the long torso, the flat feet, the round knees, the ankle bone that sticks out, the moist and limp hand of the hypocrite and the traitor. Jews usually have one arm shorter than the other. (1)
> Lavater [a Swiss theologian, 1741–1801] notes that Jews in general have a sallow complexion, a hooked, prominent nose, deep-set eyes, pronounced mouth muscles, reddish-brown frizzy hair, hardly any beard, the usual sign of an effeminate temperament. "Physical degradation," he adds, "always follows moral degradation; this is more evident with Hebrews because they are completely depraved." (35)

In the second part of *Within a Budding Grove*, "Place Names: The Place," the narrator introduces the "Jewish colony" that comes to Balbec for the summer. I will quote the Proust passage first in French because of the importance of the wordplay in the French version:

> Un jour que nous étions assis sur le sable, Saint Loup et moi, nous entendîmes d'une tente de toile contre laquelle nous étions, sortir des imprécations contre le fourmillement d'Israélites qui infestait Balbec. "On ne peut faire deux pas sans en rencontrer, disait la voix. Je ne suis pas par principe irréductiblement hostile à la nationalité juive, mais ici il y a pléthore. On n'entend que : "'Dis donc, Apraham, chai fu Chakop.' On se croirait rue d'Aboukir." L'homme qui tonnait ainsi contre Israël sortit enfin de la tente, nous levâmes les yeux sur cet antisémite. C'était mon camarade Bloch. Saint-Loup me demanda immédiatement de rappeler à celui-ci qu'ils s'étaient rencontrés au Concours général où Bloch avait eu le prix d'honneur, puis dans une Université populaire. (738)

> One day when Saint Loup and I were sitting on the sand, we heard a torrent of imprecations against the swarm of Jews that infected Balbec coming from the canvas tent against which we were leaning. "You can't take two steps without meeting them," said the voice. "I am not in principle irremediably hostile to the Jewish nation, but here there is a plethora of them. You hear nothing but: "'I say, Apraham, I've chust seen Chakop.' You'd think you were on Aboukir Street." The man who was thundering thus against Israel emerged at last from the tent, and we looked up to

behold this antisemite. It was my friend Bloch. Saint-Loup asked me immediately to remind Bloch that they had met each other at an essay contest in their baccalaureate year, where Bloch had won the first prize, and then later at a people's university course.

In the third act of *L'Eglise*, by Céline, which takes place at the League of Nations, the three directors are: Mr. Yudenzweck, director of the Department of Compromises at the League of Nations, a Jew, forty-five years old, Mr. Mosaic, director of the Department of Transitory Business, a Jew, same age, and Mr. Moses, director of the Department of Indiscretions, a Jew, same age. This is the description of Mr. Yudenzweck:

> While all this hullabaloo is taking place on stage, a little man, dressed like a Polish Jew, wearing a long, black, ankle-length coat, a little cap, with thick eye-glasses, a very hooked nose, an umbrella, spats, glides cautiously, very cautiously, coming from the audience, alongside the boxes. He climbs up toward the stage, furtively, as if he were trying to hide. . . . He is thin, very thin; smiling, very smiling. (144)

In the last part of the original 1942 edition of *Les Décombres*, "A Brief Meditation on a Few Big Themes," eliminated from the 1976 edition because of its virulent antisemitism, we find the following development on the theme of "The Ghetto":

> Each one of us will explain the Jew in his own manner: the expiation of a sin, the greatest of all sins, against God; a blood stain that cannot be removed; a mixing of races that places the Jew outside the law for all people and that a reactionary racism has retained. There will be many explanations. It makes no difference. In one way or another, *la juiverie* offers a unique example in the history of humanity of a race for whom a collective punishment is the only just punishment. The crimes of the Jews are well known to us. The first universal attempt, since antiquity, to help the Jew become a free man has produced its beautiful fruits. We have understood. After one hundred and fifty years of Jewish emancipation, these evil, impure beasts bearing with them the germs of all forms of pestilence should be placed back into the prisons where the wisdom of the ages had kept them locked up. (566)

Perhaps the most remarkable feature about these passages is the resemblance between them. From Drumont (1886), to Proust (1919), to Céline (1933), to Rebatet (1942), whatever the differences in individual styles of writing and the generic contexts in which Jews appear, it seems always to be the same Jew accompanied by the same French representative of *La France*. This representative is the narrator as well as, in the passages by Proust and Céline, another character, Robert de Saint-Loup or Bardamu, whose presence intensifies ideal "Frenchness" and exaggerates, for the narrator, the repulsive grotesqueness of the Jew.

I focus my analysis on the short passage from Proust because it contains so many of the overlapping elements that constitute the Jewish question in French writing from the belle epoque through the Shoah, because it is more ambiguous in its stance toward Jews than the blatantly antisemitic texts of Drumont, Céline, and Rebatet, and because it allows for a many-layered commentary and is therefore congenial to a pedagogical presentation.

Pedagogically speaking, what is important in the teaching of foreign language and literature—beyond promoting semiotic bliss and glossophilia—is identifying the inevitable blind spots in texts and in readers, that which we cannot "see" for ideological (that is to say, cultural) or for psychoanalytic (that is to say, individual) reasons. Antisemitism in French writing and culture from 1886 on is a fertile field for ideological investigations and for the locating of blind spots. Before moving in on literary texts and the nonconscious and unconscious patternings of antisemitism, it is essential to have done some research on nationalism and sexuality, on the simultaneous development of these two discourses and the fact that they are contemporaneous with the discourses that proclaim the death of God. National-sexual identity—to be French, Christian, heterosexual, and *père-de-famille*—constitutes a necessary bastion against the disintegration that accompanies the death of God, the decline of Christian community, the economic depression, and the growing presence, at least in Paris, of Yiddish-speaking Jews. The Yiddish-speaking Jews were a new phenomenon at the end of the nineteenth century, but they joined with older and persistent anti-Jewish stereotypes already noted in chapter 1: the chosen people, the Christ killers, the gold diggers and the usurers, the wandering Jew, the bearers and disseminators of the plague and other contagious illnesses, the capitalists, the Bolshvik revolutionaries, plotting to seize power in France and the world, the racially impure and inferior, with their distinctive odors, the proponents of and the profiteers from the Enlightenment, the murderers of Christian babies. Antisemitism did not replace anti-Judaism but rather incorporated it, reinforcing and reinvigorating an older configuration, making it accessible and usable on all sides of the political spectrum and in all classes of society. By the time of the Dreyfus case in France, beginning in 1894, and after the publication and eventual success of Edouard Drumont's *La France Juive* in 1886, the Jew is an all-purpose "significant other," accused of being so far inside as to have taken over, as Drumont's title states, and so different in nature, so dangerous to the French body politic, as to warrant exclusion and expulsion.

The passage from *Within a Budding Grove* reproduces, in a condensed narrative form, much of this sociohistorical background and adds to it an important sexual dimension. The seven sentences recount a curious episode that takes place on the beach at Balbec. The narrator, Marcel, a sensitive neurasthenic, with many resemblances, including that of his first name, to Marcel Proust, but neither Jewish nor homosexual like Proust, is sitting on the sand at Balbec, leaning against a tent (*une tente*, in French), with his aristocratic friend, a member of the illustrious Guermantes family, the Marquis Robert de Saint-Loup. During most of the novel Robert de Saint-Loup is the very epitome of Frenchness. In his stature, the coloring of his hair and eyes, his speech, his manners, his intelligence, and his association with the military, Saint-Loup is exquisitely French, with the additional qualities of gentleness and kindness. However, unlike most members of his class, he has socialist aspirations and, as we discover toward the end of the novel, in spite of his earlier heterosexual involvement with a Jewish actress, Rachel, and his marriage toward the end of the novel to the partially Jewish Gilberte Swann, he is, not unlike other members of his class in Proust's text, a homosexual.

What Saint-Loup and the narrator hear, on the beach, are "des imprécations contre le fourmillement d'Israélites qui infestait Balbec" (a series of imprecations against the swarm of Jews that infested Balbec). "Fourmillement" (swarm) and "infestait" (infested) belong to a metaphorical cluster that is common in the discourse of racial antisemitism that proliferated at the end of the nineteenth century and in the 1920s and 1930s. These words suggest numbers of Jews far beyond the demographic reality (a leitmotif of antisemitic pamphlets) and connect these great numbers to animality and to disease. Jews are like diseased animals that carry the plague, they take over, they infect, indeed they kill. This passage also reproduces the terms used in order to avoid the more pejorative *Jew(s)*: either *Israelites* or *Jewish nationality*, both terms suggesting the double allegiance of Jews to another religion and to another country. The unidentified voice ends its imprecations by imitating the pronunciation of Jews who speak a kind of French contaminated by German, Alsatian, or Yiddish. The act of overhearing—balanced in other scenes of the novel by the narrator's solitary overseeing or voyeurism—in the presence of an authentic Frenchman accentuates the emphasis placed on language as the nec plus ultra of elegance and on Jewish speech as being at the farthest remove from this aristocratic ideal. The voiced consonants *be*, *je*, and *ve*, transformed into their voiceless counterparts *pe*, *che*, and *fe*, evoke the portraits I quoted earlier from the texts by Drumont and Céline of the unassimilated Eastern European Jew in his long caftan, with his bulbous nose, his blubber lips, his cap, his gesticulations, and his smells, the personification of ghetto misery and sexual repulsion. The proper names of persons and place—Abraham, Jacob, Aboukir—suggest a continuity between the patriarchal figures of the Old Testament and the names of contemporary Jews, vacationing at Balbec (the name of a Phoenician, then a Greek, today a Lebanese city) and living in Paris on a street, the rue d'Aboukir, that runs from the Place des Victoires (it was at Aboukir in Egypt, northeast of Alexandria, that Napoleon defeated the Turks in 1799) to the Porte Saint-Denis, and that had become part of the Jewish Quarter of Paris. From Egypt to Balbec to Paris Jews have been, and always are, as the metaphors suggest, everywhere.

The last part of the episode provides a revealing and an unexpected twist. These antisemitic remarks were not proferred by a stranger or by a French Christian but by the narrator's schoolfriend Albert Bloch, one of the major Jewish characters in the novel, who will, at a later date, change his name to Jacques du Rozier, retaining, on the level of the signifier, the name of the most famous street inhabited by Jews in all of Paris, the rue des Rosiers (with an *s*). Jewish antisemitism, the hostile reaction of many assimilated Jews to their nonassimilated brethren, was an important sociological phenomenon in France from 1881 through the years when the government of Vichy deported, whenever it could, Eastern European Jews who had sought refuge in France and, up to a point, protected native French Jews. The passage ends with Robert de Saint-Loup, ever the French gentleman, establishing his prior acquaintance with Bloch in a university setting in which Jews, so another stereotype claims, frequently have the upper hand.

In this text, then, Saint-Loup stands in for *La France* and Bloch for *Le Juif* and perhaps also for the narrator. But where in the text can we locate the feminine or sexuality? It is not enough that we who have read the entire novel know that Albert Bloch's uncle, Nissim Bernard, his sister, and his cousin Esther, as well as Robert de Saint-Loup, will be revealed as homosexuals, and that a certain complicity between the characters may well be attributed to sexual preference, which Proust compares explicitly to the complicity among Jews. But there is one word, twice repeated in the text, the word *tente*, that opens another and an essential dimension. A *tente* in French is a tent, a shelter made of canvas such as one may find on elegant beaches along the Atlantic coast of France or associated with Middle Eastern nomads (including Jews) and potentates. But *tente* in French sounds exactly the same as *tante*, which usually refers to an aunt, a female relative (and Robert de Saint-Loup's aunt, Madame de Villeparisis, an old friend of the narrator's grandmother, is the person who introduces the narrator to Saint-Loup). *Tante* is also, in popular French, a slang word for a homosexual. The imprecations that come from the *tente* (tent) also come from the nephew of a *tante*. This triple direction of a word is reinforced the second time the word occurs in the text: "L'homme qui tonnait ainsi contre Israël sortit enfin de la tente, nous levâmes les yeux sur cet antisémite" (The man who was thundering against Israel finally emerged from the tent; we looked up to behold this anti-Semite). The verbally active antisemite, on the basis of what the narrator and Saint-Loup overheard, is associated with homosexual activity, "sortit de la tente," on the basis of a close reading of the text. More important, for our analysis, the representative of *La France* is a homosexual and the representative of *Le Juif* is a native French Jewish antisemite. Proust's text both recapitulates and scrambles the signs by which we usually read *La France* and *Le Juif*.

La France and *Le Juif* are thus inscribed on the conscious, nonconscious, and unconscious levels of this passage. A close reading proposes that the epitome of Frenchness, Robert de Saint-Loup, is closer to the frequently feminized Jews than anyone, including the narrator, would have suspected. Saint-Loup leans against a *tente* (a tent, an aunt, a homosexual) and is, himself, a member of the *race*, a word that Proust will use later, in *Sodom and Gomorrah* to describe the homosexual family. In Proust's novel the significant other for France is, until the last section, *The Past Recaptured*, the Jew, but, toward the end, as the Jewish characters die off or are massively assimilated into *La France*, the significant other becomes the homosexual, as much an insider as an outsider. What looks at first reading like an antisemitic caricature of Bloch (pace Seth Wolitz and *The Proustian Community* [1971] and pace Albert Sonnenfeld and his rich two-part essay, "Marcel Proust Antisemite?" [1988]) may be read alternatively as an anecdote in which the homosexual breaks up the antagonistic couple *La France* and *Le Juif* by potentially inhabiting each of them, and thus destabilizing their absolute identity. In this instance the Other of language or repression, the Other as *tante*, may be said to share the stage with the other of sociohistoric oppression, the Jew-as other of cultural studies.

The same cannot be said for the opposition between *La France* and *Le Juif* in Drumont's *La France Juive*, in Céline's *L'Eglise*, or in Rebatet's *Les Décombres*. For them *Le Juif* remains the monstrous, un*ass*imilated and un*ass*imilatable Yiddish-speaking Yudenzweck, the significant other whose shipment back to Poland, by train, with a firmly stamped label, JUIF, their texts helped make possible.

6

Getting Away with Murd(h)er—
Author's Preface and Narrator's Text:
Reading Marguerite Yourcenar's
Coup de Grâce "After Auschwitz"

> We thus propose to show how the basic and legitimate critical
> demand for *contextualization of the text* itself needs to be com-
> plemented, simultaneously, by the less familiar and yet necessary
> work of *textualization of the context*; and how this shuttle move-
> ment or this shuttle reading in the critic's work—the very *ten-
> sion between textualization and contextualization*—might yield
> new avenues of insight, both into the texts at stake and into
> their context—the political, historical, and biographical realities
> with which the texts are dynamically involved and within which
> their particular creative possibilities are themselves inscribed.
> —Shoshana Felman and Dori Laub, *Testimony*

French imaginative writing "after Auschwitz" (and this simple two-
word phrase has, since its initial coinage by Adorno in 1955, its own fas-
cinating development) was obsessed with the death camps, with the
complicity of the Vichy regime in the extermination of eighty thousand
Jews deported from France, although this had not as yet been ade-
quately analyzed except in the most obvious cases. It now seems to me
important not only to locate and identify sexist and antisemitic discourses in French literature and culture but also to uncover and con-
textualize the presence of this obsession. Thus I am involved in reading
again, but from a different perspective, a certain number of narrative
texts with which I have long been familiar. And "after Auschwitz" does
not apply exclusively to cultural production since the end of World War
II. It applies as well to texts written at any moment in the long history
of French writing, texts that are today being read in the knowledge of
"Auschwitz" by readers whose interpretive universe has been perma-
nently changed by *Auschwitz* as event and as metaphor.

The reading I propose in this chapter involves a short novel, *Coup de Grâce*, published in 1939, and a preface to this novel published twenty-three years later, in 1962.[1] Both *Coup de Grâce* and its preface were written by Marguerite Yourcenar, the pseudonymous anagram of Marguerite de Crayencour, the first woman to be elected to the French Academy since its creation three hundred and forty-five years ago. Not all of the questions that prompted my investigation receive primary attention in this essay, but I include them because they have directed my thinking: Why did Marguerite Yourcenar find it imperative to write the 1962 preface and to insist on its being read as part of *Coup de Grâce*? How does the author, in the preface, blatantly manipulate the reader? What are the connections between antisemitism, racism, classism, and sexism in the preface? What kind of political agenda does the preface propose and refuse? How are these connections maintained and reinforced in the narrative? How do they work together through the selection and ordering of events, metaphors, and metonymies, as well as the narrator's first-person discourse, to destroy the female protagonist by shooting her twice, the first time in the face? How can psychoanalytic and deconstructionist concepts such as the "repression of the feminine" help us to read together the silence surrounding the male narrator's homosexuality and the narrator's aversion for the mother figure and for Jews? What shall we do with the author's intentions and with her affirmations about nobles and nobility, about the "natural" antisemitism of her Baltic-Prussian-French aristocratic protagonist, and her generalizations about the behavior of women in love? How does the preface affect our reading of the narrative it now precedes? What are the connections between the "I" in the preface and the "I" in the narrative; between the ideology that permeates both preface and *récit*? Do the so-called realistic conventions of narrative inevitably reproduce stereotypes and clichés as has been claimed by leading contemporary literary and cultural theorists? What are the political and social consequences of rejecting these conventions? And, finally, how might we read this first-person narrative, written by a woman and narrated by an aristocratic male homosexual, after Auschwitz? My reading will explore three levels of interpretation with which we are familiar in literary studies: the intentions of the writer-author, the ideology, or the nonconscious presuppositions that inform the text, and the unconscious of the text, which we will look for in the signifiers of *Coup de Grâce*, primarily in the title. These

signifiers, more than the overt references to Eric von Lhomond's antisemitism, will lead us linguistically and textually to some of the connections between sexism, antisemitism, and nationalism with which I
began my inquiry.

I am aware that when dealing with questions of such a delicate and
powerful nature it is almost impossible to maintain a nonjudgmental
tone. Although I would rather accuse the text of reproducing an antisemitic ideology than the author of being antisemitic, it is impossible,
as my analysis will show, not to implicate the author and not to hold
her responsible. May I remind the reader in the most general way of
what was happening in Europe in 1938, the fifth year of Hitler's Third
Reich, the year of Kristallnacht, and the year Marguerite Yourcenar
wrote her novel? And may I insist more precisely on books that were
published in France between 1937 and 1939 in which antisemitism held
the center of the page, both reflecting and reinforcing its importance in
France? Two of the most significant books published during this period
include Céline's violent polemic against Jews, *Bagatelles pour un massacre* (1937), and Sartre's *récit* "L'Enfance d'un chef" (The Childhood of
a leader; 1939), which links antisemitism to a prefascist, nationalist, aesthetic sensibility.

Author's Intentions

In the Pléiade edition of her collected prose fiction, which she edited
herself, Marguerite Yourcenar insists that the preface to *Coup de Grâce*
must accompany and precede the narrative. The eight-page preface,
which in the American edition published by Farrar, Straus and Giroux
is translated by Marguerite Yourcenar's *compagne de vie* since 1937,
Grace Frick, is a curious document. It is as if the author had wanted to
present as unquestionable truths the following points: that this short
novel must be read as a human and not a political document; that the
protagonist is neither a sadist nor an antisemite; that this narrative
belongs within the double tradition of seventeenth-century French
tragedy and the Russian and French first-person *récit*. Corneille is mentioned and his insistence on the importance of the unity of peril, as is
Racine and his preface to *Bajazet*; Tolstoy's *Kreutzer Sonata* is also mentioned as well as Gide's *L'Immoraliste*. Marguerite Yourcenar does not
make the connection, however, *between* the protagonists who kill their

wives in these two récits and Eric von Lhomond who shoots Sophie de
Reval in *Coup de Grâce*. The preface justifies and defends *Coup de Grâce*
in terms of the "authenticity" of the documentation (Racine does the
same in the opening sentences of the preface to *Bajazet*) and because it
places the narrative within the most prestigious literary traditions.
Readers are called upon to read with care and to rectify the inevitable
deformation in a first-person narrative. Readers are invited to be sym-
pathetic toward the "moral nobility" of the three protagonists. Readers
are also expected to consent to generalizations in the author's preface
about the behavior of women in love and the behavior of men involved
in "chivalric dreams of comradeship."

In my efforts to locate as many as possible of the reviews that followed the publication of *Coup de Grâce* in France, Great Britain, and
the United States I have not found more than one or two reviews that
accuse the writer of antisemitism.[2] Nevertheless, it is clearly as a
response to such a charge that the preface was written. And the charge
is answered, by the author, in terms of fidelity to reality and the conventions of verisimilitude. Antisemitism, she maintains in the preface,
is a natural phenomenon; it is endemic to certain geographical areas
and certain social groups. This is why Eric von Lhomond's discourse
contains so many of the stereotypes and clichés that have developed
since the Middle Ages to depict Jews as usurers, jewellers, furriers,
omnivorous readers, obese and ugly, revolutionary and pusillanimous.

Eric von Lhomond, according to Marguerite Yourcenar's logic in the
preface, is no more responsible for his antisemitic references and allusions than he is responsible for the murder of Sophie de Reval. He is not
presented as following orders but rather as reproducing the language
inherited from his ethnic and class positions. These forms are, in her
scheme, both internalized and irrelevant. They are no more than local
color, divorced from the central dramas of *Coup de Grâce*, which are the
difficulty of narrating the past and the tragic implications of a particular amorous triangular configuration. Clearly the author is annoyed
that her 1939 narrative has been misinterpreted by some readers who
have made connections—unintended by the author—between the protagonist's attitudes toward his narrative, toward the past, toward
women, and toward Jews. She seems to suggest in the preface that what
was intended as marginal description should never have become a center of critical attention.

Marguerite Yourcenar's uneasiness is revealed throughout the preface by omissions and silences about the killing of women by their husbands and lovers, by her refusal, or inability, to understand antisemitism as anything other than a class or cultural prejudice, by her general resistance to making certain obvious connections between elements of her own narrative.

The preface to *Coup de Grâce* is followed by a brief, two-and-a-half-page, third-person narrative that sets the stage for the first-person récit. These pages give the reader abundant information: a wounded aristocratic mercenary has been fighting most recently for Franco; because of "birth and inclination" he has fought during the past fifteen years for right-wing causes in which he did not believe in Central Europe, China, South America, and Latvia; he now tells his story, in the words of the text, his "interminable confession," to two comrades while waiting for a train to Germany at the station buffet in Pisa. If the mercenary's "fractured and bandaged foot" suggests Oedipus and his complex, the presence of the Leaning Tower and of "an old beggar of a coachman blind in one eye" further suggests confusion of sexual identity that reinforces confusion of national identity and contributes to the reader's sense of a tottering phallocentric Europe. The third-person narrator sustains these ambiguities by refusing to qualify Eric as belonging either to the group of "men of feeling" or to the group of "criminals." Eric von Lhomond is presented as a victim of circumstance, subject to determinants he cannot control. He will later present himself in similar fashion.

The Nonconscious Presuppositions

Eric von Lhomond's first-person narrative, like the first-person author's preface, is an ordering and a justification of events that took place fifteen years earlier, during the civil war that followed the Russian Revolution of 1917. I will focus on the representation of women and of the feminine, with particular emphasis on the figure of the mother and the death (murder) of the main female character, Sophie de Reval. Four passages are central to my reading. The first is the presentation of Eric von Lhomond's mother, sandwiched between the description of the death of his father at Verdun, fighting for the Germans and killed, ironically, by an "African soldier fighting for France," and the description of his beloved friend Conrad, "a fixed point, a center, a heart." "As for my mother, she was half lost in dreams; she passed her time reading Buddhist scripture, or the poems of Rabindranath Tagore" (10). The second passage is the presentation of Sophie de Reval, Conrad's sister, which follows a four-page description of Eric's adolescent paradise, a golden age spent in the company of Conrad de Reval: "As for the young girl, she did not count; she was careless about her attire, and did nothing but devour books lent to her by a young Jewish student at Riga; she had no use for boys" (15).

Both the narrator's mother and Sophie are associated with books and their evil effects. The mother is "lost in dreams" and in another, foreign culture; Conrad's sister is initially coupled with "a young Jewish student," an equally foreign and dangerous influence. The verb "devour" will accompany Sophie throughout the text as an indication of the danger that the "feminine" poses for Eric.

The third passage describes a screen memory that overwhelms Eric von Lhomond during a nocturnal bombardment when Sophie, who, he tells us, is desperately in love with him, falls into his arms and he kisses her:

Most amazing of all, I accepted this gesture which she had taken nearly ten weeks to bring herself to. Now that she is dead, and that I have ceased to believe in miracles, I am glad that I kissed her lips one time at least, and her wild hair. If she were to remain like a vast country subdued by me but never possessed, I was to remember, in any case, the exact taste of her mouth that night, and the warmth of her living flesh. And if ever I could have loved Sophie utterly and simply with body and soul it was surely at that moment when we both were innocent as beings just resurrected. She was fairly throbbing against me, and no previous feminine encounter, whether with a chance pick-up, or with an avowed prostitute, had prepared me for that sudden, terrifying sweetness. Her body so yielding, yet rigid with delight, weighed in my arms almost as mysteriously as earth itself would have done had I entered some few hours before into death. I hardly know at what moment ecstasy changed into horror, releasing in me the memory of that starfish [étoile de mer] that Mother once forced into my hand on the beach at Scheveningen, almost provoking convulsions in me, to the consternation of the bathers. I wrenched myself from Sophie with a violence that must have seemed cruel to a body robbed of defense by felicity itself. She reopened her eyes (they had closed) and read in my aspect something harder to bear, doubtless, than hatred or terror, for she recoiled, covering her face with her upraised arm, like a child who is slapped, and that was the last time I ever saw her actually cry. (76–77)

I would like to insist on the bringing together, through the starfish, of Sophie and the narrator's mother, on the contamination of the one by the other, and on the way in which Eric's discourse blames the mother for his reactions of revulsion: "that starfish [*étoile de mer*] that Mother once forced into my hand." Without belaboring the obvious castration anxiety, and the fear of being devoured as well as penetrated by the maternal figure, I would like to note that the *étoile de mer* is connected through the text to a group of menacing marine animals whose effect is to terrify and repulse Eric von Lhomond: the octapuslike white gloved hands of a prostitute in Riga, the medusalike head of Sophie when she has curlers in her hair. More important still, this scene is connected to a later scene in the novel when Eric, in search of Sophie, visits the home of Mother Loew, a Jewish dressmaker and midwife in the small Jewish community in Lilienkron. Eric describes Mother Loew as an "old creature fairly drowned in her own fat" (112) whose "revolting obsequiousness blended . . . with truly Biblical hospitality" (113). Eric tells us that the "old Jewess" (116) is killed by soldiers a few weeks later, thereby placing her in the series of mutilated and tortured victims beginning with a description of the "Chinese Hand" (a special form of torture for white gloved officers) and ending with the shooting of Sophie.

The fourth passage constitues the two final paragraphs of *Coup de Grâce*. Sophie has joined a group of Bolshevik militants both out of political conviction and because she had been told that her brother Conrad and Eric were lovers. When the group to which she belongs is captured, Sophie refuses to ask for mercy and will be shot along with the others. She asks to be shot by Eric:

> One step more brought me so close to Sophie that I could almost have kissed her bared throat or laid a hand on her shoulder, now visibly shuddering, but by this time she was partly turned from me. She was breathing only slightly too fast; I clung to the thought that I had wanted to put an end to Conrad, and that this was the same thing. I fired, turning my head away like a frightened child setting off a torpedo on Christmas Eve. The first shot did no more than tear open the face, so that I shall never know (and it haunts me still) what expression Sophie would have had in death. On the second shot everything was over.

At first I thought that in asking me to perform this duty she had intended to give me a final proof of her love, the most conclusive proof of all. But I understood afterwards that she only wished to take revenge, leaving me prey to remorse. She was right in that: I do feel remorse at times. One is always trapped, somehow, in dealings with women. (150–51)

The words *remorse*—etymologically: to bite again—and *trapped* relate this final passage to the screen memory of the starfish at the beach at Scheveningen and Sophie to the narrator's mother and to Mother Loew. Or, we might say the same thing in another way: to kill Sophie is also to kill the mothers. Sophie, as a spectacle, is disturbing in much the same way as the phallic mother disturbs. With her face half blown away there is nothing to see and to know (*à voir/savoir*). And Eric, a victim of his mother's gesture in the earlier passage is, here again, a victim, "trapped" in Sophie's desire that he be her executioner.

Eric in his narrative and Marguerite Yourcenar in her preface almost succeed in attempting to close off to the reader paths of resistance to their discourse. They almost succeed in convincing us that to judge acts accomplished in a fiction is impossible, because time, memory, and the complexities of language contribute to the formation of a linguistic barrier that stands between the readers and the possibility of condemnation or praise. The nonconscious presupposition structuring *Coup de Grâce* is that the readers can never know what really happened in the confusions of a civil war, "the Baltic imbroglio" (10) and between Eric, Sophie, and Conrad. Eric von Lhomond appears as a precursor of the revisionist historians who claim that the Shoah never took place, that no one can ever know what really happened in the concentration camps. Two articles that appeared in February 1989 in the *New York Times*, one in the book review section, the other on the editorial page, reiterate my point. In a review of Charles S. Meier's *The Unmasterable Past: History, Holocaust, and German National Identity*, Richard J. Evans writes:

His (Mr. Maier's) concluding comments on the relation of the debate to the emergence of post-modernist historiography—in which more attention is paid to what people (including Hitler) thought and felt than to what they actually did—should be pondered by everyone who is thinking of jumping onto this particular contemporary intellectual bandwagon. (February 12, 1989, 28)

And John G. McGarrahan, in an editorial whose title coincides with my own, "Getting Away with Murder," writes about three cases in which "the brutal killing of a young girl by a sane, strong and rational man was found to be a not very serious crime. . . . The theme of these defenses is that it's the killer's state of mind that should determine his guilt or innocence, not his actions" (February 12, 1989)

By defending Eric von Lhomond in her 1962 preface, Marguerite Yourcenar is obliged to insist on her initial intentions and thereby to diminish the power of her narrative, the power of ideology, and the power of the reader. Her persistent denials accentuate Eric's denials and aggravate his responsibility for the killing of Sophie. Denials of the extermination of European Jews have included, among other specious arguments, one that insists on Hitler's intentions not to annihilate Jews, another that denies the possibility of establishing that an event took place when there is no one who witnessed the event, and still another that attributes the fiction of the Shoah to Zionist propaganda. These denials continue to be made in the face of considerable and varied evidence. What allows me to connect Marguerite Yourcenar and Eric von Lhomond with the revisionist historians, in spite of the obvious differences between historical events and a fictional text, is the vehemence of the denials of judeophobia and the massive silencing of Jewish suffering.

The Unconscious of the Text

There is, however, a dimension of the text beyond the author's intentions and the writer's nonconscious presuppositions. The unconscious of the text may help the reader to work against the weight of the authorial presence and against her implicit claims. If Marguerite Yourcenar and Eric von Lhomond both insist that they are outside ideology, the text of *Coup de Grâce* reveals that they are not. And here I am obliged to move between the French and the English versions.

The title, unchanged in translation except for the initial masculine article *Le* in the French, is a French expression, also used in English, that refers to a finishing blow often performed as a deliverance to a dying person or animal. Usually a coup de grâce is seen as a noble gesture. Within this text, however, the signifiers *coup* and *grâce* directly relate to the body of the old Jewess, Mother Loew, whose face is described, in French as "le visage de la vieille créature noyée dans la graisse" (an old creature fairly drowned in her own fat). *Graisse* (fat or grease) is the noun corresponding to the adjectives *gras*, masculine, and *grasse*, feminine, for fatty or greasy. And *cou* (neck) in French is a homophone for *coup* (blow). *Cou de grasse* (neck of fat woman), through the connection with Mother Loew, becomes the repulsive, excessive flesh of women, mothers, and Jews that Eric annihilates. *Le Coup de Grâce* of the French title can, in consequence, also be read as a sadistic, sexist, and antisemitic act involving both matricide and genocide.[3] In her prefatory attempts to get Eric von Lhomond off the hook, and in Eric von Lhomond's self-justifying discourse, the author, writer, and narrator may all be read as almost "getting away with murd(h)er."

Having worked through the author's intentions, the nonconscious presuppositions, and the unconscious of the text, I would like to return to my introductory remarks and to draw some conclusions and observations. It would seem inevitable that between the author's stated intentions and a reader's analysis of nonconscious presuppositions and the unconscious of the text there will be serious contradictions. Indeed, this reaffirms those truisms of contemporary criticism that insist on the blindness and the insight involved in all acts of reading, including the ones I have just performed. It would also seem inevitable that the conventions of realism as applied to the writing of fiction, in which I include Marguerite Yourcenar's claim about the "authenticity" of her récit, will result in the reproduction of a certain number of stereotypes. It is particularly difficult to avoid stereotyping and caricature in the representation of Jews. The signs of Jewishness with which most French readers are familiar partake of the grotesque and the ugly. Without these signs Jews would not necessarily be recognizable. A possible solution, then, is to avoid the conventions of realism and to work against the dominant ideology by refusing representation. Another firm conclusion is that, in French literature at least, the juxtaposition of aristocrat and Jew is bound to lead to the opposition aristocrat and Jew, which may well be the basis for the more common opposition between being French and being Jewish so fundamental to the question of French identity. In this respect it might be suggested that Marguerite Yourcenar's récit depends on the binary opposition Aryan and Semite that structures so much of the antisemitic and racist discourse in France from the middle of the nineteenth century until today.

More tentative observations concern the repression of the feminine in Eric von Lhomond, both his difficulty as narrator and the difficulty of the author as narrator to acknowledge his homosexual inclinations. Eric's infatuation with Sophie's brother, Conrad, his fixation on his adolescence with Conrad as the golden age, the utopian moment that can never return, confirm an ideological position that views the present as decadent and the future as empty. It is as if this repression of the feminine within Eric were responsible both for his attitude toward the Jewish Loew family and the shooting of Sophie. I would not venture, at this moment, even a tentative conclusion about the possible significance of this repression in the body of Marguerite Yourcenar's texts.

To conclude, my last observation touches on what I referred to earlier in the chapter as an obsession with the extermination camps, their explicit repression and the ways in which they are present, implicitly, through their absence. These remarks do not bear on the narrative of *Coup de Grâce* that was published in 1939, but they do concern the preface of 1962. I would suggest that the author-narrator's refusal to acknowledge the presence of antisemitism in her text, thereby reaffirming through her resistance the antisemitic discourse in the preface, may be linked to the knowledge and the repression of the knowledge of Auschwitz. It may seem as strange to other readers as it does to me that in 1938, when Nazi Germany was already actively persecuting Jews and antisemitic tracts were being published regularly in Germany and in France, Marguerite Yourcenar should have chosen to write a story in which antisemitism is allowable because it is professed by European aristocrats. And that in 1962, when so much was known about what had happened to European Jews under National Socialism, the preface would castigate the "naïve reader" who "might make a sadist of Eric" and "would mistake for a professional anti-Semite this aristocrat whose habitual irony towards Jews is a matter of caste" (5–6).[4] I submit that denying the importance of antisemitic discourse and its effects and denying Auschwitz are inextricably related. I submit, too, that the relationship between author-narrator and narrator-character, between Marguerite Yourcenar and Eric von Lhomond is closer than contemporary narratological theory would have us believe.

7 | The Corset and the Corpse:
Antisemitism and the Death of God

> One of the essential formulations that designate the event of
> nihilism says, "God is dead." The phrase "God is dead" is not
> an atheistic proclamation: it is a formula for the fundamental
> experience of an event in Occidental history.
> —Martin Heidegger, *Nietzsche*

> As a Schwarzwald redneck, he [Heidegger] had an ingrained dis-
> like of North German cosmopolitan mandarins. As a philoso-
> pher, he viewed the rise of ironist intellectuals—many of them
> Jews—as symptomatic of the degeneracy of what he called "the
> age of the world-picture." He thought the ironist culture of our
> century, the high culture in which Proust and Freud are central
> figures, merely the unThinking self-satisfaction of a postmeta-
> physical nihilism.
> —Richard Rorty. *Contigency, Irony, and Solidarity*

I have chosen to look at the relationship between antisemitism and the
"death of God" by examining the possible connections between the
death of God, the Jews as Christ killers, the attempted "extermination of
European Jewry," and the obsession with mortality in selected writings
of Albert Cohen, a major French Jewish "ironist intellectual" and "cosmopolitan" writer of the twentieth century, and the French existentialist
and "feminist" writer, Simone de Beauvoir. I understand the expression
death of God as an apprehension of the fundamental solitude and mean-
inglessness of the human presence in the world and as a sensibility that
develops toward the end of the nineteenth century and is articulated
most fully in the writings of Friedrich Nietzsche and Martin Heidegger,
German philosophers who have had an enduring influence on French
writing of this century. I understand the word *nihilism* in the same way
as Martin Heidegger describes Friedrich Nietzsche's understanding: "By
nihilism Nietzsche means the historical development, i.e., event, that

the uppermost values devalue themselves, that all goals are annihilated, and that all estimates of value collide against one another" (156).

The *death of God* and the term *nihilism* with which it is linked are sometimes used to denigrate literary texts considered to be "pessimistic" or philosophical concepts that insist on indeterminacy. Very different writers such as Louis-Ferdinand Céline, on the one hand, and Jacques Derrida and Paul de Man, on the other, have been accused of being nihilistic, irrational, and, therefore, dangerous.

Most writers who have explored the rise of antisemitism and that aspect of nihilism associated with the death of God suggest that increased and excessive antisemitism is in part the result of nihilism, that the rejection of the Judeo-Christian God led ineluctably to the persecution of Jews and would eventually have led as well to the persecution of all believers. The death of God and nihilism are seen as responsible for the inhumanity of human beings to each other, for the disregard of those ethical positions that had for so long been dependent on the existence of God. Many writers, unwilling to accept these nihilistic conclusions, have attempted to replace the Judeo-Christian God with other compelling figures or metaphors: the Marxist belief in social change through revolution, the socialist belief in social change through social reforms, the belief in other religious rites and practices, the variety of isms that have developed during the twentieth century, including all forms of identity politics—from antisemitisms and feminisms to Afrocentrisms—that give to their adherents a sense of mission and a sense of community.

I have adopted a different point of view on the relationship of antisemitism to the death of God and to nihilism. Rather than understanding the exacerbated antisemitism of the late nineteenth century in France and in Germany as one of the consequences of nihilism and antireligious sentiment, I understand modern antisemitism as at least partially nourished by the refusal to understand and to explore nihilism. I would argue that this refusal increases antisemitism and that the reaction against the notion of the death of God is associated and assimilated to the much older story of the killing of Christ, the death of Jesus Christ on the cross, by the Jews. *Le peuple déicide*, as the Jews have been designated for centuries in French, is perhaps the central figure in Christian antisemitism, recalled in churches throughout Christendom during the Easter service and endlessly repeated in Christian iconography. And

Christ, after all, for believing Christians, is God. Perhaps killing Jews as an act of revenge for their killing of Christ blurs the frontier that separates inevitable death from death as a punishment for murder. And so, in my argument, the death of God cry and theme is associated with this other more ancient act of destruction and desecration and Jews are made to bear the burden in the popular imagination of having killed both Christ in 33 A.D. and God in the late nineteenth century.[1]

In her essay on *Antisemitism* Hannah Arendt, in the vanguard of other political scientists and historians of the twentieth century, tends to denounce nihilism as a cause of antisemitism and antidemocratic rhetoric: "Down to our times the term Anti-Dreyfusard can still serve as a recognized name for all that is antirepublican, antidemocratic, and antisemitic" (92). Hannah Arendt always uses the word *nihilistic* pejoratively: "the nihilistic nationalism of Barrès and Maurras" (94), or "the vehement and nihilistic philosophy of spiritual self-hatred" (94), or, again, "The nihilism which characterized the nationalists was no monopoly of the Anti-Dreyfusards" (112).

My own position is closer to the one described by David Farrell Krell in his introduction to Heidegger's *Nietzsche*, volumes 1 and 2:

> Heidegger is concerned to show that all the sundry diagnoses and proffered diagnoses of nihilism are bound to fail; no, not only bound to fail, but are also likely to aggravate our situation by dangling hopes of facile solutions before our eyes. For Heidegger, nihilism results from our persistant failure to think the nothing, to confront in our thought the power of the *nihil* in human existence, which is mortal existence, and history, which is the history of the oblivion of being and the abandonment by being. Such thinking requires a protracted confrontation with the history of Western thought since Plato—which is what Heidegger's *Nietzsche* is all about—and unflinching meditation on human mortality and the finitude of time, being and propriation. If dogged thought on human mortality seems unduly pessimistic, and if thought on the history of philosophy seems onerous, Heidegger replies that our optimism always underestimates the challenge of mortal thinking and that our reluctance to take the onus of history seriously reflects nothing if not the historical "impact of nihilism itself." (xviii)

I would attribute Martin Heidegger's silence concerning the Shoah to his not having successfully undertaken an "unflinching meditation on human mortality.

In the writings of Albert Cohen antisemitism and nihilism as reiterated themes directing discourse and imagery attain a position of dominance. The same might be said of the writings of Louis-Ferdinand Céline, but with two important differences. Céline's nihilism and antisemitism do not coexist in his major fictional works as they do for Albert Cohen, and the antisemitism in Céline's pamphlets *Bagatelles pour un massacre*, *L'Ecole des cadavres* (School for corpses), *Les Beaux Draps* (A Fine mess), for example, is the antisemitism of the narrator, a delirious outpouring rather than an ironic commentary on the delirium of others.

As in Marcel Proust's *A la recherche du temps perdu*, but with greater frequency and still more abruptly and unexpectedly, death erupts onto the social scene in *Belle du Seigneur*. Maurice Zermatten, in a review of the novel in the Swiss newspaper *L'Impartial*, March 6, 1969, wrote the following:

> But *Belle du Seigneur* is not only a distressing novel about an old, banal adventure. It is also a terrifying meditation on the inanity of every human endeavor, of all ambition, all fame, and all happiness. Each page, or almost, evokes the slow breaking up of everything that lives and the inexorable progress of our death. I would say that the preoccupation of the moralist is greater than the attempt to evoke a chemically perfect love. In the most deliriously happy scenes, the novelist evokes the fat gnawing worm that works its way into the radiant bodies and already begins to destroy them. Instead of a song of triumph, we hear the great moan of death during the nights when the nightingale tries to exalt the miracle of love. And it is because of this that the novel acquires a dimension of wisdom and painful reality rarely achieved. (1020)

Examples of "the fat gnawing worm" and "the great moan of death" abound in Albert Cohen's text from the very first pages of the 999-page novel to the double suicide at the end. For the narrator, as for Solal the protagonist, the future is always evoked in terms of a body that will rot in a coffin. It is as if Albert Cohen had selected as one of the epigraphs for his novel this portion of a letter written by the writer Gustave Flaubert to his mistress, the writer Louise Colet, on the August 6 or 7, 1847:

> Since we said that we loved each other you wonder why I have reservations about adding "forever." Why? It is because I predict the future.

> Because the antithesis is constantly before my eyes. I never saw a child
> without thinking that he will become an old man nor a cradle without
> thinking of a tomb. When I contemplate a naked woman, I see her
> skeleton. That is why joyful sights make me sad and sad sights have lit-
> tle effect on me. (275)

The first of the many antitheses, the juxtaposition of a healthy young
body with the corpse to be, takes place in the opening scene of *Belle du
Seigneur*. Solal has stealthily entered Ariane Deume's bedroom and is
preparing to disguise himself as an old Jewish man. The narrator
describes Solal's reactions to seeing himself in a mirror:

> Narrow hips, a flat stomach, a broad chest, and under the tanned skin
> muscles, supple serpents intertwined. All this beauty will end up in the
> cemetary, a little green here, a little yellow there, all alone in a box falling
> apart because of humidity. The young women would be surprised if they
> saw him that way, silent and stiff in his crate. He smiled with a mild feel-
> ing of satisfaction, began to wander again, from time to time touching
> his automatic pistol. (9)

Throughout the novel Solal will see himself and others, women and
men, simultaneously in their present state and in their future decom-
position. This process is accompanied by the refrain of "Frères
humains" (Brother human beings), a refrain that underlines a literary
and a thematic continuity from the fifteenth-century poet, François
Villon, to Albert Cohen. It also underlines the particular blend of
nihilism and social criticism that is the hallmark of Cohen's writing. At
moments in the novel the seeing of the cadaver under the healthy body
is used to ironically undercut the stupidity and the boorishness of certain characters, Adrien Deume, for example. At other times it is used,
as in this opening scene, for the protagonist by the protagonist, under-
lining the common mortality of all human beings. But Adrien Deume
himself is also subject to these moments of metaphysical anguish,
thereby making it difficult for the reader to see him as a one-dimen-
sional man, to see him uniquely as a caricature of the bureaucrat eager
to advance without working, to be recognized without having accomplished anything of note.

The presence in this early scene of the "automatic pistol" and Solal's
meditation on which part of his body to aim at both foreshadows his
suicide and that of Ariane (although they will die from an overdose of

pills and not from a gunshot) and makes it clear that the rotting corpse is not necessarily a state reserved for a distant future but one that could become his body's reality at any moment. Death is not, in this novel, something that will happen to everyone at some future time, but rather something that could happen to anyone at any moment. Solal's meditation is quite explicit about why suicide might be attractive. It is not only to move a step ahead of the inevitable. It is also to get away from what the narrator refers to as "the human gang, always ready to hate, to speak ill of someone" (9). "To hate" and "to speak ill" are oblique references to antisemitism, to all the antisemitic words and gestures to which Solal is exposed.

On at least two occasions in the novel, antisemitic words and gestures and the emphasis on our common mortality come together in the same paragraph. In a very long speech delivered in the presence of Ariane, before the beginning of their liaison, in his hotel room at the Ritz in Geneva, Solal says:

> Just think, all these future cadavers in the streets, on the sidewalks, in such a rush, so busy and who don't know that the earth in which they will be buried exists, awaits them. Future cadavers, they joke, or get angry, or brag. . . . Future cadavers and nonetheless mean during their short lives, and they like to write "Death to the Jews" on the walls. Should I go around the world and speak to them? Convince them to take pity on each other, fill them with their imminent death? But there is nothing to be done, they enjoy being mean. (351–52)

Later in the novel, when Solal is alone in the streets of Paris where the walls are covered with the cry "Mort aux Juifs" (Death to the Jews), it is clear that speaking to human beings and trying to convince them to have pity for each other is a utopian plan. But faced with the effects produced on him by these antisemitic inscriptions, Solal proposes a reason for their hatred: "In fact the fear of death has given them colic of the brain, and they love their diarrhea" (859). In Albert Cohen's novel, *Belle du Seigneur*, when the fear of death is not confronted lucidly, antisemitism is not far behind.

In the fourth volume of her memoirs, *Tout Compte fait/All Said and Done*, published eight years after *Une Mort très douce/A Very Easy Death*, Simone de Beauvoir comments extensively on the books she read during the 1960s. Among them is *Belle du Seigneur*, which she praises and analyzes with sentences that could be applied mutatis mutandis to her own writing in *Une Mort très douce*:

> 1936. The sound of the Nazi boots in the streets of Berlin. In the League of Nations plump officials yawn over their files, indifferent to what is happening in the world. The hero, Solal, is very like the author; he works in the League of Nations, and he looks at his colleagues with a dismayed irony. He makes us want to laugh and weep when he describes a cocktail-party at which superiors, inferiors and equals confront one another with a vivid sense of hierarchy—never a moment's respite from circumspection and devious, wary prudence. Decorations, promotions, social success: is it not ludicrous to attach so much importance to these baubles when one is a future corpse? Cohen is obsessed by the idea that every individual is a corpse under suspended sentence. . . . I have rarely read more amusing, nor more revengeful, passages than those in which Cohen brings Deume's parents on to the scene. He is sorry for little father Deume, who drags out his useless old man's existence under the harsh rule of his wife. But he hates mother Deume: he hates her false spirituality, her stupid vanity, her hardness, her pretentious vulgarity, and her avarice. She is a perfect specimen of that grasping, selfish, hypocritical, racist bourgeoisie—the bourgeoisie that the Jew Solal feels is hunting him down.
>
> Cohen contrasts this stuffy, futile society with the noisy, carefree life of the Cephalonian Jews. (168–69)

The corset and the corpse are interconnected in this appreciation of *Belle du Seigneur*. As in her own writing, Simone de Beauvoir notes both the metaphysical tragedy and the social comedy, that which is inevitable in the human condition and that which is brought about by social institutions and class prejudice. Like Albert Cohen, Simone de Beauvoir maintains one eye on and in the tomb and the other on the "sad sights" of our oppressive social and insitutional arrangements. She is sensitive to both the corpse and the corset, to mortality and anti-semitism. There is an oscillation in Simone de Beauvoir's writings between political commitment and an absurdist vision of the human condition that seems to contradict those commitments. In a parallel manner readers and critics tend either to concentrate on her political activism and her struggles against sexism, ageism, racism, and anti-semtism, or to focus on the fact that she has been so consistently pre-occupied by questions of anguish and nothingness, by her own mortality and the mortality of others. But the unavoidable truth is that Simone de Beauvoir's texts refuse to forget either the metaphysical questioning of Being or the social questioning of the organization of power and the hierarchies of dominance.

Atheism often associated with nihilism continues to be, in Western Europe and in the United States, a difficult, even a dangerous, doctrine to affirm publicly. In the United States a right-wing political rhetoric conflates being a *nihilist,* an *atheist,* and being a *communist* with three nouns signifying demonic evil. And increasingly, so it seems, in Western Europe where Pope Jean Paul II during his visit to Austria in the summer of 1988 preached the "reevangelization" of Europe, nihilism, atheism, and Nazism have been conflated, making it possible to suggest, as did an editorial in the French newspaper *Le Monde* (June 28, 1988) that "it is the God of the Jews and the God of the Christians that the Nazi initiative wanted to eliminate." Nihilism and atheism have also been inculpated in elements of Nietzschean discourse reinterpreted by the Nazis and in the silence of the influential German philosopher Martin Heidegger regarding the extermination of European Jews. Simone de Beauvoir's explicit atheism informs all of her writings and her philosophical and political positions and may be read in relation to her revolt against her dogmatically Catholic mother, against the upper-middle-class Catholic bourgeoisie into which she was born, and against those of her contemporaries who seemed to her to be drawn by diverse forms of theism.

In Simone de Beauvoir's five novels, as in her four volumes of autobiography and her volume of short stories, she tries to capture the meanings of a life lived in time, the meaning of the passage of time, of change, mortality, death, and history. The act of writing, for Simone de Beauvoir, is linked to the desire not to lose anything of her own life. It is interesting to examine the differences between the intentions of Simone de Beauvoir and those of contemporary critics and theorists for whom the text, rather than the author, plays the principal role in the structure and the determination of meanings. The author, for Simone de Beauvoir, is not dead, nor is she essentially governed by her unconscious; the author is conscious of her intentions and responsible for them.

Simone de Beauvoir is a writer who introduces taboo topics, as well as an often new transgressive content, into traditional narrative and descriptive writing. For example, her chapter on "La lesbienne" (the

Lesbian) and on "La mère" (the mother) in *Le Deuxième Sexe / The Second Sex*; her written version of her passionate love affair with the Chicago writer Nelson Algren in *Les Mandarins*; her detailed description of the death of her mother in *Une Mort très douce* and of Jean Paul Sartre's incontinence in *La Cérémonie des adieux / Adieux*; her interest in the sexuality of aging women and men in *La Vieillesse / On Old Age*; her repeated references, explicit and implicit, to the Shoah and the Jewish question in France in her memoirs, her novels, and her play, as well as in certain articles and prefaces.

In reviewing the corpus of Simone de Beauvoir's writings and the critical commentaries it has elicited for a volume of *Critical Essays on Simone de Beauvoir*, I noted that the Jewish question is evoked frequently in Simone de Beauvoir's autobiographical writings, particularly in the volume that deals with the German Occupation of France, and that unlike many other writers of her generation, Simone de Beauvoir was not silent either about the complicity of the Vichy government in the antisemitic policies that were so fundamental to Nazism or about the importance of antisemitism in France and Western Europe. The Jewish question also figures in the form of a crucial anecdote in her novel, *Le Sang des autres / The Blood of Others* (1945), and in her only play, *Les Bouches inutiles / Useless Mouths* (1945), set in fourteenth-century Flanders, it is present as a suppressed historical referent.[2] One of the last essays written by Simone de Beauvoir before her death was the preface to Claude Lanzmann's film scenario, Shoah. There is also an essay—originally a lecture—"Solidarité d'Israël: Un Soutien critique" (Solidarity with Israel: A critical support), written in 1975 in order to explain to the French Left why she had accepted the Jerusalem Prize and why the French Left should reconsider its anti-Israel positions and support the Israeli Left.

These examples have reinforced my desire to present Simone de Beauvoir in a favorable light, not only because she is a thinker to be admired, to be argued with, and to be commented on, but because in spite of recent critical accounts insisting on how little she and Sartre did to help Jews in France during the years of the Occupation, she was nevertheless one of a relatively small group of "righteous" left-wing intellectual gentiles whose refusal to succumb to the antisemitic discourses and practices of the thirties and forties was, with one exception, constant and exemplary.[3]

At the risk of simplifying the multilayered contexts, I would like to suggest that for Simone de Beauvoir the "destruction of European Jews" (to borrow Raul Hilberg's title), was one of the structuring events inscribed in her texts along with her family configuration, the "experience" of the death of God, and her meeting, in 1929, with Jean-Paul Sartre. The destruction of European Jews haunts Simone de Beauvoir's texts (as it also haunts the texts of Samuel Beckett and Marguerite Duras), pushing her toward antifascist and anticolonialist political commitments and the maintenance of a relentless vigilance.[4] Auschwitz for Simone de Beauvoir is the "incontournable" and the "indépassable"[5] historical event—an event that cannot be skirted or gone beyond—of the twentieth century. Auschwitz can be neither ignored nor transcended. It is "there" and must somehow be included. And, moreover, it merges with her awareness of mortality so that death at Auschwitz and death as a universal occurrence always, after 1944, coexist in Simone de Beauvoir's writings. Unlike the German philosopher Martin Heidegger, for whom, it seems, the universal overshadowed the historical, Simone de Beauvoir is dedicated to maintaining both in her writings.[6]

In the second chapter of *Une Mort très douce* (1964), Simone de Beauvoir's autobiographical account of the dying and death of her mother, Françoise de Beauvoir, the narrator-protagonist interrupts the relentless description of her mother's cancer with a brief analysis of how a French baby girl born in 1887 became a constrained, conservative, and unhappy woman. The chapter illustrates the famous opening sentence of the second volume of *Le Deuxième sexe*: "On ne naît pas femme: on le devient" (One is not born, but rather one becomes a woman). The metaphor used by Simone de Beauvoir to represent the oppressive constraints imposed on her mother by the institutions of the family, the Church, and Catholic school is carried by the words *corset* and *laces*. The *corset* that oppresses the woman's body occurs twice in the chapter. Toward the beginning, "Maman started life corseted in the most rigid of principles—provincial propriety and the morals of a convent girl (33), and, at the end, "In her childhood, her body, her heart and her mind had been squeezed into an armour of principles and prohibitions. She had been taught to pull the laces hard and tight herself. A full-blooded, spirited woman lived on inside her, but a stranger to herself, deformed and mutilated" (43). The suggestion, throughout the rest of the text, is that the imposition of the corset and the pulling of the laces, at first by outside forces and later by Françoise de Beauvoir herself, are causally related to the intestinal cancer from which she died.

If the only problems were those caused by the corset, the solution would be relatively simple: to take it off, as indeed many women have done for both symbolic and hygienic reasons. Liberation from oppression is, as we know, difficult but possible. But there is another more basic problem: the presence of the corpse, the dead body of Simone de Beauvoir's mother. In the nonreligious mode that is Simone de Beauvoir's there is no liberation from the idea of mortality. My thesis, as the title of this chapter indicates, is a simple one: Simone de Beauvoir's importance, perhaps even her uniqueness as a writer during the third quarter of the twentieth century, is her double commitment, in her writings and her pronouncements, to questions of life *and* death, to the corset *and* to the corpse—her simultaneous attention to certain formulations of Heideggerean and Sartrean existentialism as well as to her own particular brand of social activism and feminism. On the one hand there is in her novels, memoirs, and essays a constant awareness of memento mori, and on the other hand a dedication to the urgent need for social change. In both cases this urgency and this commitment were nourished and sustained by Auschwitz as a fact and a metaphor that encompass the metaphysical and the social. When Jean-Paul Sartre moved from *L'Etre et le néant/Being and Nothingness* (1943), his extended analysis on what it means to be an existing, desiring, finite human being in the world, to historical and social concerns, his writings lost (or seemed to lose) their inclusion of mortality. And few "feminist" writers since 1968 with whom I am acquainted—this acquaintance is limited to the United States, France, Canada, and Great Britain—have included the question of mortality in their theoretical writings. Almost alone of her sex, Simone de Beauvoir has attempted to bring together the existential phenomenological description of a fundamental human condition with the feminist insistence on the construction of femininity and the inevitable differences among women of race, class, sexual preference, and age, anchoring both in a traumatic historical event. In "coming to feminism" after existentialism, Simone de Beauvoir lost neither the energy of her atheism nor her obsessive awareness of its implications.

The plight of the existential other, victim of racism and antisemitism, sexism and heterosexism, colonialism and imperialism, theorized in terms of power relations, has been central to the discussions within feminism since the late 1960s. But for many feminists this concern with the other and difference has been seen as antithetical to "male" meditations on mortality, death, and closure. Indeed, there has been, during the second half of the twentieth century, a massive flight by most isms, including feminisms, away from Heideggerian anguish and care as categories fundamental to human being. Simone de Beauvoir has not fled. To the contrary, she has sustained and defended the need to mourn as well as the need for a critical discourse and a discourse of possibility written in a language accessible to most readers, a language whose effects would be powerful enough to "move" and to "convince" and thereby constitute a call to individual and collective rethinking and action. A similar investment in questions of life and death can be found today in France only in texts by theologians.

I would like to examine a little-known text by Simone de Beauvoir, written in 1975 at the moment when UNESCO excommunicated Israel and when Simone de Beauvoir, who had refused all prizes after she received the Goncourt prize for *Les Mandarins* in 1954, agreed to go to Jerusalem to accept the "prix de Jérusalem." In November of 1974 Simone de Beauvoir and thirty intellectuals, including Raymond Aron, Jean-Paul Sartre, Eugene Ionesco, and Arthur Rubinstein, signed a manifesto in which they accused UNESCO of spiritually abolishing Israel. In December of 1974 Simone de Beauvoir, Sartre, and Ionesco announced that they would no longer participate in the activities of UNESCO because of its anti-Israel resolutions. On January 14, 1975, the award was announced in the French newspaper *Le Monde* and on April 23 of the same year Simone de Beauvoir received the award at the opening of the International Book Fair in Jerusalem. This prize, which is given to writers who promote the notion of the freedom of the individual, had been previously awarded to Bertrand Russell, Max Frisch, André Schwarz-Bart, Ignazio Silone, Jorge Luis Borges, and Eugene Ionesco. And, finally, on May 6, 1975, Simone de Beauvoir gave a lecture at a meeting organized by the Cercle Bernard Lazare in Paris, later published in *Les Cahiers Bernard Lazare*, entitled "Solidaire d'Israël: un soutien critique" and reprinted in Claude Francis and Fernande Gontier's indispensable book *Les Ecrits de Simone de Beauvoir* (1979).

Politically what is at stake for Simone de Beauvoir in this text is her public stance as an activist in French left-wing movements. Already, in

1975, signs of support for Israel were considered by the Left to be politically incorrect. Simone de Beauvoir's intentions in this article are
fourfold: to convince the French Left to reconsider its positions vis-à-
vis Israel and to support the Israeli Left; to show that Israel is not a
monolithic state, that within Israel there is a Left and a Right, a spectrum of political and religious convictions; to reiterate the meanings
that she attaches to the Shoah and therefore to the continued existence
of the state of Israel; and to affirm the possibility of both support and
criticism.

This ten-page article is a summary, or so I will read it, of Simone de
Beauvoir's intentions and her nonconscious presuppositions. In a more
traditional mode of explication it is also a summary of Simone de Beauvoir's thematic concerns and rhetorical strategies, her generosity and her
limitations as a thinker and a writer. Her intervention in the long and
persistent history of antisemitic acts and writings in France constitutes
an important moment in what is still an ongoing debate involving
today, as it did in earlier periods, the question of French identity.

If we begin with a study of the thematic concerns and the rhetorical
strategies employed by Simone de Beauvoir in this article, we come to
what are, I think, fairly obvious conclusions. Her article is an attempt
to convince the French Left to reconsider its position on Israel by insisting on her experience, as a French leftist, during the Occupation and
during her subsequent trips to Israel. Simone de Beauvoir's arguments
are, in every instance, based on what she *saw*: her Jewish friends who
were deported by the Nazis and never returned; the dangerous isolation
of Israel and the Israeli Left; the transformation of the land in Israel by
the work of the Jewish settlers. Her primary strategy is the use of the
pronoun *I*— "I" as a witness, as an intellectual, as a repository and a
guarantee of empirical truths. The article has a beginning, a middle,
and an end; it is a superior example of the French exercise known as the
dissertation française. It begins with the question "Why am I here and
why did I go to Israel?" (522) and it ends, optimistically, "for the future
. . . the happy existence of the country" (532). Thematically and rhetor-
ically, then, the article poses a number of recognizable contemporary
(for 1975) problems, examines them, and proposes other ways of dealing with them. But the contrast between the nonconscious presuppositions that structure the text and the unconscious propositions that
emerge from a symptomatic reading of the text produce a less positive,

more anguished perspective on Israel, the French Left, antisemitism, and Simone de Beauvoir's relationship to them. The reassurance provided by visual evidence and her belief in social change clash with the critique of the antisemitism and the romanticism of the French Left and raise the question of her own identity. If the French Left is also antisemitic, to what audience does she then address her writings? Still more poignantly, the reader is struck by the tension between the argument that Simone de Beauvoir refuses, the religious, fundamentalist argument that asserts Israel's claim to the land, and the argument that she accepts, based on Berthold Brecht's claim in *The Chalk Circle*, that the land belongs to those who labor to improve it.

Like the young Jewish "lycéen" to whose anguished letter she refers in her article, Simone de Beauvoir fears, and perhaps has already experienced, rejection and name-calling from the French Left. Her final argument, "This country must continue to exist, that is a certainty for me," is certainly not one that would convince an antiempirical Left. For Simone de Beauvoir, and once again I am simplifying, seeing is believing. It is interesting to contrast this cliché of Western metaphysics with her earlier concern in this article that a "suppression symbolique" of Israel by UNESCO "implies a deep desire, conscious or unconscious, for annihilation" (522). Simone de Beauvoir reasons on both sides of the philosophical-political spectrum: she seems to advocate inductive and deductive approaches, as they are needed or useful.

There is a central and long passage in this text, in which the Shoah and its aftermath are recorded through Simone de Beauvoir's direct experience of it:

> Thus, I could see with my own eyes—what I had anticipated when I signed with others a manifesto against the UNESCO resolution—that it was indeed a plot destined to push Israel ever deeper into isolation, destined as I said earlier, to negate Israel symbolically while waiting to accept that Israel be negated materially and really. The idea of the annihilation of Israel is an idea that fills me with horror. I am not Jewish, but I lived through the Nazi Occupation from 1940 to 1944 and I followed almost day by day the horrors of the Holocaust; I followed the persecutions to which the Jews, as victims, were subjected. It is not necessary to have personal ties with someone in order to feel the horror of the Holocaust, but it happened that I had a rather large number of Jewish friends and that almost all of them were taken away; they were deported and

they never came back. I lived through the Occupation and the persecution of the Jews in a state of profound horror; but this horror had something logical about it because they were persecuted by enemies, by Nazis,
a group of horrible people whose business it was to annihilate and per-
secute Jews.

What was even more painful, if I can express myself in this manner,
were the events that followed. We thought in 1944–1945 that the night-
mare was over and that the Jews would be able to breathe again, would
be able to live in some way or another in freedom, with rights equal to
those of other human beings. And what did we see? We saw the survivors
of the camps, the rare survivors, who were thrown into other camps; or
they were obliged to wander over the seas without anyone wanting to
receive them; and I found that all the more scandalous because it was our
allies, the English in particular, who were responsible for all this misery,
all this misfortune. We also learned what the responsibility of the Amer-
icans had been in the Holocaust; they had refused to raise their immigration quota, they had not allowed Jews to enter as massively as was
necessary in order for them to escape the Nazi persecutions. What a
scandal to see the complicity of all the allied countries (including
France) contributing to the misfortune of the Jewish people. (523–24)

The strengths and the weaknesses of this article, and of many of Simone
de Beauvoir's essays and documentary writings, are obvious and do not
require further elaboration here. What is more interesting, and I think
more important, is why Simone de Beauvoir is different, why, unlike
most post-Heideggerians in France, and this category includes many of
the major writers considered under the rubric of poststructuralism,
deconstruction, and post-Lacanian psychoanalysis, she is willing to *look
at* the Shoah, to place it in a central position in her texts? Why was
Simone de Beauvoir not silent? Why did Simone de Beauvoir not forget? Why did Simone de Beauvoir, in spite of the parenthetical
"(including France)" not deny?

I would like to propose two very different hypotheses as ways of
approaching Simone de Beauvoir's "difference." The first hypothesis,
which in no way contradicts the second, is that Simone de Beauvoir
had, in 1940, a number of Jewish friends, and that in 1952 she began a
liaison with Claude Lanzmann whose adult life has been in large part
devoted to resurrecting the deliberately covered traces of the destruction of French and European Jews. Affectively, then, Simone de Beauvoir was close to Jews; she not only saw them disappear but she also fol-

lowed, through Lanzmann, the implications and the consequences of their disappearance.

The second hypothesis relates to Simone de Beauvoir's reiterated position on equality, her suspicion of feminist theories of difference, her antagonism toward feminist attempts to define and describe a "feminine" identity. On the post-1968 feminist scene, in both France and the United States, Simone de Beauvoir has often been accused of representing an outmoded version of feminism. Her refusal to privilege difference as a major category for discussing male and female, masculine and feminine, woman and man has been vigorously attacked and denigrated by those feminists eager to establish differences, and, through differences, to recognize either fixed or constructed identities. If we transpose her feminist arguments to the Jewish question, some of the advantages of Simone de Beauvoir's position are immediately discernible. For her the differences in historical experiences between Jews and non-Jews in no way constitute a Jewish identity and differences become neither exotic nor irremediable: they are rather precise, explainable in common sense language. There is no attempt in her writings, whether on women or on Jews, to create mysterious privileged beings. An emphasis on difference that leads to an obsession with identity is neither a progressive concept nor a productive one for Simone de Beauvoir.

Experientially and intellectually, Simone de Beauvoir was prepared to *see* and to empathize with the suffering of French Jews and to remember what that suffering had been. But, most important, and this will bring me toward my conclusion, Simone de Beauvoir's theory of language and communication, so opposed to that of Heideggereans, Lacanians, and Derrideans, made it possible and imperative for her to write about Auschwitz. Heidegger's silence, which has been at the center of heated discussion on the intellectual scene in France, may be analyzed not only in terms of Heidegger's particular brand of national socialism but more significantly in relation to his theory of language. If we compare Heidegger's 1946 essay "Brief über den Humanismus"/"Letter on Humanism)," which he sent to his French disciple Jean Beaufret in 1946, and which was published in 1947, with the writings of Simone de Beauvoir and Jean-Paul Sartre during this same period, we will, I think, have a better understanding of what is implied in Heidegger's silence and in Beauvoir's and Sartre's attempts to confront the Shoah in words.

(Parenthetically, let us note that Jean Beaufret also supported the revisionist historians' declaration that no Jews were gassed at Auschwitz.)

First, a few titles. In 1945, Simone de Beauvoir's novel *Le Sang des autres* and her play *Les Bouches inutiles* were published and in 1946 Jean-Paul Sartre's extended essay *Réflexions sur la question juive* appeared. I have not as yet been able to determine the possible relationship between the publication of Heidegger's letter of 1946—it was sent to Beaufret in December—and the earlier publication in the same year of Sartre's essay. It would be essential to know whether or not Sartre's analysis of the Jewish question reinforced Heidegger's intention to critique Sartrean existentialism and its emphasis on a notion of "engagement" or commitment. If indeed it could be shown that Heidegger had read *Réflexions sur la question juive* before answering Beaufret's questions about his relationship to Sartrean existentialism, one would be able to suggest that Heidegger's letter against existentialist humanism, his critique of Sartre's essay *L'Existentialisme est un humanisme*, also of 1946, were in some measure an apology for his own increasingly thunderous silence. In his *Martin Heidegger* (1978) George Steiner writes:

> The "Letter on Humanism" sets out the idiom and motifs that were to dominate Heidegger's postwar teachings and publications. It is composed in the evident shadow of national and professional debacle, and is meant to refute Sartre's existentialism, which albeit derivative from *Sein und Zeit* [*Being and Time*] at cardinal points, had proclaimed itself to be a politically engaged "humanism." Heidegger now postulates the absolute primacy of language: "Language is the house of Being. Man dwells in this house. Those who think (*die Denkenden*) and those who create poetry (*die Dichtenden*) are the custodians of the dwelling. (127)

In his rigorous and careful attention to Being, Heidegger is led to forget the Shoah. But for Simone de Beauvoir, as for Sartre, language does not occupy the position of "absolute primacy." The Shoah did not happen in language, or, to quote Tzvetan Todorov in the *Times Literary Supplement*, "Absolute truth may not exist, but the extermination of the Jews is unquestionably a truth and not an interpretation" (June 17–23, 1988, 684). Auschwitz poses a conundrum for those who rail against the referential fallacy. There is a disturbing parallel between the Nazi attempt to eradicate all traces of the Shoah, the Nazi euphemisms that took the place of such words as corpses, death, gas chambers, the displacements, the metonymies for not naming what they were indeed doing, and theories of language that insist on undecidability, metaphoricity, and figuration, thereby making it impossible to report on "real" happenings in the world.

Simone de Beauvoir would not deny that language has a life of its own and may introduce effects and possibilities that the writer does not control. However, her frequently repeated conception of language as a means of attempting to communicate what one has seen and felt is appropriate and courageous as a response to such overwhelming historical events as the Shoah.

I would like to stress, in my brief conclusion, the uniqueness of writers like Simone de Beauvoir and Albert Cohen taking on these questions, questions of life and death, confronting everyday mortality and anguish as well as Auschwitz. I am convinced that questions of life and death are the essential questions, and that many of us have been prevented by diverse combinations of social and literary theory from incorporating them into our work. These questions that are raised in the writings of Simone de Beauvoir and Albert Cohen have now become unavoidable. I am willing to run the risk of appearing to some avantgarde critics politically incorrect or intellectually naive by suggesting that these questions should not be left to the theologians.

Cendres Juives: Jews Writing in French "After Auschwitz"

> Because he was a Jew my father died at Auschwitz: how can one
> not say it? And how can it be said?
> —Sarah Kofman, *Paroles suffoquées*

> Do you see that chimney over there? Do you see it? Do you see
> the flames? (Yes, we saw the flames). Over there, that's where
> they're going to take you. That's your grave, over there. Haven't
> you understood yet? Sons of bitches, don't you understand any-
> thing? You're going to be burned. Burned to a cinder. Turned
> into ashes.
> —Elie Wiesel, *Night*

The title of this chapter is a deliberate attempt to work against the question of who is or is not Jewish, who is or is not French, by focusing not
on the official religious or national identity of the writer but on his or
her confession of Jewishness and relation to the French language. My
title is also a deliberate attempt to work against the notion of a universal and always-the-same Jew, by focusing on a variety of writers and
writings, by insisting on a plural *Jews*.[1]

Jews writing in French after Auschwitz may be divided roughly into
two groups: those who write about Auschwitz, and those who write
about how to write about Auschwitz. I say "roughly" because there are
in the first group writers who, without abandoning the Real (I am thinking particularly of the historian Pierre Vidal-Naquet in his essays *Les
Assassins de la mémoire/Assassins of Memory* [1987]) never lose sight of the
inevitable mediation of writing, that is to say of rhetoric and discourse.

The first group—those who write about Auschwitz—includes
among others, in alphabetical order, Nadine Fresco, Marek Halter,
Serge Klarsfeld, Annie Kriegel, André Schwarz-Bart, Pierre Vidal-
Naquet, Georges Wellers, Elie Wiesel. Whether they produce fictional
representations of Auschwitz based on personal or documentary mate-

rial, essays documenting what happened at Auschwitz, or essays contradicting and contesting the revisionist historians, these writers write within a tradition that does not necessarily put into question the relation between words and things, between the text and the *hors texte*. I would consider as belonging primarily, if not exclusively, to this first group the two generations of Jewish intellectuals engaged in preserving the remains of Eastern European Jewish culture through the revival of Judaic studies, particularly Emmanuel Lévinas, about whom Judith Friedlander writes in *Vilna on the Seine* (1990).

The second group, those who write about how to write about Auschwitz, includes, again among others and in alphabetical order, Robert Bober, Hélène Cixous, Jacques Derrida, Serge Doubrovsky, Jean-Pierre Faye, Alain Finkielkraut, Edmond Jabès, Sarah Kofman, Claude Lanzmann, Patrick Modiano, Georges Perec. Some members of this second group maintain significant connections with the existential-phenomenological, philosophical style and themes of Martin Heidegger, Maurice Blanchot and/or with deconstruction, poststructuralism, and psychoanalysis. All of the members of this second group have manifested their dissatisfaction with the mimetic principles that sustain the fictional and historical narratives produced by members of the first group.

As examples, and for my analysis of these two groups, I have selected three texts by writers of the first group and four texts by writers of the second group. In several of these seven texts the word *cendre* (ash or cinder), singular, or *cendres* (ashes or cinders), plural, used as metaphor and/or symbol, is accompanied by the theme of mourning. These are texts in which the writers work through their own mourning—for an individual Jew or for Jews in general—a mourning that in some cases continues the mourning begun at the end of the nineteenth century for the death of God. In their texts the French word *cendre(s)* may function as a figure for both or either death and rebirth, for mourning and celebration, for Jews who were exterminated in gas chambers and in ovens, and for the philosophical problem of the trace. *Cendre(s)* points not only to the product of incineration and its dispersion, but to anonymity and also to the figure of the Phoenix, reborn from its own ashes. I shall argue that the figure or figures of the Phoenix may take unexpected forms, transforming the Heideggerean analysis of the Being-toward-death into a Being-toward-the-other, transforming the historical-social-ethical question of the extermination of the Jews into a philosophical-poetic-linguistic question of presence and absence. These texts are, more or less in the order in which I shall discuss them, from the first group: *La Nuit/Night* by Elie Wiesel (1958), *Le Dernier des Justes/The Last of the Just* by André Schwarz-Bart (1959), and *Difficile Liberté: Essais sur le Judaïsme/Difficult Freedom: Essays on Judaism* by Emmanuel Lévinas (1963); from the second group: the scenario from the film *Shoah* by Claude Lanzmann (1985), *Paroles suffoquées* (Suffocated words) by Sarah Kofman (1987), *W ou le souvenir d'enfance* (W or the memory of childhood) by Georges Perec (1975), *Feu la cendre/Cinders* (or, The Recently dead cinders) by Jacques Derrida (1987).

Toward the end of Claude Lanzmann's film, *Shoah*, there is a sequence in which the political scientist, Raul Hilberg, highlights one aspect of the language problem that haunts those who attempt to write about the Shoah and who are conscious of the danger of reproducing stereotypical figures and clichés:

> This is the *Fahrplanordnung* 587, which is typical for special trains. The number of the order goes to show you how many of them there were. Underneath: —"Only for internal use." But this turns out to be a very low classification for secrecy. And the fact that in this entire document, which after all deals with death trains, one cannot see—not only on this one, one cannot see it on the others—the word *geheim*, "secret," is astonishing to me. That they would not have done that is very astonishing. On second thought, I believe that had they labeled it secret, they would have invited a great many inquiries from people who got hold of it. They would then have raised more questions; they would have focused attention on the thing. And the key to the entire operation from the psychological standpoint was never to utter the words that would be appropriate to the action being taken. Say nothing; do these things; do not describe them. (138–39)

Claude Lanzmann's mission as researcher, cinematographer, editor, and lucid yet empathetic inquisitor in the film *Shoah* is to uncover the covered traces, to decode the coded expressions, to replace euphemisms with dysphemisms, with words that describe as accurately as possible the "things" that were done. The film *Shoah* exterminates the Jews for a second time in the presence of spectators for whom the veil of secrecy has been lifted. Claude Lanzmann's relentless questioning and pursuit of recurring detail is a systematic attempt to work against the camouflage of events and places through language, to work against litotes, allusion, obliqueness. And yet the camouflage of language, the use of litotes, allusion, and obliqueness are precisely the strategies of poststructuralism and deconstruction in their deliberate refusal of the conventions of realistic description and narrative representation. Were the Nazis poststructuralists and deconstructors *avant la lettre* in their desire "never to utter the words that would be appropriate to the action being taken"? Or, more worrisome still for certain critics, and as we have seen earlier in this book, were and are Heideggereans and poststructuralists engaged in an intellectual enterprise that involves inherently dangerous modes of thought? Does an obsession with the primacy of language and etymology lead inevitably to extermination? Does questioning direct access to the Real imply a trivialization of reality and suffering? Does an investigation of historical narrative imply a turning away from historicity? What happens to the Jewish question in French writing when it is viewed in the light or the glare of the humanism/antihumanism exchange? How does the putting into question of the status of subjects and agents affect the Jewish question? These are some of the questions that have been raised in preceding chapters and that also inform this chapter, questions to which I will propose neither answers nor solutions but to which I will add other equally crucial questions.

In *Night* by Elie Wiesel and the last chapter of *The Last of the Just* by André Schwarz-Bart, writers and narrators attempt to memorialize and to mourn through familiar narrative strategies. In spite of the differences in length, style, and intention, both of these novels contain a certain number of identical elements in the representation of Auschwitz and *cendres juives*: the description of a small shtetl of Eastern Europe and/or a Jewish ghetto in a large Western European city; the presence of the Gestapo, the local police, and the Jewish officials in charge of deportations; the young, innocent hero-narrator; the voyage by train from the shtetl or, in France, from Drancy near Paris, to Auschwitz, a voyage made in anxiety, anguish, humiliation, and physical suffering both individual and collective; the arrival at Auschwitz at night with the howling dogs, the barked orders in German, the selection, the smoke, and the odors; the "experience" of those who are immediately gassed and/or those who are forced to work in the camps; and finally the cendres juives that the protagonists become or that the protagonists witness and whose provenance—the ovens in which members of their families from whom they were separated shortly before were burned—they sud-

denly understand. In *The Last of the Just*, as in the final scenes of other
novels in which the protagonists walk into one of the gas chambers at
Auschwitz, someone sings, in Hebrew, the prayer or profession of faith
that Orthodox Jews recite three or four times a day and that dying Jews,
whether or not they are Orthodox, frequently recite on their deathbed,
Shema Israel (Hear, o Israel, the Eternal is our God, the Eternal is One).
It is finally this affirmation of faith in God, this affirmation of monotheism in Hebrew, that defines the Jewish presence. Thus the representation in fiction of Auschwitz has become fixed and codified, inevitable
and unchanging. And yet it might be said that the tragic mode is
averted by the words of the Shema, for if God is listening, or if the Jews
who intone the Shema think that God is listening, the Jews are not
alone, their agony is not without a witness. These conventional narratives are thus informed by an equally conventional and reassuring metaphysical apparatus from which God is never entirely absent.[2]

God is also always present in the writings of the philosopher
Emmanuel Lévinas and in his unabashedly Jewish apologetics. In
Judith Friedlander's book, *Vilna on the Seine* (1990), an account of the
revival of Judaic studies in France after 1968, Emmanuel Lévinas is
given a leading role as a member of the older generation educated in
both European and Jewish cultures. My comments will bear on only
one of his books, *Difficult Freedom: Essays on Judaism*, a collection of
essays written between 1945 and 1960, and also on an essay entitled "La
Renaissance culturelle juive en Europe occidentale" (The Jewish cultural renaissance in Western Europe) published in 1968. I do not consider Emmanuel Lévinas to be representative of all French Jewish religious thinkers, nor do I place myself, in relation to his writing, in a
position other than that of a compassionate lay reader.

We find at the core of Lévinas's essays an investigation of violence, of
all those acts that threaten the rights of the Other. The Other is a face
to whom words are addressed. Lévinas denounces the naked violence
haunting the Occident; he rejects the claims of the Logos to unify and
totalize, to produce a homogeneous image of man and of the world.
Lévinas writes against his early teachers Husserl and Heidegger. In the
words of Seán Hand, Lévinas's "post-national ethics stands as the ultimate and exemplary challenge to the Solitude of Being, a rigorous and
moving testimony of one's infinite obligation to the other person" (v).

For Lévinas Judaism, or rather biblical and Talmudic studies, represents the source of an ethics of exigency:

> In the aftermath of Hitler's exterminations, which were able to take place in a Europe that had been evangelized for fifteen centuries, Judaism turned inwards towards its origins. Up to that point, Christianity had accustomed Western Judaism to thinking of these origins as having dried up or as having been submerged under more lively tides. (xiii)

My appropriation of Emmanuel Lévinas draws from what I will call tentatively his critique of Christianocentrism, a critique that provides a way of speaking critically about Christian culture.

In several of his essays in *Difficult Freedom*, Lévinas reminds his readers of the "fraternal contact" that many Jews had with Christians during the Nazi period, "Christians who opened their hearts to them—which is to say, risked everything for their sake" (xiii). In spite of this frequent reminder, Lévinas nevertheless raises serious questions about the inevitable presence of Christian culture and the impossibility of escaping from it even in contemporary secular states. The separation of church and state in France, according to Lévinas, has not dissipated this religious "Christian atmosphere," which we take in, like the air we breathe, without realizing it. He notes that French legal time and calendar are punctuated by Catholic holidays, that towns are built around cathedrals or churches, and that French art, literature, and ethics have been and continue to be nourished by Christian themes. The only way of freeing oneself from Christianity, he suggests, is through immersion in the Hebrew language. It is the forgetting of Hebrew, according to Lévinas, that is in part responsible for our neglecting of ethical questions. Lévinas consistently represents Christianity as the conqueror of the Occident, and Judaism, to his continuing astonishment, as that which has always refused to recognizie the conquest. The Wandering Jew becomes the emblematic figure of that refusal.

It is possible to see in Emmanuel Lévinas's critique of Christianocentrism a parallel with the critique of phallocentrism. It may well be that women and Jews, as psychoanalytic theory and analyses of ideology suggest, occupy a similar position within both the unconscious and the nonconscious of texts and images. Within French culture, from the end of the nineteenth century until 1944, the figures of *Le Juif* and *La*

France provide an intriguing clue to the relationship between woman and Jew. Because *Le Juif*, as I have noted in chapter 5, was frequently portrayed as fat, with a bulbous nose and blubber lips, sexually perverse, effeminate, and cowardly, there are resemblances between *Le Juif* and the feminine grotesque. And because *La France* was frequently portrayed as tall, erect, brandishing a flag, leading the troups with her often exposed phallic breasts, there are resemblances between *La France* and the virile.

A radical solution to this perpetuation of stereotypes and clichés, and another way of reading cendres juives, is proposed by Emmanuel Lévinas in at least two of his essays. In "How is Judaism Possible?" Lévinas writes, "It is the spread of Christian culture everywhere that gives Christianity its impact, not the pious sermons and the parish bulletin. We are the only ones in the world to want a religion without culture" (247). And in "The Jewish Cultural Renaissance in Continental Europe" Lévinas strongly affirms the importance of Hebrew studies:

> What we expect from a return to Hebrew learning is that we will receive the light of the world through Hebrew, through the arabesques that are often drawn by the square letters of the prophetic, talmudic, rabbinical, and poetic texts, in the same way as we receive the light through the stained glass windows of the cathedrals or through the poetic lines of Corneille, Racine, or Victor Hugo. (25)

What Emmanuel Lévinas seems to be proposing is that, at the very least, Judaism in France separate itself from the term *Judeo-Christian tradition* and claim its uniqueness: the indispensable association of study, *conscience* (consciousness and conscience), and justice. Judaism, for Emmanuel Lévinas, refuses the seduction of myths, mysteries, and the supposed magical power of the sacraments. For him Judaism counteracts the violence that is at the heart of Christianity. In *Difficult Freedom* Lévinas is less concerned with writing about Auschwitz than with coming to terms with what made Auschwitz possible. He does this by raising the "Christian Question" and displacing the meaning of cendres from death, through violence toward Others, to rebirth, through Talmudic texts that emphasize the ethical relationship to the Other.

In certain respects Sarah Kofman's *Paroles suffoquées* is a paradigmatic text for Jews writing in French after Auschwitz. Like many texts written or edited by Jews and focusing on the Shoah—for example,

Edmond Fleg's *Anthologie Juive* (Jewish anthology), Elie Wiesel's *Night*, André Schwarz-Bart's *The Last of the Just,* Serge Klarsfeld's *Memorial to the Jews Deported from France 1942–1944,* Pierre Vidal-Naquet's *Assassins of Memory*—*Paroles suffoquées* is dedicated to a family member who died at Auschwitz. In *Mourning and Melancholia* (1917) Sigmund Freud writes: "Mourning impels the ego to give up the object by declaring the object to be dead and offering the ego the inducement of continuing to live" (257). It is interesting to note that in *Paroles suffoquées,* as in the other texts, the ending marks a reversal, a movement from absorption in and identification with the dead body to detachment and new signs of life. Sarah Kofman suggests gingerly on the last page of her text "the possibility of a new ethic."

Through direct quotations and multiple references, Sarah Kofman also incorporates fragments from texts by Theodor Adorno and Jean-François Lyotard. But most of her quotations are from Maurice Blanchot's *L'Ecriture du désastre/Writing the Disaster* (1980) and from Roger Antelme's *L'Espèce humaine/The Human Species* (1947), a book on his experience as a non-Jew in German concentration camps. What is essential for Sarah Kofman, as it is for Maurice Blanchot, Roger Antelme, and Claude Lanzmann, is to write endlessly about writing about Auschwitz, in order not to forget what happened at Auschwitz, while respecting the proscription against representation that follows Talmudic law as well as poststructuralist directions within contemporary literary theorizing. The problem remains for Sarah Kofman: how to write about Auschwitz without betraying Auschwitz? Without telling a story, "a story before Auschwitz . . . even if it were the story of a Passion, the passion of Christ" (46). Sarah Kofman does not tell a story, but she mingles philosophical inquiry, citations, and anecdotal fragments. Readers piece together the following events: her father was a rabbi, arrested in Paris on July 16, 1942, deported from Drancy to Auschwitz and buried alive, so witnesses relate, because he insisted on observing the Sabbath and on saying prayers for both the victims and their tormentors. He insisted on maintaining a relationship in language with God. He and his words were literally suffocated, and Sarah Kofman's writing mimes this suffocation by attempting to translate intensity and silence with the aid of quotations: "To be obliged to speak without being able to speak nor be heard, such is the ethical exigency which Roger Antelme obeys in *The Human Species*" (46). *Paroles suffoquées* is a text on Auschwitz and writing, separately and together, a book in which the anecdotal referent survives.

The anecdotal referent also survives in Georges Perec's *Wou le souvenir d'enfance*. This is a narrative in two parts, marked by three different kinds of type: italic characters for the narration of the voyage to W, a fictional island situated by the narrator in the archipelago of the Tierra del Fuego; the description of life on W, an allegory of the concentration camp universe in the imaginary of a boy; typographically normal characters for the autobiographical account of the narrator's childhood, between 1936 and 1949; bold characters for the two brief central texts that recount the death of his father, in the French army, the day after the Armistice in 1940 and the death of his mother, at Auschwitz, following her deportation on February 11, 1943, from the camp at Drancy in the convoy number 47.[3] Here, the work of mourning consists in projecting the narrator's affect onto the constructed decor of a terrifying narrative at once familiar and strange. The three and a half pages that tell the story of the narrator's Polish-born mother's life and death (what he knows of them) are remarkable for their sparseness and their precision. These are the last four sentences: "She was caught in a police raid with her sister, my aunt. She was interned at Drancy on January 23, 1943, and deported on February 11 in the direction of Auschwitz. She saw her native land before she died. She died without understanding" (48–49). Although the word *Auschwitz* appears only once in *Wou le souvenir d'enfance*, as the presumed end of his mother's voyage, Auschwitz indirectly and unremittingly permeates the entire text.

There are no anecdotes, no narrative, no history in Jacques Derrida's *Cinders* other than, in the prologue, two indications concerning the genesis of this text. The first, and for my purpose the most significant, relates the mysterious coming of a sentence into the writer's consciousness, a sentence that had haunted him for over fifteen years (earlier than 1972), a sentence rich in semantic and thematic ambiguities: "Il y a là cendre" (There is ash there; 21). The semantic ambiguity resides in the difference between hearing and reading the sentence, between the adverb *là* (there), with its *accent grave* (its grave accent, already funereal), and the feminine definite article *la* (the). There is also a phonetic similarity prolonged throughout the text by the words *cendre* and *centre* (center). Thematic ambiguities and questions abound, nourished by familiar Derridean themes: the trace and dissemination, the disjunction

between the words of a text and the things to which they refer, the inde-
cision and the indetermination of meaning. And there is the heavy debt
to Martin Heidegger evident in the sentence that haunts the narrator(s)
of *Cinders* with its references to *es gibt* (there is) and *da* (there), the *da*
of *dasein*, the very core of Heideggeer's thinking on Being. The reader
of Derrida's text is alerted then, from the beginning, to the presence of
such Heideggerean themes as astonishment and the need to be attentive to the call of Being, the opening of the question—here of cendre—
by the interrogation of a word, and the emphasis on language as, in
Heidegger's words, "the house of the truth of Being" (43). A debt to
Heidegger in 1987, the year during which the Heidegger debate raged
in France focusing on the relationship between Heidegger's thought, his
adherence to the Nazi party from 1933 to 1945, and his persistent silence
concerning the Shoah, is a particularly heavy debt to bear for a "Jewish"
writer who will at the same time acknowledge the debt and include, in
his meditation on cendre, references to the Shoah. Derrida's own contribution to the Heidegger debates includes a lecture published as an
extended essay in 1987, *De l'esprit. Heidegger et la question/On Spirit:
Heidegger and the Question*. The essay begins with the following sentence: "I will speak of the ghostly, of flame and of ashes" (11). Both Heidegger and the Shoah are at the center of Derrida's other texts written
during the late 1980s.

The second anecdote relates that *Cinders* was written in response to
a request, made in 1980, by Derrida's friends at the journal *Anima* for a
text on the theme of la cendre. Both of these anecdotes suggest the
importance of an outside: the first, an outside of consciousness and the
second, the world outside the writer. As if Jacques Derrida were
solicited by his unconscious and by his friends to produce a text in
which *cendre*, as signifier and signified, would be both in the background and highlighted.

The prologue, unlike most other texts by Jacques Derrida, gives us
serious clues about its own genesis. It also describes the text in some
detail, and insists on the relationship between the text to be read and
the text to be listened to as a cassette, recorded with the voices of the
author and of actress Carole Bousquet, and made available, like the
printed text, by the édition des femmes. It is worth asking why Jacques
Derrida surrounds this particular text with so much context, why he is
so specific about the occasions that prompted its writing?

Cinders, like Jacques Derrida's text *Glas*, is a double text. On the right-hand side of the page, an indeterminate number of voices engage in a polylogue, a conversation in which gender and identity are deliberately confused. Sometimes the voices suggest a love duo, at other times a series of hopeless soliloquies. All imaginable themes associated with cendre appear and disappear: from the more abstract and philosophical considerations of trace and remains, of being and nothingness, to the more concrete associations with the Holocaust, with Germans, and with Jews.

On the left-hand side of the page there are quotations from other texts by Jacques Derrida in which *cendre* is a central signifier: *La Dissémination* (1972), *Glas* (1974), *La Carte postale* (1980). An attentive reader will also hear echoes of *Cinders* in *Schibboleth: Pour Paul Celan* (1986), *De l'esprit: Heidegger et la question* (1987), and "Paul de Man's War," (1988). Deconstruction is haunted by death, temporality, and mourning, as is the thought of Jacques Derrida's principal philosophical mentor, Martin Heidegger. The ashes of the Holocaust mingle with the ashes of other dead in other places, for example with those of Paul de Man (216, 230), mingle with the theme of death and mourning, and with the ontological question of being as it had been thought before the Shoah changed the terms of the meditation on death for many Jews and non-Jews writing in French after Auschwitz. Jacques Derrida is in a unique category. He is a Jew writing in French after Auschwitz for whom the Shoah is always present but rarely appears as such, never appears as anecdote or as representation but always already transformed into trace, dissemination; it remains hauntingly, in the prismatic fragmentation of his texts.

I offer a possible reading of *Cinders*. I remain respectful of Jacques Derrida's insistence, here and elsewhere, on polysemy and heterogeneity in texts. Nonetheless, I propose to read the *cendre* of *Cinders* as *cendres juives*. Furthermore, I would suggest that this text has its place in the curious polylogue in France, Western Europe, and the United States that has engaged revisionist historians—those who claim that the Jews were not deliberately gassed in the extermination camps of Poland by the Nazis but rather died in the concentration camps of diverse illnesses—and such eminent philosophers and linguists as Jean-François Lyotard in France and Noam Chomsky in the United Sates. For Lyotard in *Le Différend/The Differend* (1983) the revisionist thesis becomes the occasion of philosophical debate: how can one determine what did take place, how can one weigh the rhetorical evidence when there is no one to bear witness? For Chomsky, who wrote the preface to Robert Faurisson's *Mémoire en défense: Contre ceux qui m'accusent de falsifier l'Histoire* (*Defense brief: against those who accuse me of falsifying history*; 1980), the revisionist thesis became the occasion of political debate: the necessity of upholding free speech, of upholding the right to publish the most outrageous positions.

Jacques Derrida's text enters poetically rather than polemically into the debate, suggesting that the protagonist—the voice and the voices—like Hamlet in *Hamlet*, has a debt, an obligation toward the specter that is the cendre. The cendre, again like the ghost in *Hamlet*, contains a secret. But unlike the ghost, it cannot speak; it can only be spoken about. The secret is never divulged anecdotally, but it is alluded to, even played with:

> You just said that he could not have an "up to date" phrase for this cinder word. Yes, there is perhaps only one worth publishing, it would tell of the all-burning, otherwise called holocaust and the crematory oven, in German in all the Jewish languages of the world. (57)
>
> Above the sacred place, incense again, but no monument, no Phoenix, no erection that stands—or falls—the cinder without ascension, the cinders love me, they change sex, they re-cinder themselves, they androgynocide themselves. (61)

Derrida's word games and puns, in Ned Lukacher's translation, do not trivialize the Shoah, do not negate or minimize the event. Rather the plays on words, the words within words, emphasize the notion that in 1987 what remains are words, like traces, with their secrets, their etymologies, their histories. These words that haunt us, like the word *cendre*, must be attended to, interrogated. This kind of interrogation, when it is philosophical, linguistic, poetic, as it is in the text of *Cinders*, has among its many effects the deepening and broadening of our meditation on the Shoah, its reality and its textuality.

There is a curious irony in this inquiry into Jews writing in French after Auschwitz. Although Martin Heidegger was silent about the Shoah, several of his French disciples and students, whether non-Jews like Maurice Blanchot, Jean-François Lyotard, and Philippe Lacoue-Labarthe, or Jews like Jacques Derrida, Sarah Kofman, Emmanuel Lévinas, and Alain Finkielkraut, have incorporated the extermination of the Jews into their meditation on Being-toward-death; or rather, their meditation on our primordial anxiety has been inflected by the Shoah. Heidegger's silence, even more than his National Socialist affiliation, has been and is being referred to by writers on both sides of the Atlantic, Jewish and non-Jewish, to condemn his pernicious influence on contemporary modes of thought. And yet it is precisely those texts, like *Cinders*, where Heidegger's thought and poetic style are most recognizable, that, through metaphoric indirection, produce an effect of horror and of silence acceptable to my expectations, at least, of writing after Auschwitz. If there is a lesson about "culture" to be learned from these examples, it is that the intellectual inheritance of some Jews writing in French after Auschwitz is strongly rooted in German thought.

9 | Marrano as Metaphor

MARRANE n.—1690; "Spanish," XVe; esp. *marrano*, term of insult, "pig" (X^e), arabic *moharramah* "something forbidden by religion."

    Didact. A Jew from Spain or Portugal forced to convert to Christianity, and who remained faithful to Judaism.

                                          —*Le Grand Robert*

marrano also *marano n-s usu cap* [Sp *marrano*, lit., pig, prob. fr. *Ar mahram* something prohibited; fr. the fact that the eating of pork is outlawed by the Jewish and Muslim religions]: a Christianized Jew or Moor of medieval Spain; *esp*: one who accepted conversion only to escape persecution.

                —*Webster's Third New International Dictionary*

This chapter deals with aspects of the question of Jewish identity, a pressing question "after Auschwitz" although not entirely because of Auschwitz. The question of Jewish identity—what it means to say "I am a Jew" or "I am Jewish" and what it means for someone who is not Jewish to say "You/They are Jews" or "You/They are Jewish"—has been a significant question in France, Western Europe, and the United States, particularly since the offical proclamation of the emancipation of the Jews in France in 1791. As I have noted, this question is related to other discourses and areas of historical, anthropological, and sociological investigation that include the history, the evolution, and the consequences of the concepts of race and racism in particular places and contexts and over time, the waning of religious belief, the question of the assimilation of subordinate groups to the language and culture of dominant groups, the fear of assimilation through intermarriage as another more subtle form of annihilation, the question of inclusion, exclusion, and immigration. The question of Jewish identity is also related to the construction of stereotypes, both negative and positive, by Jews and non-Jews, including those that construct Jews as Christ killers, restless wanderers, dangerous revolutionaries, materialistic, lascivious, superior thinkers, intellectual leaders, and so forth. Jewish identity further involves the question of secularism, of Jewish heretics, of Marranos and crypto-Jews, and of the notion of a Jewish community. Identity, as a more general philosophical and psychoanalytic problem, raises questions of the self, of subjectivity, and of language. The reader will already have noticed the difficulty of remaining within the hexagon with this topic, or even of remaining within a strictly Jewish or Judaic frame.

I have been struck over and over again in my readings by the degree to which French Jews from the mid-nineteenth century until today, writing about the Jewish presence or question in French society and culture, were Christianized, Frenchified, Europeanized by their education, their libraries, their mode of thinking, even when, or perhaps especially when, they were trying to come to terms with the question of Jewish identity. In his book on *The Politics of Assimilation: The French Jewish Community in France at the Time of the Dreyfus Affair* (1969, 1980) Michael Marrus, the noted historian, writes about the desire among many Jews at the end of the nineteenth century in France to construct, to believe in, to praise, only occasionally to denigrate, the notion of a Jewish "race." Marrus understands this desire as the need to express feelings of Jewish identity, a sense of community, a sense of "some common historical fate," and "a solidarity of origin." Like many historians writing after Auschwitz and interested in France and French Jews from the time of the Dreyfus case until today, Michael Marrus tends to blame the seductions of assimilation for many of the disasters that have befallen Jews in France, including the horrors of the Shoah. In the introduction to *The Politics of Assimilation* Michael Marrus writes:

> Assimilation, we have found, lies at the heart of our problem. Any effort to describe the Jewish community in France at the end of the nineteenth century faces the fact that the Jews of France were highly assimilated into French life and that, at the same time, their assimilation was never complete, and was thus a continuing problem. By "assimilation" we are referring here to the process by which individuals of Jewish background assumed an *identity* which is essentially French. Such identification may take a number of different forms: Jews may intermarry with other Frenchmen, may accept the basic civil allegiance demanded of French citizens, may engage in extensive social interaction with other Frenchmen, and may otherwise move towards a situation in which, in the

expression of the time, they were "Frenchmen like any other." Assimilation has many different forms and degrees, and we shall not enter here
into a full discussion of this problem. Rather we have a particular aspect
of assimilation in mind.

The particular object of our inquiry is "the politics of assimilation." By
this we mean the way in which French Jews translated their identification with France and with French life into perspectives upon and activity in public affairs. Largely excluded from this discussion is any analysis of the personal behaviour of individual Jews, their modes of social
intercourse, and their private responses to various aspects of French life.
Where such questions are relevant to individual biographies they will be
discussed, but our central purpose is to highlight Jewish thought and
activity on broader, public questions. Attention is therefore directed
towards issues of national political concern, specifically politics, public
policy, and, of course, the important issue of anti-Semitism. (2–3)

This chapter, "Marrano as Metaphor," attempts to open two important and related areas of questioning: one concerns the limits and limitations of historical research and historiography as the unique mode of
discourse in the investigation of the Jewish question and of the peren-
nity of antisemitism, particularly when, as in the writing of Michael
Marrus quoted above, the "private," the "personal," the "modes of social
intercourse" by which I understand language are deliberately if not
completely excluded. The other concerns the place of the literary text
in historical studies. I will argue that the literary text can complicate
audaciously and fruitfully, and go beyond the didactic discourses of history, through the rhetorical effects of figures of speech and narrative
strategies. I shall illustrate this power and function of words in literary
texts by placing at the heart of this chapter several passages from Albert
Cohen's novel *Belle du Seigneur* (1968) and one passage from Nathalie
Sarraute's autobiographical novel *Enfance/Childhood* (1983).

"Marrano as Metaphor" also contains another agenda. My curious
title announces an argument that may be controversial. What I shall
attempt to show is that secular Jews in France, Western Europe, and the
United States, particularly in urban areas, throughout most of the nineteenth century and all of the twentieth, although they were Europeanized and Christianized, remained crypto-Jews in the same way that
many of the Jews who converted to Catholicism in Spain and Portugal
in the fifteenth century, known in French as *marrane* from the Spanish

word for pig, *marrano*, remained crypto-Jews. Once again, passages from *Belle du Seigneur* and a vignette from *Enfance* will play a central role in the development of this agenda.

Four quotations direct my argument. Each of these quotations takes a very different position on the question of secular Jews and their double belonging to both a Christian and a Jewish culture. The first quotation is from a letter written by the French "Jewish" philosopher Simone Weil to the Minister of Education under the Vichy government in November of 1940. It is a response to Vichy's silence regarding her request to secure a teaching job. She imagines that the silence is related to the Statute on Jews under which she would be considered Jewish and therefore forbidden to teach. Her letter is an attempt to argue that the statute does not apply to her because her culture is entirely French, Catholic, and Greek:

> Finally, the concept of heredity may be applied to a race, but it is difficult to apply it to a religion. I myself, who profess no religion and never have, have certainly inherited nothing from the Jewish religion. Since I practically learned to read from Racine, Pascal, and other French writers of the 17th century, since my spirit was thus impregnated at an age when I had not even heard talk of "Jews," I would say that if there is a religious tradition which I regard as my patrimony, it is the Catholic tradition. In short: mine is the Christian, French, Greek tradition. The Hebraic tradition is alien to me, and no Statute can make it otherwise." (Coles 46)

Simone Weil's position is further expanded upon by H. L. Finch in the *Times Literary Supplement*:

> Jewishness was never an issue for Simone Weil. "I was born, I grew up, and I always remained within the Christian inspiration," she wrote in her *Spiritual Autobiography*. She was a French woman and therefore a "Christian by culture," and she simply did not recognize the category of "biological Judaism," which for her was not significantly different from Hitler's "racial Jewishness." The two things she *really* hated were egocentricity and ethnocentricity, the one the sin of the Christians, the other the sin of the Jews. If she hated "biological Judiasm," it would have been because it led to ethnocentricity. (15)

The second quotation is from an essay entitled "How is Judaism Possible?" (1959) by the French Jewish philosopher Emmanuel Lévinas, an essay to which I have referred in chapter 8. Although Emmanuel Lévinas makes some of the same points as Simone Weil about the dominance of French Christian and Catholic culture, his interpretation of this situation is very different:

> There is in fact a sense of inequality between Christianity—which, even in the secular state, is present everywhere—and Judaism, which does not dare to show its face out of doors, held back as it is by scruples about being indiscreet enough to break the pact created by Emancipation. The non-religious City incorporated into its secularized substance the forms of Catholic life. Between the strictly rational order of political existence and the mystical order of belief are realities intermediary to the diffuse state, realities that are half-rational, half-religious. They permeate this political life. They float around in it like lymphatic matter. The churches are integrated into landscapes that always seem to be waiting for them and to sustain them. We give no more thought to this Christian atmosphere than to the air we breathe. The juridical separation of Church from State did nothing to dispell it. The rhythm of legal time is scanned by Catholic feast days, cathedrals determine towns and sites. Art, literature and morality whose basis classically lives off Christian themes are still nurtured by these themes. . . . The entry of Jews into the national life of European states led them to breathe an atmosphere completely impregnated with Christian essence, and that heralded the baptisms. It is not the local church priest who has converted our children and brothers, it is Pascal, Bossuet and Racine; it is the people who built Chartres Cathedral with them. Judaism understood as a Synagogue is reduced to an abstract confession that does not even earn a civil status. We are limited to it only by moving family memories, popular melodies and a few recipes. (246–47)

Emmanuel Lévinas's main arguments in this quotation may be recapitulated as follows: France is only nominally a secular state. In fact, French culture, literature, and daily life are saturated with Catholic symbols and events. Jewish children are informed at an early age by the words of such writers as Pascal, Bossuet, and Racine, are visually and spiritually uplifted and seduced by such artistic forms as the Cathedral of Chartres. Judaism, on the other hand, is a private affair, or it is awakened only on the High Holy Days. This is a situation that Emmanuel Lévinas, in this essay, unlike Simone Weil in her letter, deplores. He would like to have Judaism, at least for Jews, be as much a part of cultural, literary, and daily life as Christianity is now for both Christians and Jews. In her book *Vilna on the Seine: Jewish Intellectuals in France*

Since 1968 (1990) Judith Friedlander describes the attempts by Jewish philosophers, intellectuals, and writers, including Emmanuel Lévinas, to revive and promote Jewish Talmudic and rabbinical culture in France after Auschwitz.

The third quotation is from Isaac Deutscher's essay "The Non-Jewish Jew," based on a lecture given during Jewish Book Week to the World Jewish Congress in February of 1958. Isaac Deutscher is interested in Jewish heretics, those who go "beyond the boundaries of Jewry" (26):

> The Jewish heretic who transcends Jewry belongs to a Jewish tradition. You may, if you like, see Akher (Elisha ben Abiyuh, the teacher of Rabbi Meir, co-author of the *Mishna*) as a prototype of those great revolutionaries of modern thought: Spinoza, Heine, Marx, Rosa Luxemburg, Trotsky, and Freud. You may, if you wish to, place them within a Jewish tradition. They all went beyond the boundaries of Jewry. They all found Jewry too narrow, too archaic, and too constricting. They all looked for ideals and fulfillment beyond it, and they represent the sum and substance of much that is greatest in modern thought, the sum and substance of the most profound upheavals that have taken place in philosophy, sociology, economics, and politics in the last three centuries.
>
> Did they have anything in common with one another? Have they perhaps impressed mankind's thought so greatly because of their special "Jewish genius"? I do not believe in the exclusive genius of any race. Yet I think that in some ways they were very Jewish indeed. They had in themselves something of the quintessence of Jewish life and of the Jewish intellect. They were a priori exceptional in that as Jews they dwelt on the borderlines of various civilizations, religions, and national cultures. They were born and brought up on the borderlines of various epochs. Their mind matured where the most diverse cultural influences crossed and fertilized each other. They lived on the margins or in the nooks and crannies of their respective nations. Each of them was in society and yet not in it, of it and yet not of it. It was this that enables them to rise in thought above their societies, above their nations, above their times and generations, and to strike out mentally into wide new horizons and far into the future." (26–27)

In a similar vein, but with a precise reference to Marranos, the fourth quotation is taken from the first volume of *Spinoza and Other Heretics*, "The Marrano of Reason," (1989) written by the Israeli Jewish philosopher Yirmiyahu Yovel:

Marranos were former Jews in Spain and Portugal who had forcibly converted to Christianity. For generations, however, many of them maintained a crypto-Jewish life in secret, an experience that produced many
dualities—an opposition between the inner and outer life and a mixture
of the two religions that, in certain cases, led to the breakdown of both
Christian and Jewish beliefs. It also made disguises, including the linguistic masks of equivocation and dual language, necessary for survival.
In this present book, I analyze this Marrano experience and identify
several characteristic Marrano patterns that recur in Spinoza's case,
although they are translated into a new, secular, and rationalistic context. These Marrano patterns include a this-worldly disposition; a split
religious identity; a metaphysical skepticism; a quest for alternative sal-
vation through methods that oppose the official doctrine; an opposition
between the inner and outer life, and a tendency toward dual language
and equivocation. By closely examining other cases of Marrano intellectuals—both in the early phases of Marranism and among Spinoza's contemporaries—I show the recurrent nature of these patterns and how
they are expressed in Spinoza while being transformed from transcen-
dent historical religion to the domain of reason and immanence. Hence
my calling Spinoza the Marrano of Reason." (ix–x)

In opposition to Emmanuel Lévinas, and like Isaac Deutscher
before him, Yirmiyahu Yovel views Spinoza's Marranism (what Isaac
Deutscher would have called his non-Jewish Jewishness) as the origin
of a rich tradition among secular Jews, a tradition that extends from
Baruch Spinoza through Heinrich Heine, Karl Marx, and Rosa Luxemburg to Sigmund Freud. I would add to Deutscher and Yovel's lists
the names of Hannah Arendt and George Steiner and, within the
French tradition, the novelist Albert Cohen, perhaps the philosopher
Simone Weil—although her infatuation with Christianity and her bla-
tant anti-Judaic bias might disqualify her from this list—the philosophers Jacques Derrida, Sarah Kofman, and Alain Finkielkraut, the
political scientist Raymond Aron, the writers Nathalie Sarraute and
Hélène Cixous, the cinematographer Claude Lanzmann, the poet
Alain Bosquet, and the Catholic prelate, Cardinal Jean-Marie Aaron
Lustiger.

Both Isaac Deutscher and Yirmiyahu Yovel, although in different
rhetorical modes, give value to the variety and multiplicity of "civiliza-
tions, religions, and national cultures" and suggest the superiority of
those Jews who were able to transcend the single language and the rigid

constraints of any one social, cultural, or religious order. This is not, nor
has it ever been, a position that religious Jews or Jews (with or without
religious belief) who are striving for the preservation and the strengthening of Jewish identity and community regard with particular favor.
As the reader may imagine from what has preceded, it is a position that
I espouse with fervor.

I have selected two French writers through whom I will continue to
develop the notion that secular Europeanized and Christianized Jews
today are crypto-Jews, that this is a good rather than a bad thing, and
that appropriate literary texts have a significant role to play in exploring the question of Jewish identity.

We can locate in the life history and the writing of both Albert
Cohen (1895–1981) and Nathalie Sarraute (born in 1903) those "characteristic Marrano patterns . . . translated into a new, secular, and rationalistic context" that according to Yirmiyahu Yovel "recur in Spinoza's
case" (x). These patterns include "a this-worldly disposition; a split religious identity; a metaphysical skepticism; a quest for alternative salva-
tion through methods that oppose the official doctrine; an opposition
between the inner and outer life, and a tendancy toward dual language
and equivocation" (x).

I shall begin with what I consider to be relevant biographical information. Both Albert Cohen and Nathalie Sarraute were born outside
metropolitan France into Jewish families: Albert Cohen into the Jewish
community on the island of Corfu and Nathalie Sarraute in Ivanovo,
Russia. Both came to France at an early age, having had as their mother
tongue a language other than French. Both were obliged to leave their
country of origin, Albert Cohen at the age of five, because of the difficulties his parents experienced as members of the small Jewish community on the island and for financial reasons; Nathalie Sarraute at first, at
the age of two, because of internal strife between her parents, and later,
at the age of six, because of continuing familial strife and also because
her father's brother had been implicated in an attempt to kill the Tsar.
Albert Cohen's first school in Marseilles was a primary school run by
Catholic nuns, whereas for Nathalie Sarraute, her father's second wife
was Russian Orthodox, and the maid who took care of her in her
father's Paris appartment was Catholic. These two cases exemplify
Emmanuel Lévinas's description of how a "Christian atmosphere," and
"Catholic life" permeate and dominate French culture and the Jewish

children who live in it. But it is in the patterns of the writing of Albert Cohen and Nathalie Sarraute that I find most strongly marked the splits in religious identity, the oppositions to official doctrines, the presence of dual language and equivocation, those qualities that have led to my referring to them as *Marranos*, twentieth-century Jews who are also Christianized.

Belle du Seigneur is generally regarded as Albert Cohen's most important novel. Published originally in 1968, *Belle du Seigneur* received rave reviews in leading French newspapers and literary journals. In 1986 it was republished in the prestigious Pléiade edition.

I concur with much of the hyperbole that has been lavished on this long 999-page novel, divided into seven parts and 106 chapters that cover approximately two years, from 1936 to 1938, in the life and death by suicide of Solal des Solal and Ariane Deume. *Belle du Seigneur* may be considered a microcosm of the Jewish presence in French writing.

The novel contains the discourses of antisemitism, the discourses of philosemitism, references to major events of Jewish and antisemitic history in Europe from the Middle Ages to Hitler, assimilationist and anti-assimilationist Jewish characters and discourses, a variety of Jews including types and individuals, secular and Orthodox, Sephardic and Ashkenazic, as well as examples of interactions between Jews and Christians. It is as if the novel had been written by a secular Jew, a religious Jew, and a secular Christian. Solal des Solal, the protagonist, feels himself to be strongly Jewish when he is cut off from human society. Although Solal appears to lose his acute consciousness of his Jewishness when he is sequestered with his Christian (Protestant) lover, Ariane Deume, the narrator, ever vigilant, never allows the reader to forget the Jewish presence and the Jewish difference.

In the opening scene of *Belle du Seigneur* Solal is introduced in his double role as a youthful Don Juan, certain of his victory over Ariane Deume whom he plans to abduct from the bedroom of her house outside Geneva, and as "handsome and no less noble than his ancester Aaron, brother of Moses" (7). Once he has entered Ariane's bedroom Solal disguises himself as "an old Jew, poor and ugly, but not without dignity. After all, that is how he will be later. Even if he is not already buried and rotting, there will be no more handsome Solal in twenty years" (27). From the very beginning of the novel the narrator provides the reader with a double vision of being human in terms of desire, love, masculinity and femininity, agressivity, cruelty, inevitable aging and mortality, and being Jewish in terms of an ancient tradition that will be for many readers both somewhat familiar and somewhat exotic. Throughout the novel Solal remains deeply attached to his Jewish tradition, which he recreates by describing his disguises:

> And I disguise myself as the kind of Jew I love, with a beard and touching ritual curls and a fur hat, with shuffling feet, a bent back and a simple umbrella, an old Jew of very ancient nobility, o love of mine, bearer of the Law, Israel the savior, and I walk the streets in the evening in order to be mocked, proud of being mocked by them. (357)

These evocations of Solal's Jewishness are usually, as in this instance, lyrical passages that suggest a loving tenderness rarely sensed by the reader in Solal's or the narrator's descriptions of his encounters with or imaginings of Ariane. It is frequent, as in the lengthy monologue in which Solal speaks his passion for Ariane, to find the Jewish tradition used to strengthen and to elaborate on this passion:

> Yes, no one before you, no one after you, I swear by the holy Book of the Law that I kiss when it passes solemnly near me at the synagogue, draped in gold and velvet, holy commandments of that God in whom I do not believe but whom I revere, extravagantly proud of my God, God of Israel, and I am thrilled to the marrow when I hear His name and His words. (394)

It is important to note that Solal believes neither in love as *amour passion*, nor in God, but that he says the words and performs the rituals of a passionate lover and of a believing Jew.

Perhaps the most powerful evocation of what Jewishness means to Solal and what it means to those who see him as Jewish occurs toward the end of the novel when Solal, unable to bear the agonizing boredom of his folie à deux with Ariane, leaves their hideaway in Agay on the Mediterranean and takes a room in Paris at the Hotel George V.

Alone in his hotel room, and alone on the streets of Paris, having lost his position with the League of Nations in Geneva and his French naturalization, Solal becomes a wandering Jew. The only activity in which he would be able to engage in the social world is business and usury, making money, dealing with money. But the only desire he has, the fantasm that dominates all others, is to dress as an Orthodox Jew for prayers. Before leaving Paris to rejoin Ariane in Agay, Solal puts on his

false nose, opens his suitcase and dons the ritual prayer shawl and phy-
lacteries, says the official Jewish benediction, and then puts on the
Purim crown that was given to him by the Jewish gnome Rachel in
Berlin. This solo act is a prelude to the final scene of this chapter, in
which Solal, having checked his luggage at the train station, sees,
emerging from the station, a group of religious Jews:

> He recognizes them as they come out of the station one after the other,
> in groups of two or three, some in broad black felt hats pulled down too
> far and with their ears sticking out, others in flat caps of velvet trimmed
> with fur, all in interminable black coats, the old ones with their umbrel-
> las closed, weighed down by suitcases, their backs bent, shuffling their
> feet, discussing with passion. He recognizes them, recognizes his dearly
> beloved fathers and subjects, humble and majestic, the pious of strict
> obedience, the unshakeable, the faithful with their black beards and
> temporary hanging locks, all of a piece and absolute, strangers to their
> own exile, strong in their strangeness, mocked and mocking, going
> straight on their path, proud of their truth, mocked and despised, the
> great ones among his people, having come from the Eternal One and
> from His Sinai, bearers of His Law. (869–70)

Solal follows his "dearly beloved fathers and subjects" to Kohn's
restaurant where they eat while he watches them (as the narrator
watches him watching) and where he sees a very old man, in the back
of the restaurant, reading and praying, his bust moving up and down.
Solal, too, prays with the same movements, praising God in Hebrew.

This passage, which is two pages long in the Pléiade edition, is an
excellent example of how Albert Cohen's writing transforms recognizable signs and stereotypes, how the use of repetition and Biblical intertexts and a variety of style levels give us the familiar figure of the Orthodox Jew and at the same time propose to us a tender and lyrical relationship to this figure. The fragility of these old Jewish men is
emphasized by the historical moment. The reader recognizes that they
will be prime victims for the extermination camps yet to come.

In Solal's very long monologue without punctuation that follows this
scene, their fragility is further underlined by Solal's musings on the existence of antisemites and on the grandeur of pious Jews:

> Because there is nothing because the universe is not governed and hides
> no meaning other than its stupid existence under the dismal eye of noth-
> ingness and in truth this is our greatness this obedience to a Law that

nothing justifies or sanctions, nothing but our crazy will without hope
and without reward. (904)

From Solal's perspective, which is also the narrator's and we must
assume is also Albert Cohen's, the stature of these pious figures is
enhanced by the fact that they take their stand and insist on it in a
meaningless universe.

I maintain that a literary text like *Belle du Seigneur* has a far greater
potential for disturbing and unsettling fixed models and paradigms
than didactic essays written by historians or political scientists. Of
course, it is possible within a novel as vast in its scope and as varied in
its narrative techniques as *Belle du Seigneur* to include didactic presen-
tations from the point of view of the narrator and/or the characters that
provide multiple illuminations of complex problems. The Jewish presence in this extended narrative, this piece of imaginative fiction, opens
suggestively and in depth the reader's comprehension of and empathy
for the sorrows and joys of being in general and being Jewish in particular. In the introduction to his essays included in the volume *Contingency, Irony, and Solidarity*, the philosopher Richard Rorty writes:

> In my utopia, human solidarity would be seen not as a fact to be recog-
> nized by clearing away "prejudice" or burrowing down to previously hid-
> den depths but, rather as a goal to be achieved. It is to be achieved not
> by inquiry but by imagination, the imaginative ability to see strange
> people as fellow sufferers. Solidarity is not discovered by reflection but
> created. It is created by increasing our sensitivity to the particular details
> of the pain and humiliation of other, unfamiliar sorts of people. Such
> increased sensitivity makes it more difficult to marginalize people dif-
> ferent from ourselves by thinking, "They do not feel it as *we* would," or
> "There must always be suffering so why not let *them* suffer."
>
> This process of coming to see other human beings as "one of us"
> rather than as "them" is a matter of detailed description of what unfa-
> miliar people are like and of redescription of what we ourselves are like.
> This is a task not for theory but for genres such as ethnography, the
> journalist's report, the comic book, the docudrama, and especially, the
> novel. Fiction like that of Dickens, Olive Schreiner, or Richard Wright
> gives us the details about kinds of suffering being endured by people to
> whom we had previously not attended. Fiction like that of Choderlos de
> Laclos, Henry James, or Nabokov gives us the details about what sorts
> of cruelty we ourselves are capable of, and thereby lets us redescribe our-

selves. That is why the novel, the movie, and the TV program have, gradually but steadily, replaced the sermon and the treatise as the principal vehicles of moral change and progress. (xvi)

Although I cannot subscribe entirely to Richard Rorty's overly utopian vision, I do agree with the importance he ascribes to the imagination and to the novel as the means par excellence of nourishment for the imagination. I would propose that a novel like *Belle du Seigneur* participates in the two kinds of fiction Rorty delineates: fiction that describes the suffering of people different from ourselves and fiction that describes our own cruelties. And further I would propose that this is so precisely because the weltanschauung that directs the novel is *marrano*, that is to say, is both Jewish and not Jewish, both Jewish and Christian or, better still, both Jewish and European. Hannah Arendt, in her essay "Rosa Luxemburg" from *Men in Dark Times* (1966), reminds us of Nietzsche's assertion "that the positions and function of the Jewish people in Europe predestined them to become the 'good Europeans' *par excellence*." Hannah Arendt, in the same essay, insists that

> The Jewish middle classes of Paris and London, Berlin and Vienna, Warsaw and Moscow, were in fact neither cosmopolitan nor international, though the intellectuals among them thought of themselves in these terms. They were European, something that could be said of no other group. (42)

The label "European" is as appropriate for Albert Cohen as it was for Rosa Luxemburg, and it is substantiated in both cases by their degree of plurilingualism and the number of European countries in which they lived.

The same status of Marrano and European could by claimed for the writer Nathalie Sarraute. The writer-narrator in *Enfance*, published twenty-two years after *Belle du Seigneur*, only once refers to herself as being a Jew. This happens in the vignette in which she performs as a Christian. In one of the last vignettes in the text, the narrator, interrupted by her interlocutor, recounts going to Catholic church with the housemaid, Adèle, and attending Russian Orthodox services with her stepmother's mother: "Adèle sometimes used to take me to church in Montrouge, where I made the same gestures as she did" (207).

The first part of the vignette focuses on gestures, the gestures made by Catholics in their church. The young girl accompanying her housemaid to church imitates the gestures as signs of politeness rather than as signs signifying belief. Not only does the young girl not believe, but she notifies us that the maid, Adèle, is also of a "this-worldly disposition." Nor is the Russian mother of the child's stepmother any more of a believer, even though the gestures she makes at the Russian Orthodox church, gestures that are imitated by the narrator and that require prostrating the body on the floor of the church, are even more dramatic than the Catholic gestures. The Russian Orthodox experience, carried by sounds and lights, and the child's love for her childhood memories of Russia, bring Russia to both stepgrandmother and narrator. These gestures may be related to superstition, as the narrator suggests, but their very performance has multiple poetic and human effects.

In the second half of the vignette the interlocutor reminds the narrator that she is not Christian, that she is neither Catholic nor Russian Orthodox. The interlocutor seems surprised that no one in the narrator's family either spoke to her about the religion "of your ancestors" or spoke to her about being Jewish. The reader then learns from the narrator that her real mother did not want to discuss the matter of religion, and that her father, a "freethinker" in the tradition of Russian Jewish atheists, would never have made distinctions between Jews and non-Jews. And this tradition to which the Russian father adheres is the same tradition that supports the secular state schools in France, the schools that the narrator-writer attends. This is the liberal world of assimilation in which religion is the equivalent of superstition, in which there are no differences and everyone is French.

The last sentence of the vignette begins with a "But," a conjunction announcing a contradiction, that prepares the reader for yet another way of thinking about being Jewish:

> But later, every time this question came up, I always saw my father immediately declare, shout from the housetops, that he was Jewish. He thought that it was vile, that it was stupid, to be ashamed of it, and he used to say: How many horrors and ignominious acts, how many lies and servile acts, has it taken to achieve this result: that people are secretly ashamed of their ancestors and feel of greater value in their own eyes if they can manage to claim others, no matter which, so long as they are not those. "Don't you agree?" he sometimes said to me, much later, "that all the same, when you come to think of it . . . "Yes, I did agree." (209)

The "later," that follows the "But" may stand for "after Auschwitz," since Nathalie Sarraute's father lived through the war and died in 1949. History thus intervenes discreetly in the narrative, propelling her father, and herself in imitation of her father, to declare through an utterance, even though they do not perform it with gestures, their Jewishness. Their verbal behavior echoes the pronouncement of Sigmund Freud (but not of Simone Weil) before Auschwitz and that of many secular Jews after Auschwitz: "My language . . . is German, my culture, my attainments are German," wrote Freud. "I considered myself German intellectually, until I noticed the growth of anti-Semitic prejudices in Germany and German Austria. Since that time, I prefer to call myself a Jew" (Gilman, *Freud, Race, and Gender* 16). This particular speech act on the part of assimilated Jewish nonbelievers in the face of hostility during and after the outbreaks of fierce antisemitism in Europe during the late 1930s and the 1940s was not uncommon.

For a young, handsome, secular Jewish man to disguise himself as an old pious Jew is as ambiguous a gesture as for a Jewish child to make the sign of the cross and prostrate herself on the floor of a church. I like to think of the tradition out of which Albert Cohen and Nathalie Sarraute write as the same tradition as the one Yovel Yirmiyahu posits for Baruch Spinoza, the tradition of Marranism in which Jewish and Christian cultures mingle, in which both are recognized as being present albeit in different degrees, and neither is denied, although crossing over from one to the other is considered a transgression by strict Jews and official Christians. Marranism in Cohen and Sarraute implies multiple languages, countries, and cultural traditions, a refusal of separatism, a going beyond the discourses of history. This is, I think, the best of the contemporary Jewish tradition and one that makes itself felt more readily through literature than through the binary thinking and the arguments that direct most of academic historical and sociological writing on the Jewish question. I also think that in France, where assimilation has been such a powerful force for almost two hundred years, *Marrano* is a particularly "useful" (Rorty 9) metaphor for trying to come to terms with the presence and the question of secular Jews. *Marrano* allows us to understand the *Juifemme* (I am a Jewish woman) of Hélène Cixous ("Sorties" 187), the "Ich bleibe also Jude" (I remain therefore a Jew) of Jacques Derrida (*Circonfession* 279), even the "parce que je suis juif" (because I am a Jew) of Cardinal Jean-Marie Aaron Lustiger (65), the "moi, intellectuelle juive qui ait survécu à Auschwitz" (me, a Jewish intellectual who survived Auschwitz) of Sarah Kofman (*Paroles suffoquées*, 13), the "Juif imaginaire" (imaginary Jew) of Alain Finkielkraut as metaphors for the multiple ways of acknowledging being a Jew and therefore the multiple ways of understanding Jewishness outside the synagogue, outside the Jewish confessional community.

Albert Cohen and Nathalie Sarraute, in very different kinds of writings, construct ambiguous, equivocal representations of Jews, allowing neither stereotypes nor identity politics to direct their discourse or their fictions.

10 | *Juifemme*

Bit by bit the question formulated itself in my mind: what is left of identity when both language and religion are gone.
—H. Stuart Hughes, *Prisoners of Hope: The Silver Age of Italian Jewry, 1924–1974*

My title, *Juifemme*, a French portmanteau word, is taken from a subheading in Hélène Cixous's essay "Sorties" (Ways out), the second part of *La Jeune Née/The Newly Born Woman*, written in collaboration with Catherine Clément and published during the annus mirabilis of theoretical writing by women in France, 1974–1975. I understand the word *Juifemme* as used by Hélène Cixous to be a conscious attempt to write against the fixed ethnic and gender meanings of fundamentalist or identity politics, to undercut the many dogmas and pieties that inform being Jewish or being woman, and to propose other ways of figuring identity. For my purposes, *Juifemme* displaces being Jewish from the domain of religious questions to the domain of philosophical or political, or literary, or linguistic questions. In order to do justice to my title, I have divided this chapter into three parts that correspond to three different modes of engaging, in an autobiographical mode, the reconfiguring of (my) Jewish (European and) American identity: the personal, the political, and the poetic.

The Personal

Since childhood, Sigmund Freud has been a constant figure in my affective and my intellectual life, a figure associated with family members, particularly one uncle, interminably analyzed, who was my first mentor. For most members of my secular Jewish family "enlightenment consciousness which defined religion as the ultimate enemy" (Diller 29) was replaced in the early 1930s by Freudian psychoanalysis, which played the role of governing principle, frame of reference, and endless source of Jewish pride. This role continued through my own analysis, from age thirteen to seventeen, and beyond adolescence, into my young adult life. It colored my encounters with religion, socialism, and feminism on the one hand, antisemitism and racism on the other, not to mention my work in French language, literature, and culture and my engagements with people whom I have loved. I would like to explore briefly different moments of this relationship with Sigmund Freud in an attempt to understand why I continue to find it so exciting, and how Freud's Jewish atheism and my own, how being, like Freud, a secular, godless Jew, is central not only to my Jewishness but to my sense of Who and What I Am.

First of all, my awareness as a child that only boys and men were really Jews: boys were circumcised, some boys wore yarmulkes, some boys had bar mitzvahs. You could see, if you looked at their penises, that boys and men were Jews. I could hear that my maternal grandmother was Jewish, because every morning and every evening she recited prayers in Hebrew and Yiddish. But hearing is not seeing. On my mother's side of the family the women, my mother and her sisters, had all been on the stage: acting, singing, playing the piano, and dancing. Not one of them "performed Jewishness," that is to say, dressed or talked or behaved like the Jewish mothers and relatives of my Jewish friends on the south shore of Long Island or on Riverside Drive in New York City. And, most important for my understanding, we were not Christians. We did not observe Christian holidays, we were different from, superior to, the "goyim" (the word applied exclusively to Christian women) who were, in spite of much evidence to the contrary, represented in my mother's discourse as blond and dumb. If in my imaginary Jews were men, goyim were women. This curious binary opposition was reinforced by my "phallic" mother's talent for telling stories, Jewish stories, that were often dirty jokes, with the punch line in Yiddish. At gatherings of family and friends, my mother, as storyteller, was the central figure. Her stories, which provoked howls of laughter from most listeners, were usually at the expense of ridiculous, impotent, henpecked Ashkenazi Jewish men, either Litvaks or Galitzianers. The "little yiddle" (my mother's words) was the focus and the butt of her humor. And then there were the rabbis, whom my mother referred to as the wild ones, in their long coats and wide-brimmed fur hats, who presided over the seders we attended during Pesach with my maternal grandmother at Jewish hotels in the Rockaways. Their performances were commented on with denigrating humor by my mother, next to whom I sat during the meals. Until I encountered Sigmund Freud in my uncle's library and overheard whispered comments about my uncle's analysis, Jews were all pathetic, comic, slightly repulsive male characters. The picture becomes clearer: Jews are unattractive men; we are not Christian; goyim are dumb, blond women; we are Jewish. To be a Jew is not the same as being Jewish. Sigmund Freud was Jewish.

To be Jewish like Freud was to be intelligent, liberal, generous, talented, bright, superior, European, cosmopolitan, and irreligious. *The Future of an Illusion* (1927) was the Torah in our house. My mother frequently repeated Karl Marx's slogan, "Religion is the opiate of the masses," but it was Freud, not Moses and not Marx, who was the giver of laws. And if Freud rather than Marx was the central figure in our household, it is in great part because, as Yosef Hayim Yerushalmi has understood so well in *Freud's Moses: Judaism Terminable and Interminable* (1991), for both Freud and my mother "'Jewishness' can be transmitted independently of 'Judaism,' the former is interminable even if the latter be terminated." (90)

And so this transmission of Jewishness continues through me, with occasional eruptions of Judaism. I transmit Jewishness by saying and repeating, "I am Jewish" in social situations when I consider it appropriate to mark a difference or raise the question. This is, in the groups within which I move in the United States and in France, a frequent occurrence. And the reaction I hear most often is: How can you be Jewish without being a practicing Jew or even believing in God? My response is not simple nor is it usually convincing to my interlocutors. I am Jewish precisely because I am not a believer, because I associate from early childhood the courage not to believe with being Jewish; I am Jewish because of familial ties and loyalties; I am Jewish because of the memory, transmitted to me by members of my family, of suffering and pain; I am Jewish because I can still hear my maternal grandmother's voice in Yiddish. My mother died in October of 1981 and was buried in my father's family plot—the Jacob Marks plot—at Beth El Cemetery in Piramus, New Jersey. The rabbi, hastily found for the occasion and coached by me on what not to say, called for someone to read the graveside Kaddish. I am an only child, divorced and unmarried, and I stepped forward with the righteous gentile woman with whom I live, and we read together the transliterated version of the prayer. *Juifemme* indeed.

Why I love French may be as relevant to this chapter and, indeed, to this book, as noted in chapter 1, as how I am Jewish. I suspect that in my imaginary, French has been for a very long time the antithesis of Jewish and, particularly, of Yiddish. When I was a child my mother, who was a singer, sang frequently in French (and also in German, Italian, Russian, English, and Yiddish). I remember specifically her singing "Parlez-moi d'amour" (Speak to me of love) and reciting almost each night at my bedside: "Je t'aime comme de la crème, je t'adore comme de l'or" (I love you as I love cream, I love you as I love gold). When I was a child French was the language of desire and of love. It was associated with elegance and freethinking. During the Second World War these older associations were augmented by media images of the fall of France, the German's marching down the Champs Elysées while French men and women cried, and the heroes and heroines of the Resistance. I wonder if perhaps I came to French to escape or to hide from Jewishness and from Yiddish,[1] and if this is indeed the case, how ironic, then, that in the last decade of my career as a professor of French and Women's Studies I came to the Jewish question and the Jewish presence in French writing.

The Political

In the preface and in chapter 5, "*La France* et *Le Juif*: Identity and a Significant Other," I noted my witnessing of media reactions in France to the trial of Klaus Barbie and to the presentation of Claude Lanzmann's film *Shoah* on French television during the summer of 1987. I also noted the ongoing discussion of and preoccupation with names—Jewish names—during the Barbie trial and in antisemitic books and pamphlets.

The preoccupation of the antisemites with identifying Jews is matched by the preoccupation of some French Jews with "coming out" as Jews and "outing" other Jews. If many antisemites in France want to know who is and who isn't Jewish, so do some French Jews. The question of identity has become a central factor in cultural and social as well as political and religious life in France as well as in the United States. If antisemites have their favorite stereotype of what constitutes Jewishness, so do some *French* Jews. And their stereotype frequently includes the obligation to be a practicing Jew.[2] An active relation to the religion of Judaism is tending to become a sine qua non of Jewishness. Thus far I have spoken of France, but I would now like to give two brief examples from the United States that are equally disturbing, as least for those whose Jewishness resembles mine.

The first example is from a course I taught at the University of Wisconsin-Madison during the spring semester of 1991, through the Women's Studies Program and cross-listed with our nascent Jewish Studies Program, titled "Jewish Women: Writers, Intellectuals, Activists." Many of the Jewish women in the class, about twenty-eight of the forty-five students, were unwilling to accept Rosa Luxemburg, Hannah Arendt, and Simone Weil as "Jewish." Any serious questioning of Judaism by nonpracticing, nonobservant, nonreligious Jews—the students' criticisms did not cover the work of Judith Plaskow for example—was considered antisemitic and was immediately and categorically rejected.

The second example comes from an article that appeared in the *Capital Times* of Madison, Wisconsin, October 19–20, 1990, on the efforts of Rabbi Ephraim Buchwald "to bring the non-religious and the unaffiliated . . . the marginal Jews . . . back into active faith" (9A). In this sentence "non-religious, "unaffiliated" and "marginal" are synonyms. I do not contest the desire to proselytize. But, once again, as with my Jewish students, I challenge (and I resent) the refusal to recognize nonreligious, unaffiliated, marginal Jews as Jewish, the refusal even to consider the possible coexistence of *assimilation* (a word that is on its way to becoming the epitome of evil in Jewish Studies) and *Jewishness*.

In a letter to Kurt Blumenfeld about the assimilationist position, Hannah Arendt wrote: "In a society on the whole hostile to the Jews—and that situation obtained in all countries in which Jews lived, down to the twentieth century—it is possible to assimilate only by assimilating anti-Semitism also."[3] This is an ironic and a profound comment, and it is essential to my understanding of assimilation. I do not think that it is possible to live in any contemporary Western society without assimilating antisemitism, whatever one's religious beliefs and practices may be. Antisemitism is too pervasive, in overlapping areas of language and culture, not to become part of discourses and feelings. But at the same time it is, as least for Jews, the coming to terms with the existence of antisemitism outside and inside, that is an important component of "being" Jewish in the late twentieth century.

Juifemme puts into motion *I, Jew-Jewish,* and *Woman.* What and Who am I? Is the difference only between *Jew-Jewish* and *Woman* or is it also among Jews, among women, and among competing theories of the subject? Are we, if we insist on one of these terms alone, *Jew* or *woman,* running the risk of reproducing, as Jean-François Lyotard suggests (in the words of Eric Santner), those narcissistic patterns that are partially responsable for Nazism as is any attempt to refuse nomadism and fragmentation and to insist upon a return to roots?[4]

In the November/December 1991 issue of *Tikkun,* Ilene Philipson in an essay entitled "What's the Big I.D.? The Politics of the Authentic Self" "attacks" (editor Michael Lerner's word) identity politics: "At the foundation of identity politics is a fundamental belief in the necessity of expressing an identifiable 'authentic self,' and this belief increasingly has become the means through which individuals interpret their own experience and give it social expression" (51). Ilene Philipson is in turn attacked (or at least severely criticized) by Henry Louis Gates, Jr., Ellen Willis, David Biale, and Arthur Waskow. I am interested in changing the terms of this debate and of investigating what happens when we create, as Hélène Cixous has, a portmanteau word that attempts, poetically and ironically, to transcend the separate strands that constitue contemporary identity politics, for example, *Juifemme*?

The Poetical

Juifemme is, at first glance, the coming together of two French words *juif,* a generic, male Jew, and *femme,* woman. It recalls the sixteenth-century spelling *Juifves,* as in the title of Robert Garnier's play *Les Juifves,* in which masculine and feminine endings are present in a single word. In *Juifemme,* depending on how you look at it, there is either a lost *f* or only one *f* that belongs to both words. If the *f* belongs to *juif* then it is *âme,* the soul, that follows. If the *f* belongs to *femme,* then there is a drift toward words that mean I am, I have pleasure, I hear.

Both *juif* and *femme* are words with a troubled history. *Juif* was the word stamped by the Vichy government on the identity cards of Jews in France, making it easier for the Nazis to round them up. *Juif* in exotic lettering, parodying the letters of the Hebrew alphabet or Gothic script, and never the feminine *juive,* also appeared on the yellow star that Jews were required to wear sewn onto their outer garments in the Occupied Zone. *Femme,* meaning both woman and wife in French, may be interpreted as incorporating the subservient and the property status of woman into the assignment of sex and gender.

The French Jewish writer Albert Cohen, in a text entitled "Jour de mes dix ans" (The Day of my tenth birthday), tells the story of his encounter in Paris with an antisemitic street hawker who verbally harrasses him. At the end of his narrative Cohen writes:

> From the day of this encounter, I could not look at a newspaper without immediately noting the word *juif,* immediately at the first glance. And I even notice the words that resemble this terrible word, this sad and beautiful word, I notice immediately *juin* (June) and *suif* (suet, mutton fat) and, in English, I notice immediately few, dew, jewel. (467–68)

For Albert Cohen paranomasia and rhyme expand the possibilities of making visible the inner obsession with the word *Juif,* Jew.

Hélène Cixous's delight in the play of the signifier, in portmanteau words, is of another kind, and echoes the delight of her major intertextual reference, James Joyce, whose famous coupling in *Ulysses* (1922), "Jewgreek is greekjew. Extremes meet" (493), is quoted by Jacques Derrida at the end of his essay "Violence and Metaphysics" (1966), on the French Jewish philosopher Emmanuel Lévinas. In "Sorties" the heading "Juifemme" is preceded by the heading "L'Aube du Phallocentrisme" (The Dawn of phallocentrism) and two quotations from Sigmund Freud's *Moses and Monotheism,* and it is followed by references to Kafka's *Before the Law,* a parable through which Cixous reads the birth of phallocentrism and its devastating effects on Jew and woman. The beauty of the portmanteau word is not that it to brings together what has been separate (as in "Jewgreek," "Greekjew"), and not, as I interpret it, that it performs an *aufhebung,* that it makes a synthesis. *Juifemme* is more than, different from, Jew and woman, or Jewoman. It is a rich poetic word in which the sounds of *Je,* I, and *jouir,* to have pleasure, and *ouir,* to hear (*Je suis femme* and *je jouis* and "*j'ouis*") as well as the visual juxtaposition of *juif,* a Jewish man, and *femme,* woman, prevent any one-way meaning of sex, gender, subjectivity, or religious belonging—any coincidence of hearing and seeing. As Jean-François Lyotard proposes in his essay "Jewish Oedipus," hearing rather than seeing occupies a primary position in both Hebrew ethics, in which representation is forbidden, and in psychoanalysis. What one hears does seem to open more possibilities in *Juifemme* than what one sees.[5]

If I have chosen a portmanteau word, in French, to carry my deliberately ambivalent messages, it is because, like Jacques Derrida, I suffer from a "mal de l'appartenance," a belonging sickness. Let me begin to end with a quotation from Derrida's "Curriculum vitae" (1991), which we find at the end of the double text *Circonfession* (Circumfession), a confessional text by Jacques Derrida written as a counterpoint to Geoffrey Bennington's text, "Derridabase," in a book whose title is *Jacques Derrida,* by Geoffrey Bennington and Jacques Derrida.

> It is undoubtedly during those years (1942–1943 in Algeria, North Africa) that J.D. was stamped as "belonging" in this curious manner to Judaism: a wound, certainly, a painful sensitivity schooled in antisemitism as in all forms of racism, the response of a flayed victim to xenophobia, but also an impatience with gregarious identification, with the militantism of belonging in general, even with Jewish belonging. In short, a double refusal, of which we have so many signs, and much before *Circonfession.* (Let me say in passing that J.D. suprised me less than he believed or pretended to believe in exhibiting his circumcision in these pages: for a long time, he has been speaking only of his circumcision, I can prove this with supporting quotations from such places where he names it as *Glas, La Carte Postale, Schibboleth* [in particular], *Ulysse Gramophone.* As to what can tie the "this is my body and I give it to you" of the Eucharist to the exhibiting of the circumcised body, we can add to the above texts the seminar that J.D., so they tell me, is devoting to "the rhetoric of cannibalism," to what he refers to as "the loving" of "the loving-eating-the other" and, of course, to the big question of transsubstantiation). This belonging sickness, one might almost say identification sickess, affects the entire corpus of J.D.'s work in which "the deconstruction of one's own" is, it seems to me, at the heart of his afflicted thought. (300–1)

Circonfession is also a portmanteau word, a new word formed from the mingling of circumcision and confession. Like *Juifemme,* for Cixous, it allows Derrida to engage in autobiographical play referentially and poetically. *Circonfession* announces his Jewishness and his masculinity and also subverts them, playing with them literarily and literally through multiple echoes of Saint Augustine's *Confessions.* Saint Augustine, philosopher and bishop of Hippo, was also, like Derrida, from North Africa and also had a dying mother. Derrida's parents, Aimé Derrida and Georgette Esther Safar, lived on the rue Saint-Augustin in Algiers from 1923 until 1934, three years after the birth of Jacques (Jackie) Elie Derrida. But there are also echoes of Jean-Jacques Rousseau's *Confessions,* a classic of French literature (but Rousseau was Swiss), in which Rousseau confesses to many major and minor "sins," including the pleasure he received when his foster mother whipped his buttocks. This, in French, is a *fessée,* and it has become, for readers of Rousseau, an integral part of what is involved in the *Confessions* and in the act of confessing. The portmanteau word that Derrida selected is a sign that Derrida, like Cixous, will not stop at either of the signifiers, in his case "circumcision" or "confession," in her case "Jewish" or "woman," and will not elaborate didactically on being a circumcised Jewish man.

Geoffrey Bennington's J. D. suffers from the xenophobia of antisemites and suffers also from the injunction to be Jewish by accepting to be part of a group already constituted and defined as Jewish. "Identification sickness" may however be a misnomer, or at any rate an improper analogy for "belonging sickness." One might identify, one might recognize similarities, without wishing or accepting to belong. Identifying and recognizing—and these are not the same—are psychological, philosophical stances whereas belonging is a social position, and involves an obligation to follow preexisting discourses, institutions, and practices. This "belonging sickness," which I and others seem to share with Jacques Derrida as diagnosed by Geoffrey Bennington and Jacques Derrida, is the refusal of identity politics and ultimately of stereotypes. It is the acceptance of being Jewish and being assimilated, of being Jewish and being other(s) at the same time.

Two recent books that I read with a certain ethnic intensity but little intellectual pleasure and one book that I read with ethnic intensity and enormous intellectual pleasure will help me make my points in another mode. The books are Letty Cottin Pogrebin's *Deborah, Golda, and Me: Being Female and Jewish in America* (1991), Alan M. Dershowitz's *Chutzpah* (1991), and Yirmiyahu Yovel's *Spinoza and Other Heretics* (1989). Differences in genre and intention notwithstanding, the autobiographical texts by Pogrebin and Dershowitz inevitably tend toward narcissism and exhibitionism, whereas the philosophical volume on Spinoza maintains a very different style level throughout. I found Pogrebin's account particularly disturbing because she seems to know intuitively how women and Jews should think and behave. Nothing could be further from Hélène Cixous's *Juifemme* than Pogrebin's search for "a comfortable collective identity" (xiv) that includes being female and Jewish in America. Dershowitz is considerably more open than Pogrebin to differences—political, philosophical, ethnic—and to questions that challenge any simple answers. His sixth chapter, "Visiting Synagogues Around the World: Exploring the Different Meanings of Jewishness," repeats in varying formulations "that the Jewish way is not a singular road, but rather an almost endless series of interconnecting paths with a common origin and an uncertain and unknowable destination—or destinations" (206). My preference for Yovel's *Spinoza and Other Heretics* will come as no surprise to the readers of this book. Spinoza is represented by Yovel as a heretical Jew who abandoned the normative Jewish practices of his time and refused to convert to Christianity. Spinoza is the Jew who, according to Yovel, prefigures contemporary Judaism, which is determined by the way Jews live rather than by an obligatory model which all Jews must follow (265). Yovel's "Spinoza" resembles my "Freud."

Before Auschwitz, two of the main protagonists in European narrative fiction were assimilated Jews, Leopold Bloom and Charles Swann, distinguished by their cultural and "racial" differences from the Christian cultures in which they lived. After Auschwitz, in texts by Paul Celan, Edmond Jabès, Jacques Derrida, and Hélène Cixous, the trope of the wandering marked Jew and the poet as wanderer erases the racial connotations in favor of estrangement so that anyone, in Hélène Cixous's words, "can be a Jew, anyone who is sensitive to the cut, to what by marking a limit, produces otherness" (*Readings*, 147).[6] We are not by law or by nature Juifemme, but we may choose to be so.

What remains most important for me is the construction of a discourse that sustains both the particular and the general, the political and the poetic, the social and the ontological, i.e., the question of being Jewish and being a woman, and the question of being. At the beginning of this chapter, I noted that I came to questions of Jewishness through the Shoah. It would be more accurate to state that in the beginning was an obsession with death and absence to which the Jewish story became attached.

The earliest ontological experience that I remember occurred at the age of four at the time of my maternal grandfather's death. I was sitting at the piano and saying over and over again, "Dead forever and ever," and trying to comprehend "forever." The second revelation was occasioned by the taste of bacon (not a neutral food in this context), for which I had an inordinate fondness, and my attempts at comprehending where the taste went when it was no longer in my mouth, the complete absence of what had been so overwhelmingly present. Before I was consciously aware of "being" Jewish or "being" a woman, I was aware of "being" and the possibility of not "being." This has remained over the years as the most constant of my experiences and of my intellectual concerns.

During my years at college, when I was freer from the turmoils of adolescence, the literary and philosophical texts that most deeply affected my intellectual growth and my affective life were passages from François Villon's *Testament*, from Blaise Pascal's *Pensées*, French lyrical poetry from Baudelaire to Bonnefoy, Tolstoy's *Death of Ivan Illych*, the long passage on the death of the grandmother in Marcel Proust's *Remembrance of Things Past*, passages in Colette's first-person writings on old age, and, in general, novels and biographical writing that tell the story of a life in and through time.

This has not changed, but the specific areas of inquiry have. I am therefore obliged to admit that had it not been for the Second World War and the Shoah, I would not have turned my research efforts so passionately to the Jewish question and the Jewish presence in French writing and, by extension, in other languages, literatures, cultures, and in myself. In all honesty I must conclude that the *Je suis* (I am) that we understand but neither hear nor see matters more to me now, and always has, than what we hear and see in *Juifemme*.

Notes

Preface

1. This metonymic use of the German word for the major Polish extermination camp, concentration camp, and work camp as a synonym for *Holocaust* or *Shoah* is frequent in both scholarly and poetic writing.

2. Scholarship on the Shoah, the Vichy government, and the years of the German Occupation of France during World War II has had, in the past ten years, as one of its central themes, the importance and the analysis of memory and remembering. I recommend, among other books listed in the bibliography, Rousso's *Le Syndrôme de Vichy / The Vichy Syndrome*. I also recommend the works cited in the bibliography by Blanchot, Derrida, Felman, and Kofman on the complexities of remembering and the dangers of commemorating.

3. Titles of French books are translated into English the first time they appear in my book. Thereafter, unless the English title is well known, I have used the French title. Titles that are translated but not italicized indicate that the book has not been translated and published in English, or is not available in English.

4. "Issues, Terms, and Contexts," de Lauretis's introduction to *Feminist Studies/Critical Studies*, 1986.

5. I prefer the word *Auschwitz*, the German name for the Polish town in which the largest of the extermination-concentration-labor camps was located, to either the Hebrew word *Shoah* (destruction, catastrophe) or the Greek word *Holocaust* (burnt offering). The Hebrew word is troublesome not only because it might seem to exclude the murder and pain of non-Jews but more particularly because it does exclude the Yiddish *hurbn* (destruction, catastrophe).

Holocaust is even more problematic. To refer to the destruction of the Jews in terms of a biblical sacrifice seems to perpetuate, albeit unwittingly, a form of Christian antisemitism, as if the Jews were expiating their role in the death of Jesus Christ. However, because all three terms—*Auschwitz, Shoah,* and *Holocaust*—are used in the texts on which I will be commenting, I also use these terms at different moments when it seems appropriate to do so. The term *Shoah* was used increasingly in France after the opening of Claude Lanzmann's film *Shoah* in 1985.

1 | Theoretical Considerations

Unless otherwise indicated, all translations from the French are my own.

1. For a discussion of this refusal, see de Man's essay, "The Resistance to Theory," pp. 3–20.

2. In a similar vein, Kofman writes at the beginning of *Le Mépris des Juifs* about the branding of Nietzsche:

> The fashion of the moment seems to have decided in favor of the anti-semitism of the philosopher, accused in the hastiest and grossest way (without a serious examination of the texts in their plurality and complexity) of having been the mouthpiece, indeed the father, of Nazism and to be held responsible—no more no less—among other things, for Auschwitz. (p. 12)

2 | Jewish Biblical Literature in French Literature: *Les Juifves* and Esther

1. I will refer to Jewish Holy Scriptures as the Old Testament when I am discussing a Christian perspective or manner of speaking common in Western culture.

2. I am not attempting to be complete in my coverage. I am leaving out French translations of Jewish Holy Scriptures including translations by Jacques Lefèvre d'Etaples (1530), Pierre-Robert Olivétan (1535), a translation printed in London in 1550, and, closer in time to us, the translation by the Chanoine Crampon (1960) and the *Bible de Jérusalem* (1986). I am also leaving out French literary texts informed by Jewish Holy Scriptures, among which some of the best known are: *Le Jeu d'Adam,* Marot's *Psaumes, Les Tragiques* by Agrippa d'Aubigné, *Saül le furieux* by Jean de la Taille, *Abraham sacrifiant* by Théodore de Bèze, Louis des Masures's *David combattant, David triomphant,*

David fugitif, Aman by André de Rivaudeau, Antoine de Montchrestien's *Les Tragédies*, passages in Pascal's *Pensées* and in Bossuet's sermons, Saint Amant's *Moyse Sauvé*, Racine's *Athalie*, nineteenth-century poems such as Alfred de Vigny's "Moïse" and "La Colère de Samson," Victor Hugo's "Booz endormi," twentieth-century rewritings of the story of the garden of Eden by Jules Supervielle in *La Première famille* and Monique Wittig in *Les Guérillères*.

3. This psalm is referred to in the French *Bible de Jérusalem* as the "Ballade de l'exilé." In English it is one of the most beautiful of the Biblical psalms. I quote from the translation in the Masoretic text: "By the rivers of Babylon, / There we sat down, yea, we wept, / When we remembered Zion" (Psalm 137).

4. See notes to *Esther* in Raymond Picard's *Oeuvres complètes*, vol. 1, Bibliothèque de la Pléiade.

5. For a much fuller treatment of some of these questions, I direct the reader to Moore's discussion of "Esther, Additions to" and "Esther, Book of."

6. Esther's Jewishness was not forgotten by the collaborationist press during the Occupation. In a September 1942 issue of *Je Suis Partout*, P. A. Cousteau published an article in which he referred to Racine's Esther as a "petite garce juive" (a little Jewish bitch) and suggested that the play be eliminated from school reading lists. I found this reference in Elizabeth Brunazzi's article "The Question of Colette and Collaboration" in *Tulsa Studies in Women's Literature* (Fall 1994), 13(2):284.

3 | "Sapho 1900": Imaginary Renée Viviens, Charles Maurras, and the Rear of the Belle Epoque

1. See Gubar, "Sapphistries."

2. The edition of Maurras that I have used is: *L'Avenir de l'intelligence*, suivi de *August Comte, Le Romantisme féminin, Mademoiselle Monk, L'Invocation à Minerve*.

3. The *Grand Robert* dictionary gives the Greek etymology (*metoikos*, from *meta* and *oikos maison* "Qui change de maison" (who changes house). In ancient Greek the word designated a foreigner living in Greece who did not have *droit de cité*. The *Grand Robert* notes that the word is used by Charles Maurras from 1894 on to refer to a foreigner living in France, and that since 1894 (the date at which Captain Alfred Dreyfus was convicted of treason) the word has acquired a strong xenophobic if not racist meaning.

4. It is also the key word in Soller's novel, *Femmes/Women*.

5. Colette, in her 1928 portrait of Renée Vivien, incorporated in 1932 as a chapter of *Ces Plaisirs . . .*, renamed in 1941 *Le Pur et l'impur*, insists on the childish, puerile behavior of Renée Vivien and represents both her anguish and her sexuality as eccentric and unhealthy. Indeed, although her style bears little

resemblance to that of Charles Maurras, Colette reproduces, through elaborate anecdotes, Maurras's ideological positions. Toward the beginning of her texts, Colette refers to "the hidden tragic melancholy that throbs in the poetry of Renée Vivien" (*The Pure and the Impure*, 80). But because Colette and Renée Vivien never talked together about their writing and because Colette only occasionaly saw Renée Vivien in the act of writing, Renée Vivien, the writer, is absent. Colette focuses on Renée Vivien's face, her lisp, her claustrophobic apartments, her eating and her drinking habits, and her manner of speaking about her Lesbian love affairs. Colette's Renée Vivien is only incidentally a writer. She is, rather, an exemplary dark figure of the belle epoque and, as Colette's definitive title suggests—corroborating Charles Maurras's conclusions—one of the impure.

6. Rubin fails to mention that the title of the novel is a quotation from the thirtieth canto of "Purgatory" in Dante's *The Divine Comedy*. The essential reversal in the text is that a woman, a Beatrice, appears not to the male narrator, Dante, but to the female narrator of *A Woman Appeared to Me*.

7. These words are from the quotation in Maurras's *L'Avenir de l'intelligence* cited on page oo of this chapter.

4 | Jewish Literature and Jewish Writing in French Literature: Albert Cohen and the *Revue Juive*

1. Albert Cohen's play, *Ezéchiel*, published by Gallimard in 1956, stages a confrontation between Ezekiel and Jeremiah in which the future of the Jews and the coming of the Messiah is projected by the force of Ezekiel's desire and will.

2. Israel in this context refers to the Jews as a people.

5 | *La France* et *Le Juif*: Identity and a Significant Other

1. The figures I am using come from different sources, hence the word *approximately*. I direct my readers to the following entries in the bibliography: Dawidowicz, *The War Against the Jews*, Gilbert, *The Holocaust*, Hilberg, *La Destruction des juifs européens*, Klarsfeld, *Memorial to the Jews Deported from France 1942–1944*, Michael Marrus, *The Holocaust in History*.

2. During the 1980s in France *memory* and *remembering* became key words in writing about the fate and the resistance of Jews in France during the German Occupation. I refer readers to two books noted in the bibliography: Rousso's *The Vichy Syndrome: History and Memory in France Since 1944* (French edition 1987 and 1990; English translation 1991) and Vidal-Naquet's *Assassins of Memory* (French edition 1987; English translation 1992).

Toward the beginning of his fourth chapter, "Obsessions (After 1974): Jewish Memory," Henry Rousso writes:

> Still, while economic factors may have influenced what I have called the Vichy syndrome, other factors had a more direct bearing on its evolution. Foremost among these was a reawakening of Jewish memory, a phenomenon by no means confined to France. In the wake of a series of crises in the Middle East and the emergence of new forms of anti-semitism, Jewish consciousness was heightened around the world. Memories of the genocide—the Shoah—were at the heart of this change. (132)

3. See note 5 of the preface.

4. The reader may wish to look again at the long Robbe-Grillet quotation in chapter 1, "Theoretical Considerations."

6 | "Getting Away with Murd(h)er"—Author's Preface and Narrator's Text: Reading Marguerite Yourcenar's *Coup de Grâce* "Afte Auschwitz."

I dedicate this reading to the graduate students at the University of Wisconsin-Madison in the seminar on "Littérature et Idéologie," spring 1989.

1. The French edition I have used is *Marguerite Yourcenar Oeuvres Romanesques*, pp. 77–157. The English-language edition to which all subsequent quotations will refer is *Coup de Grâce*, translated by Grace Frick, in collaboration with the author.

2. The English translation omits at least one reference to Jews that exists in the French version, suggesting that the author and the translator were conscious of possible reader reactions in the United States. "Trois mois d'été humide et ouaté de brouillard, bourdonnant d'offres de marchands juifs venus de New York pour acheter dans de bonnes conditions leurs bijoux aux émigrés russes" (92). The English version reads: "Three months of dank and foggy summer, buzzing with dealers from New York who had come to buy jewels at a profit from Russian refugees" (pp. 17–18). But in English *Jews* are present in *jewels*.

3. I would not eliminate the possibility of reading *Coup de Grâce* as "The Neck [*cou*] of Grace," Marguerite Yourcenar's companion and translator, Grace Frick. I would also like to acknowledge a suggestion made by my colleague, Professor Martine Debaisieux, who, having read the chapter, made a connection between the sounds of the title and

Coude de Grâce (Elbow of grace). This connection is particularly interesting because the funny bone in French is sometimes referred to as *le petit juif* (the little jew). In addition, I acknowledge a further suggestion made by my colleague, Professor Yvonne Ozzello, who reminded me that elbow grease in French is *de l'huile de coude*.

4. I intend, at some future date, to compare the manner in which Jacques Derrida, in "Comme le bruit de la mer au fond d'un coquillage: La Guerre de Paul de Man," trans. Peggy Kamuf, "Like the Sound of the Sea Deep within a Shell: Paul de Man's War," *Critical Inquiry* (Spring 1988), 14(3):590–652, defends Paul de Man and comments on the newspaper articles written by de Man for Belgian newspapers between 1939 and 1943, with Marguerite Yourcenar's apology for Eric von Lhomond in her 1962 preface.

7 | The Corset and the Corpse: Antisemitism and the Death of God

1. In the first volume of his *Antisemitism in Modern France* Robert Byrnes writes:

> There are elements in the history of the Jews, however, which have made their history far more tragic than even that of the Irish and Polish people in the modern era. To begin with, it has been commonly believed now for almost two thousand years by billions of people that "the Jews," corrupted by their own vices and the perversities of their religion, are responsible for the death of their own Messiah and the Christian God. Moreover, Christians throughout the Christian era have been particularly horrified because "the Jews" have forever refused to recognize the divinity of their victim. Freud once asserted that there is a corollary from this: every Christian is turned against the Jews because "the Jews" will not admit they killed God and are therefore not cleansed, which makes them even more objects of revulsion.
>
> The interpretation of this tragic incident has had appalling consequences. This interpretation has been a real basis for some antisemitism, not in the esoteric definitions given by the psychologists on the various complexes which have derived from this incident, but in the sheer fact that there have been clear antisemitic overtones in the drama of Calvary as it has been presented in Christian religious instructions and services. The ascribing of this act, which must remain incredible to every Christian, to a whole people, "the Jews," has provided a fertile soil for antisemitism for those Christians who have been little influenced by the true Christian values and Christian spirit but who have been

affected by the tone of some of their literature concerning Christ's life and death. (72)

See Sigmund Freud, *Moses and Monotheism*, 215–216 for an excellent analysis and description of the consequences of the deicide accusation.

2. In her article on "Simone de Beauvoir and 'the Woman Question': *Les Bouches inutiles*" Virginia Fichera writes, "Simone de Beauvoir's play, by recreating the situation of the Vichy government's participation in the Holocaust using women in the place of Jews, adds a new dimension to an analysis of legitimation and government" (p. 62). I would also direct the reader to Marianne DeKoven's essay, "History as Suppressed Referent in Modern Fiction."

3. In his article on "L'Université française sous l'occupation" Pascal Ory writes:

> On October 21, 1940, collaboration between the French university system and discrimination against Jews began. A circular sent by the state to all public educational institutions asked the provosts and heads of academic units to furnish a list of those civil servants "who were generally considered to be or considered by you personally to be Jewish." . . . In the beginning the Board of Education trusted the loyalty of its personnel. Oaths of not being Jewish multiplied.

To the great displeasure of Jean-Paul Sartre, Simone de Beauvoir signed the declaration that she was not a Jew.

4. The Shoah may even be present at the conclusion of her first novel, *L'Invitée/She Came to Stay* (1943), when Françoise, the narrator, unable to maintain the tension brought about by a ménage à trois, kills the consciousness of a young woman by turning on a gas oven.

5. Words used by Marguerite Duras during a television interview, summer 1988, to refer to Auschwitz.

6. There might be an interesting set of parallel lines to investigate: those who, like Heidegger, critical of both the Jewish and the Christian traditions *and* humanism became Nazis and those who, critical of these same traditions, like Simone de Beauvoir, became feminists.

8 | *Cendres Juives*: Jews Writing in French "After Auschwitz"

The quotations from texts by Derrida, Lanzmann, Lévinas, and Wiesel are from available English translations noted in the bibliography. All other translations are my own.

1. It is not irrelevant to note here, as at the beginning of this book, that the writer writing describes herself as an atheist and a Jew.

2. Serge Doubrovsky's "autofiction" *Le Livre brisé* (The Shattered Book:

1989) maintains a delicate balance between the genre with which it is traditionally associated and the questions it raises that threaten the integrity of the genre. Here *cendres juives* are introduced as one element among others in an extended work of mourning. Mourning for the narrator's youth, for his idol, Jean-Paul Sartre, for his mother, for his divorced wife, Claudia, and his ex-mistress, Rachel, for his dead Austrian wife, Ilse, for her still-born baby, for his own past, for what he can and cannot remember. His non-Jewish wife, Ilse, is incinerated and buried in a Jewish cemetery, in passages dominated by the metaphor of Auschwitz.

3. For both Sarah Kofman's father and George Perec's mother, Serge Klarsfeld's *Memorial to the Jews Deported from France, 1942–1944* provides confirmation of their deportation: their names, place of birth, and the number of their convoy.

10 | *Juifemme*

1. This chapter was written before I had read Alice Kaplan's *French Lessons*. On the last page of her "memoir" she asks the question: "Why did I hide in French?" (216). I suspect that for Alice Kaplan, as for myself, French was both a hiding place and a "coming out."

2. "Les 100 Juifs Qui Comptent en France," *Passages*, 1989. See also "Les Juifs en France en 1994," *L'Express*, 9–15 juin, 1994, pp. 60–73, and "Juifs de France," *Le Nouvel Observateur*, 9–15 juin, 1994, pp. 92–94.

3. Quoted in Young-Bruehl, *Hannah Arendt*, p. 92.

4. Santner, *Stranded Objects*, pp. 8–9.

5. Lyotard, "Jewish Oedipus."

6. Cixous. *Readings*, p. 147.

Bibliography

Alter, Robert, and Frank Kermode, eds. *The Literary Guide to the Bible*. Cambridge: Harvard University Press, 1987.

Annales d'Histoire Révisionniste. Nos. 1, 2, 4. Paris: Nouvelles Messageries de la Presse Parisienne, 1987–1988.

Antelme, Robert. *L'Espèce humaine*. Paris: Gallimard, 1957.

Aragon, Louis. *Le Musée Grévin*. Paris: Minuit, 1946.

Arendt, Hannah. *Antisemitism*. New York: Harcourt, Brace and World, 1968.

— *Men in Dark Times*. New York: Harcourt, Brace and World, 1968.

— *Rahel Varnhagen*. New York: Harcourt Brace Jovanovich, 1974.

Aschheim, Steven E. *Brothers and Strangers*. Madison: University of Wisconsin Press, 1982.

Auerbach, Erich. *Mimesis*. New York: Anchor, 1957.

— "Figura." *Scenes from the Drama of European Literature*, pp. 11–76. New York: Meridien, 1959.

Avni, Ora. "Patrick Modiano: A French Jew?" In Alan Astro, ed., *Discourses of Jewish Identity in Twentieth Century France*. *Yale French Studies* (1994), no. 85, pp. 227–47.

Azéma, Jean Pierre, and François Bédarida, eds. *Vichy et les Français*. Paris: Fayard, 1992.

Barbey d'Aurevilly, Jules. *Les Bas-bleus*. Paris: Société Générale de Librairie Catholique, 1878.

Barthes, Roland. *Sur Racine*. Paris: Seuil, 1963.

— "The Struggle with the Angel. Textual Analysis of Genesis 32:22–32." *Image*

Music Text, pp. 125–41. Trans. Stephen Heath. New York: Hill and Wang, 1977.

Beauvoir, Simone de. *L'Invitée*. Paris: Gallimard, 1943.

— *Les Bouches inutiles*. Paris: Gallimard, 1945.

— *Le Sang des Autres*. Paris: Gallimard, 1945.

— "Littérature et Métaphysique." *L'Existentialisme et la sagesse des nations*. Paris: Nagel, 1948.

— *Le Deuxième sexe*. Paris: Gallimard, 1949.

— *The Second Sex*. Trans. H. M. Parshley. New York: Knopf, 1952.

— *Les Mandarins*. Paris: Gallimard, 1954.

— *Mémoires d'une jeune fille rangée*. Paris: Gallimard, 1958.

— *La Force de l'âge*. Paris: Gallimard, 1960.

— *The Prime of Life*. Trans. Peter Green. New York: Lancer Books, 1962.

— *La Force des choses*. Paris: Gallimard, 1963.

— *Une Mort très douce*. Paris: Gallimard, 1964.

— *Force of Circumstance*. Trans. Richard Howard. Harmondsworth: Penguin, 1968.

— *La Vieillesse*. Paris: Gallimard, 1970.

— *Tout Compte fait*. Paris: Gallimard, 1972.

— *Memoirs of a Dutiful Daughter*. Trans. James Kirkup. New York: Harper and Row, 1974.

— *All Said and Done*. Trans. Patrick O'Brian. New York: Warner, 1976.

— "Solidaire d'Israël: un soutien critique." *Les Ecrits de Simone de Beauvoir*. Ed. Claude Francis and Fernande Gautier. Paris: Gallimard, 1979.

— *La Cérémonie des adieux*. Paris: Gallimard, 1981.

— *Who Shall Die?* Trans. Claude Francis and Fernande Gontier. Florissant, Mo.: River, 1983.

— *The Blood of Others*. Trans. Yvonne Moyse and Roger Senhouse. New York: Pantheon, 1984.

— *She Came to Stay*. Trans. Yvonne Moyse and Roger Senhouse. London: Fontana, 1984.

— *A Very Easy Death*. Trans. Patrick O'Brian. New York: Pantheon, 1985.

— *Adieux: A Farewell to Sartre*. Trans. Patrick O'Brian. Harmondsworth: Penguin, 1986.

— *The Mandarins*. Trans. Leonard Friedman. London: Fontana, 1986.

— *Old Age*. Trans. Patrick O'Brian. Harmondsworth: Penguin, 1986.

— *The Prime of Life*. Trans. Harmondsworth: Penguin, 1988.

Bennington, Geoffrey, and Jacques Derrida. *Jacques Derrida: Derridabase Circonfession*. Paris: Seuil, 1991.

— *Jacques Derrida*. Trans. Geoffrey Bennington. Chicago: University of Chicago Press, 1983.

Berkovitz, Jay R. *The Shaping of Jewish Identity in Nineteenth-Century France*. Detroit: Wayne State University Press, 1989.

Bernanos, Georges. *La Grande Peur des Bien-Pensants*. Paris: Grasset, 1969.

— *Les Grands Cimetières sous la Lune*. Paris: Plon, 1977.

Billy, André. *L'Epoque 1900: 1885–1905*. Paris: Tallandier, 1951.

Birnbaum, Pierre. *Un Mythe politique: La "République juive"*. Paris: Fayard, 1988.

Blanchot, Maurice. *L'Écriture du désastre*. Paris: Gallimard, 1980.

— *The Writing of the Disaster*. Trans. Ann Smock. Lincoln: University of Nebraska Press, 1986.

Bober, Robert. *Quoi de neuf sur la guerre?* Paris: P.O.L., 1993.

Bosquet, Alain. *Un Détenu à Auschwitz*. Paris: Gallimard, 1991.

Boyarin, Jonathan. *Polish Jews in Paris: The Ethnography of Memory*. Bloomington: Indiana University Press, 1991.

— *Storm from Paradise: The Politics of Jewish Memory*. Minneapolis: University of Minnesota Press, 1992.

Brasillach, Robert. *Notre Avant-Guerre*. Paris: Plon, 1981.

Brownstein, Rachel M. *Tragic Muse*. New York: Knopf, 1993.

Bredin, Jean-Denis. *L'Affaire*. Paris: Julliard, 1983.

Byrnes, Robert F. *Antisemitism in Modern France*. Vol. 1. *The Prologue to the Dreyfus Affair*. New Brunswick, N.J.: Rutgers University Press, 1950.

Caylus, Mme de. *Souvenirs*. Quoted by Maurice Rat, *Théâtre complet: Racine*. Paris: Garnier, 1960.

Céline, Louis-Ferdinand. *Bagatelles pour un massacre*. Paris: Denoël, 1937.

— *L'Eglise*. Paris: Gallimard, 1952.

— *Voyage au bout de la nuit*. Paris: Gallimard, 1952.

Chemouni, Jacquy. "Au-delà de la psychanalyse: L'identité juive." *Frénésie* (1986), 7:99–124.

Cixous, Hélène. "Sorties." *La Jeune Née*. Paris: Union Générale d'Editions, 1975.

— "Poésie e(s)t Politique." *Des Femmes en Mouvements Hebdo* (November 30 – December 7, 1979), 4:29–32.

— "Sorties/Out and Out/Attacks/Ways Out/Forays." Trans. Betsy Wing. *The Newly Born Woman*. Minneapolis: University of Minnesota Press, 1986.

— *Readings: The Poetics of Blanchot, Joyce, Kafka, Kleist, Lispector, and Tsvetayeva*. Ed. and trans. Verena Andermatt Conley. Minneapolis: University of Minnesota Press, 1991.

Cohen, Albert. *Solal*. Paris: Gallimard, 1930.

— *Mangeclous*. Paris: Gallimard, 1938.

— *Le Livre de ma mère*. Paris: Gallimard, 1954.

— *Ezéchiel*. Paris: Gallimard, 1956.

— *Belle du Seigneur*. Ed. Christel Peyrefitte and Bella Cohen. Paris: Gallimard, 1968.

— *O vous, frères humains*. Paris: Gallimard, 1972.

— *Oeuvres*. Ed. Christel Peyrefitte and Bella Cohen. Paris: Gallimard, 1993.

Cohen, Albert, ed. "Déclaration." *La Revue Juive*, pp. 5–13. Paris: Gallimard, Jan. 1925.

Cohen, Derek, and Deborah Hiller, eds. *Jewish Presences in English Literature*. Montreal and Kingston: McGill-Queen's University Press, 1990.

Coles, Robert. *Simone Weil*. Reading, Mass.: Addison-Wesley, 1987.

Colette. *Le Pur et l'impur*. Paris: Aux Armes de France [Calmann Lévy], 1941.

— *The Pure and the Impure*. Trans. Herma Briffault. New York: Farrar Straus and Giroux, 1978.

Compagnon, Antoine. *Proust: Between Two Centuries*. Trans. Richard Goodkin. New York: Columbia University Press, 1992.

Davis, Natalie Zemon. "Rabelais Among the Censors (1940s, 1540s)." *Representations* (Fall 1990), 32:1–32.

Dawidowicz, Lucy S. *The War Against the Jews, 1933–1945*. New York: Bantam, 1976.

— *The Holocaust and the Historians*. Cambridge: Harvard University Press, 1981.

Debré, Moses. *The Image of the Jew in French Literature from 1800 to 1908*. Trans. Gertrude Hirschler. New York: Ktav, 1970.

Deguy, Michel. "Le Sozi de Heidegger." *Le Débat* (January-February 1988), no. 48. Paris: Gallimard.

DeKoven, Marianne. "History as Suppressed Referent in Modernist Fiction." *ELH* (Spring 1984), 51(1):137–52.

Derrida, Jacques. "Edmond Jabès et la question du livre," "Violence et métaphysique: Essai sur la pensée d'Emmanuel Lévinas." *L'Écriture et la différence*. Paris: Seuil, 1967.

— *Writing and Difference*. Trans. Alan Bass. Chicago: University of Chicago Press, 1978.

— *De l'esprit: Heidegger et la question*. Paris: Galilée, 1987.

— *Feu la cendre*. Paris: des Femmes, 1987.

— "La Guerre de Paul de Man." *Mémoires pour Paul de Man*. Paris: Galilée, 1988.

— "Like the Sound of the Sea Deep Within a Shell." Trans. Peggy Kamuf. *Critical Inquiry* (Spring 1988), 14(3):590–652.

— *Of Spirit: Heidegger and the Question*. Trans. Geoffrey Bennington and Rachel Bowlby. Chicago: University of Chicago Press, 1989.

— *Cinders*. Trans. Ned Lukacher. Lincoln: University of Nebraska Press, 1991.

Dershowitz, Alan M. *Chutzpah*. Boston: Little, Brown, 1991.

Deutscher, Isaac. "The Non-Jewish Jew." *The Non-Jewish Jew*, pp. 25–41. London: Oxford University Press, 1968.

Dijkstra, Bram. *Idols of Perversity: Fantasies of Feminine Evil in Fin-de-Siècle Culture.* New York and Oxford: Oxford University Press, 1986.

Diller, Jerry Victor. *Freud's Jewish Identity*. London and Toronto: Associated University Presses, 1991.

Di Mauro, Damon. "Entre l'ombre et la réalité: Etude sur *Les Juifves* de Robert Garnier." Ph.D. diss., University of Wisconsin-Madison, 1991.

Dioudonnat, Pierre-Maris. *Je Suis Partout 1930–1944.* Paris: Table Ronde, 1973.

Drumont, Edouard. *La France Juive.* 2 vols. Paris: Trident, 1986.

Duras, Marguerite. *La Douleur.* Paris: P.O.L., 1985.

— *The War: A Memoir.* Trans. Barbara Bray. New York: Pantheon, 1986.

Fackenheim, Emil L. *The Jewish Bible After the Holocaust: A Re-reading.* Bloomington: Indiana University Press, 1990.

Faderman, Lilian. *Surpassing the Love of Men.* New York: William Morrow, 1981.

Faye, Jean Pierre. *Migrations du récit sur le peuple juif.* Paris: Pierre Belfond, 1974.

Feigelson, Ralph. *Ecrivains juifs de langue française.* Paris: Jean Grassin, 1960.

Felman, Shoshana, and Dori Laub. *Testimony.* New York: Routledge, 1992.

Fichera, Virginia. "Simone de Beauvoir and 'the Woman Question': *Les Bouches inutiles*." In Hélène Wenzel, ed., *Simone de Beauvoir: Witness to a Century, Yale French Studies* (1986), no. 72, pp. 51–64. Repr. in Elaine Marks, ed., *Critical Essays on Simone de Beauvoir*, pp. 246–58. Boston: G. K. Hall, 1987.

Finch, H. L. "Letters to the Editor." *Times Literary Supplement*, July 23, 1993, p. 15.

Finkielkraut, Alain. *Le Juif imaginaire.* Paris: Seuil, 1980.

— *La Mémoire vaine.* Paris: Gallimard, 1989.

— *Remembering in Vain: The Klaus Barbie Trial and Crimes Against Humanity.* Trans. Roxanne Lapidus, with Sima Godfrey. New York: Columbia University Press, 1992.

Flaubert, Gustave. *Correspondance.* Ed. Jean Bruneau. Vol. 1. Paris: Gallimard, 1973.

Fleg, Edmond. *Moïse.* Paris: Gallimard, 1928.

Fleg, Edmond, ed. *Anthologie juive.* Paris: Flammarion, 1951.

Fox, Michael V. *Character and Ideology in the Book of Esther.* Columbia, S.C.: University of South Carolina Press, 1991.

Freedman, David Noel, ed. *The Anchor Bible Dictionary.* 6 vols. New York: Doubleday, 1992.

Fresco, Nadine. "Parcours du ressentiment." *Lignes*, February 2, 1988, pp. 29–72.

Freud, Sigmund. *Moses and Monotheism*. Trans. Katherine Jones. New York: Vintage Books, 1939.

— *Moses and Monotheism*. In *The Standard Edition of the Complete Psychological Works of Sigmund Freud*, pp. 1–137. Trans. James Strachey et al. Vol. 23. [1937–1939.] London: Hogarth Press, 1981.

— "Mourning and Melancholia." In *The Standard Edition of the Complete Works of Sigmund Freud*, pp. 237–58. Trans. James Strachey et al. Vol. 14. London: Hogarth Press, 1981.

— "The Future of an Illusion." *The Standard Edition of the Complete Works of Sigmund Freud*, pp. 1–56. Trans. James Strachey et al. Vol. 21. London: Hogarth Press, 1981.

Friedlander, Judith. *Vilna on the Seine*. New Haven: Yale University Press, 1990.

Friedlander, Saul, ed. *Probing the Limits of Representation: Nazism and the "Final Solution."* Cambridge: Harvard University Press, 1992.

Frye, Northrop. *The Great Code: The Bible and Literature*. New York: Harcourt Brace Jovanovich, 1982.

Garnier, Robert. *Les Juifves*. Ed. and introduction by Marcel Hervier. Paris: Classiques Garnier, 1964.

Gérard, André-Marie, ed. *Dictionnaire de la bible*. Paris: Robert Laffont, 1989.

Gide, André. *Journal: 1889–1939*. Paris: Gallimard. Bibliothèque de la Pléiade, 1948.

— *The Journals of André Gide*. Trans. and ed. Justin O'Brien. 2 vols. New York: Vintage, 1956.

Gilbert, Martin. *The Holocaust*. New York: Henry Holt, 1985.

Gilman, Sander. *Jewish Self-Hatred*. Baltimore: Johns Hopkins University Press, 1986.

— *Freud, Race, and Gender*. Princeton: Princeton University Press, 1993.

Goitein, Denise R. "French Literature." *Encyclopaedia Judaica*, 7:138–51. 16 vols. Jerusalem: Keter Publishing House, 1982.

Gold, Arthur, and Robert Fizdale. *The Divine Sarah*. New York: Knopf, 1991.

Golencer-Schroeter, Helen. *Albert Cohen, Albert Memmi, and Elie Wiesel and the Dilemma of Jewish Identity in French Literature and Culture*. Ph.D. diss., University of Utah, 1989. 9016335. Ann Arbor: UMI, 1992.

Goujon, Jean-Paul. *Tes Blessures sont plus douces que leurs caresses*. Paris: Régine Deforges, 1986.

Gould, Eric, ed. *The Sin of the Book: Edmond Jabès*. Lincoln: University of Nebraska Press, 1985.

Gubar, Susan. "Sapphistries," *Signs* (Autumn 1984), 10(1):43–62.

Gygès. *Les Juifs dans la France d'aujourd'hui*. Paris: Documents et Témoignages, 1985.

Hahn, Reynaldo. *La Grande Sarah*. Paris: Hachette, 1930.

Heidegger, Martin. "Letter on Humanism." *Martin Heidegger: Basic Writings*. New York: Harper and Row, 1977.

— *Nietzsche*. Translated by David Farrell Krell. 4 vols. New York: Harper Collins, 1991.

Hilberg, Raul. *La Destruction des juifs d'Europe*. Paris: Fayard, 1988.

Hirsch, David H. *The Deconstruction of Literature: Criticism After Auschwitz*. Hanover, N.H.: University Press of New England, 1991.

Hollier, Denis, ed. *A New History of French Literature*. Cambridge: Harvard University Press, 1989.

The Holy Bible. Rev. standard version. Camden: New Jersey, 1952.

The Holy Scriptures. According to the Masoretic text. Philadelphia: Jewish Publication Society of America, 1955.

Hughes, H. Stuart. *Prisoners of Hope: The Silver Age of Italian Jewry, 1924–1974*. Cambridge: Harvard University Press, 1983.

Hyman, Paula. *From Dreyfus to Vichy*. New York: Columbia University Press, 1979.

Ikor, Roger. *Lettre ouverte aux Juifs*. Paris: Albin Michel, 1970.

Israel, Jonathan I. *European Jewry in the Age of Mercantilism, 1550–1750*. Oxford: Clarendon Press, 1989.

Jabès, Edmond. *Le Livre des questions*. Paris: Gallimard, 1963.

Jankélévitch, Vladimir. *L'Imprescriptible*. Seuil, 1986.

Jasinski, René. *Autour de l'Esther racinienne*. Paris: Nizet, 1985.

Johnson, Paul. *A History of the Jews*. New York: Harper Perennial, 1988.

Kaplan, Alice Yaeger. *French Lessons*. Chicago: University of Chicago Press, 1993.

Kaplan, Alice Yaeger, ed. *Anti-Semite and Jew: The Aesthetics and Politics of an Ethnic Identity*. *Substance* 49, Vol. 15, no. 1, 1986.

— *Reproductions of Banality: Fascism, Literature and French Intellectual Life*. Minneapolis: University of Minnesota Press, 1986.

Klarsfeld, Serge. *Memorial to the Jews Deported from France, 1942–1944*. New York: Beate Klarsfeld Foundation, 1983.

Klein, Luce A. *Portrait de la Juive dans la littérature française*. Paris: Nizet, 1970.

Kofman, Sarah. *L'Énigme de la femme*. Paris: Galilée, 1980.

— *Paroles suffoquées*. Paris: Galilée, 1987.

— *Le Mépris des Juifs*. Paris: Galilée, 1994.

— *Rue Ordener Rue Labat*. Paris: Galilée, 1994.

Krell, David Farrell. *Intimations of Mortality*. University Park: Pennsylvania State University Press, 1986.

Kristeva, Julia. "The Pain of Sorrow in the Modern World: The Works of Marguerite Duras." Trans. Katharine A. Jensen. *PMLA* (March 1987), 102(2)138–52.

— *Pouvoirs de l'horreur*. Paris: Editions du Seuil, 1980.

— *Powers of Horror*. Trans. Leon Roudiez. New York: Columbia University Press, 1982.

— *Etrangers à nous-mêmes*. Paris: Fayard, 1988.

— *Strangers to Ourselves*. Trans. Leon Roudiez. New York: Columbia University Press, 1991.

— *Le Temps sensible: Proust et l'expérience littéraire*. Paris: Gallimard, 1994.

Lacoue-Labarthe, Philippe. *La Fiction du politique*. Paris: Christian Bourgois, 1987.

Lacouture, Jean. *Léon Blum*. Paris: Editions du Seuil, 1979.

Lambropoulos, Vassilis. *The Rise of Eurocentrism*. Princeton: Princeton University Press, 1993.

Lanson, Gustave. *Histoire de la littérature française*. Paris: Hachette, 1894.

Lanzmann, Claude. *Shoah*. Preface by Simone de Beauvoir. Paris: Fayard, 1985.

— *Shoah*. Trans. A. Whitelaw and W. Byron. New York: Pantheon, 1985.

Lauretis, Teresa de, ed. "Feminist Studies/Critical Studies: Issues, Terms, and Contexts." *Feminist Studies/Critical Studies*. Bloomington: Indiana University Press, 1986.

Lehrmann, Chanan. *L'Élément juif dans la littérature française*. 2 vols. Paris: Albin Michel, 1960.

Le Monde Juif. Paris: Centre de Documentation Juive Contemporaine. Nos. 79–143. 1975–1993.

Lévinas, Emmanuel. "La Renaissance culturelle juive en Europe continentale." In Moshe Davis, Shaül Esh, Max Gottschalk, and Emmanuel Lévinas, eds., *Le Renouveau de la culture juive*. Brussels: Editions de l'Institut de Sociologie de l'Université Libre de Bruxelles, 1968.

— *Noms propres*. Paris: Livre de Poche, 1987.

— *Difficile liberté*. [Paris: Albin Michel, 1963, 1976.] Paris: Livre de Poche, 1988.

— *Difficult Freedom*. Trans. Seán Hand. Baltimore: Johns Hopkins University Press, 1990.

Lévy, Bernard-Henri. *L'Idéologie française*. Paris: Grasset, 1981.

Lévy, Claude, and Paul Tillard. *La Grande Rafle du Vel D'Hiv*. Paris: Laffont, 1992.

Lipstadt, Deborah. *Denying the Holocaust: The Growing Assault on Truth and Memory*. New York: Macmillan, 1993.

Loewenstein, Rodolphe. *Psychanalyse de l'antisémitisme*. Paris: Presses Universitaires de France, 1952.

Lustiger, Jean-Marie. *Le Choix de Dieu*. Interviews with Jean-Louis Missika and Dominique Wolton. Paris: Fallois, 1987,

Lyotard, Jean-François. "Jewish Oedipus." Trans. Susan Hanson. *Genre* (Fall 1977), vol. 10, no. 3.

— "Discussions, ou: phraser 'après Auschwitz.'" In Philippe Lacoue-Labarthe and Jean-Luc Nancy, eds., *Les Fins de l'homme: à partir du travail de Jacques Derrida*. Colloque de Cerisy. Paris: Galilée, 1981.

— *The Differend: Phrases in Dispute*. Trans. George Van Den Abbeele. Minneapolis: University of Minnesota Press, 1983.

— *Heidegger et "les juifs"*. Paris: Galilée, 1988.

— *Heidegger and "the Jews"*. Trans. Andreas Michel and Mark S. Roberts. Foreword by David Carroll. Minneapolis: University of Minnesota Press, 1990.

Malino, Frances, and Bernard Wasserstein, eds. *The Jews in Modern France*. Hanover, N.H.: University Press of New England, 1985.

Man, Paul de. "The Resistance to Theory." In Barbara Johnson, ed., *The Pedagogical Imperative: Teaching as a Literary Genre*. *Yale French Studies* (1982), pp. 3–20.

— *Wartime Journalism, 1939–1943*. Ed. Werner Hamacher, Neil Hertz, and Thomas Keenan. Lincoln: University of Nebraska Press, 1988.

Marks, Elaine, ed. *Critical Essays on Simone de Beauvoir*. Boston: G. K. Hall, 1987.

Maurras, Charles. *L'Avenir de l'intelligence* suivi de *Auguste Comte, Le Romantisme féminin, Mademoiselle Monk, L'Invocation à Minerve*. Paris: Flammarion, 1927.

Marrus, Michael R. *The Politics of Assimilation: The French Jewish Community at the Time of the Dreyfus Affair*. Oxford: Clarendon Press, 1980.

— *The Holocaust in History*. Hanover, N.H.: University Press of New England, 1987.

Marrus, Michael R., and Robert O. Paxton. *Vichy France and the Jews*. New York: Basic Books, 1981.

Mehlman, Jeffrey. *Legacies of Anti-Semitism*. Minneapolis: University of Minnesota Press, 1983.

— *Legs de l'antisémitisme en France*. Trans. Jeffrey Mehlman. Paris: Denoël, 1984.

— "Perspectives on De Man and *Le Soir*." *Responses: On Paul de Man's Wartime Journalism*. Ed. Werner Hamacher, Neil Hertz, and Thomas Keenan. Lincoln: University of Nebraska Press, 1989.

Merle, Robert. *La Mort est mon métier*. Paris: Gallimard, 1993.

Modiano, Patrick. *La Place de l'étoile*. Paris: Gallimard, 1968.

Moore, Carey. "Esther, Additions to" and "Esther, Book of" in *The Anchor Bible Dictionary*, 2:626–43. New York: Doubleday, 1992.

Morin, Edgar. *La Rumeur d'Orléans*. Paris: Seuil, 1969.

Mosse, George L. *German Jews Beyond Judaism.* Bloomington: Indiana University Press, 1985.

Orcibal, Jean. *La Genèse d'Esther et d'Athalie.* Paris, 1950.

Ory, Pascal. "L'Université française sous l'occupation." *La France et la Question Juive, 1940–1944.* Paris: Sylvie Messinger, 1981.

O'Sullivan, Tim, John Hartley, Danny Saunders, and John Fiske. *Key Concepts in Communication.* London and New York: Methuen, 1983.

Passages 14. "Les 100 Juifs qui Comptent." February 1989.

Péguy, Charles. *Notre jeunesse.* Paris: Gallimard, 1933.

Perec, Georges. *W ou le souvenir d'enfance.* Paris: Denoël, 1975.

Philippe, Béatrice. *Etre juif dans la société française du moyen-âge jusqu'à nos jours.* Paris: Montalba, 1979.

— *Les Juifs dans le monde contemporain.* Paris: MA Editions, 1986.

— *Les Juifs à Paris à la Belle Epoque.* Paris: Albin Michel, 1992.

Pogrebin, Letty Cottin. *Deborah, Golda, and Me: Being Female and Jewish in America.* New York: Crown, 1991.

Pronier, Ernest. *Sarah Bernhardt.* Genève: Alex. Jullien, n.d.

Proust, Marcel. *A la recherche du temps perdu.* Ed. Pierre Clarac and André Ferré. 3 vols. Paris: Gallimard, Bibliothèque de la Pléiade, 1954.

— *Remembrance of Things Past.* Trans. C. K. Scott Moncrieff and Frederick A. Blossom. 2 vols. New York: Random House, 1934.

—*Contre Sainte-Beuve.* Paris: Gallimard, Bibliothèque de la Pléiade, 1954.

"Que faire de Vichy?" Special issue of *Esprit* (May 1992), no. 181.

Racine, Jean. *Esther. Oeuvres complètes.* Vol. 1. Ed. Raymond Picard. Paris: Gallimard, Bibliothèque de la Pléiade, 1950.

— *Esther.* Ed. Gabriel Spillebout. Paris: Bordas, 1985.

— *Esther.* Ed. Jean Borie. Paris: Larousse, 1986.

Rand, Nicholas. "The Truth of Heidegger's 'Logos': Hiding in Translation." *PMLA* (1990), 105:436–47.

Rebatet, Lucien. *Les Décombres.* Paris: Denoël, 1942.

— *Mémoires d'un fasciste.* 2 vols. *Les Décombres.* Vol. 1. Paris: Jean-Jacques Pauvert, 1976.

Recanti, Jean. *Profils Juifs de Marcel Proust.* Paris: Buchet/Chastel. 1979.

Rémy, Dominique. *Les Lois de Vichy.* Paris: Romillat, 1992.

Robbe-Grillet. *Le Miroir qui revient.* Paris: Minuit, 1984.

Rorty, Richard. *Contingency, Irony, and Solidarity.* Cambridge: Cambridge University Press, 1989.

— *Essays on Heidegger and Others.* Cambridge: Cambridge University Press, 1991.

Rousso, Henry. *Le Syndrôme de Vichy: De 1944 à nos jours.* Paris: Seuil, 1987, 1990.

— *The Vichy Syndrome: History and Memory in France Since 1944*. Trans. Arthur Goldhammer. Cambridge: Harvard University Press, 1991.

Rubenstein, Diane. *What's Left: The Ecole Normale Supérieure and the Right*. Madison: University of Wisconsin Press, 1990.

Santner, Eric. *Stranded Objects*. Ithaca: Cornell University Press, 1990.

Sarraute, Nathalie. *Enfance*. Paris: Gallimard, 1983.

— *Childhood*. Trans. Barbara Wright. New York: Braziller, 1984.

Sartre, Jean-Paul. "L'Enfance d'un chef." *Le Mur*. Paris: Gallimard, 1938.

— *L'Existentialisme est un humanisme*. Paris: Nagel, 1946.

— *Réflexions sur la question juive*. Paris: Gallimard, 1946.

— *Anti-Semite and Jew*. Trans. George J. Becker. New York: Schocken, 1965.

Schwarz-Bart, André. *Le Dernier des Justes*. Paris: Seuil, 1959.

— *The Last of the Just*. Trans. Stephen Becker. New York: Atheneum, 1973.

Sévigné, Madame de. *Lettres choisies*. Ed. Emile Feuillatre. Nouveaux Classiques Larousse. Paris: Larousse, 1971.

— *Correspondance*. Ed. Roger Duchêne. 3 vols. Paris: Gallimard, 1978.

Singer, Claude. *Vichy, L'Université et Les Juifs*. Paris: Belles Lettres, 1992.

Skinner, Cornelia Otis. *Madame Sarah*. Boston: Houghton Mifflin, 1967.

Slama, Béatrice. "De la 'littérature féminine' à 'l'écrire femme.'" *Littérature* (December 1981), vol. 44.

Sollers, Philippe. *Femmes*. Paris: Gallimard, 1983.

— *Women*. Trans. Barbara Bray. New York: Columbia University Press, 1990.

Sonnenfeld, Albert. "Marcel Proust Antisémite?" *The French Review*, October 1988, pp. 25–40; December 1988, pp. 275–82.

Spire, André. *Quelques Juifs*. Paris: Mercure de France. 1913.

Steiner, George. *Martin Heidegger*. Chicago: University of Chicago Press, 1978.

Sternhell, Zeev. *La Droite révolutionnaire: Les Origines françaises du fascisme, 1885–1914*. Paris: Seuil, 1978.

— "Les origines intellectuelles du racisme en France." *L'Histoire*, November 17, 1979, pp. 106–14.

Toussenel, Alphonse. *Les Juifs Rois de L'Epoque*. Paris: Trident, 1988.

Vidal-Naquet, Pierre. *Les Assassins de la mémoire*. Paris: Découverte, 1987.

— "Le Défi de la Shoah." *Les Temps Modernes* (October 1988), no. 507, pp. 62–74.

— *Assassins of Memory*. Trans. Jeffrey Mehlman. New York: Columbia University Press, 1992.

Vivien, Renée. *La Dame à la louve*. Paris: Lemerre, 1904.

— *Une Femme m'apparut*. Paris: Lemerre, 1904.

— *A Woman Appeared to Me*. Trans. Jeannette H. Foster. Preface by Gayle Rubin. Tallahassee, Fla.: Naiad Press, 1976.

— *Anne Boleyn*. Paris: A L'Ecart, 1982.

— *The Woman and the Wolf and Other Stories*. New York: Gay Presses, 1983.

— *Oeuvre poétique complète de Renée Vivien: 1877–1909*. Ed. Jean-Paul Goujon. Paris: Régine Deforges, 1986.

Wardi, Charlotte. *Le Juif dans le Roman Français, 1933–1948*. Paris: Nizet, 1973.

Weber, Eugen. *My France: Politics, Culture, Myth*. Cambridge: Harvard University Press, 1991.

Wenzel, Hélène, ed. *Simone de Beavoir: Witness to a Century. Yale French Studies* (1987), no. 72.

Wiesel, Elie. *La Nuit*. Paris: Minuit, 1958.

— *Night*. Trans. Stella Rodway. New York: Bantam, 1986.

Wilson, Edmund. *Axel's Castle*. New York: Scribner's, 1931.

Winock, Michel. *Edouard Drumont et Cie. Antisémitisme et fascisme en France*. Paris: Seuil, 1982.

Wolitz, Seth. *The Proustian Community*. New York: New York University Press, 1971.

Yerushalmi, Yosef Hayim. *Freud's Moses: Judaism Terminable and Interminable*. New Haven: Yale University Press, 1991.

Young-Bruehl, Elizabeth. *Hannah Arendt: For Love of the World*. New Haven: Yale University Press, 1982.

Yourcenar, Marguerite. *Le Coup de Grâce*. Paris: Gallimard, 1939.

— *Coup de Grâce*. Trans. Grace Frick, in collaboration with the author. New York: Farrar, Straus and Giroux, 1981.

— *Oeuvres Romanesques*. Paris: Gallimard, 1982.

Yovel, Yirmiyahu. *The Marrano of Reason*. Vol. 1. *Spinoza and Other Heretics*. 2 vols. Princeton: Princeton University Press, 1989.

Index

Abjection, Jewishness and, 10
Action Française, 72
Activist, de Beauvoir as, 107–8
Adorno, Theodor, 121
Aesthetic, Jewish, Cohen and, 64
"After Auschwitz": Jewish identity, 127;
	Jews writing in French, 114–26; read-
	ings, 85–95
Ahasuerus, king of Persia, 30–32
Algren, Nelson, de Beauvoir and, 104
Allied countries, and Holocaust, 110
Alter, Robert, 24
American literature, "other" in, 74
Anglo-American literature, "other" in, 74
Anguish: de Beauvoir and, 107; meta-
	physical, of Jews, 4
Annals of Revisionist History, x
Antelme, Roger, *The Human Species*, 121
Anti-Jewish persecutions, documenta-
	tion of, x–xi
Anti-Judaism, antisemitism and, 80–81
Antisemitism, 6, 8–10, 81; and assimila-
	tion, 147–48; Babylonian captivity
	and, 28; as castration anxiety, 9; of
	Céline, 9–10; Christian, 7, 40, 97–98,
	156*n*5; in Cohen's writings, 99, 101;

contextualization of, 85–95; and
	death of God, 97–113; de Beauvoir
	and, 102, 104, 108; Derrida and, 151;
	Drumont and, 70; in Europe, 64, 65;
	in France, 1–4, 71, 80, 94, 146–47; of
	French Left, 108–9; in French litera-
	ture, 87; in French university system,
	161*n*3; Freud and, 9; heterogeneity of,
	7; Holocaust and, 74, 156*n*5; Jewish
	literature and, 61; Lunel and, 67;
	Madame de Sévigné and, 34–35; of
	Maurras, 48, 52; as mental illness,
	8–9; militant, 7; of Nietzsche, 156*n*2;
	nihilism and, xiii, 97; "ordinary," 3;
	and prejudice against women, 53–54;
	in Proust's works, 38–40; Racine's
	Esther and, 35–36; racist, 7, 81; and
	repression of the feminine, 94; right-
	wing, 4, 7, 8; of Robbe-Grillet's par-
	ents, 3–5; of secular Jews, 147; in sev-
	enteenth century, 28; stereotypes of,
	78–80; in twentieth-century litera-
	ture, French, 10–13; verbally para-
	noid, 7; Yourcenar and, 88–89, 94;
	Zionism and, 64
Arabs, in France, 72

Arendt, Hannah, xvii, 133; *Antisemitism*, 98; and assimilation, 147; *Men in Dark Times*, 139

Arnauld, Antoine, 42

Aron, Raymond, 107, 133

Aschheim, Steven, 77

Ashkenazic Jews, xi, 68

Assimilated Jews: antisemitism of, 82; as fictional protagonists, 152

Assimilation, xviii, 40–41, 140–41, 151; of antisemitism, 147–48; and fate of Jews, 61–62; fear of, 127; and Jewishness, 147; Marranism, 141; Marrus's view of, 128–29

Atheism, 103; of de Beauvoir, 106; Jewishness and, 145

Aubigné, Agrippa d', 28

Augustine, Saint, *Confessions*, 151

Auschwitz, 70, 155–56n5; de Beauvoir and, 105, 106; denial of, 2, 112; knowledge of, 95; as metaphor, 85; writing about, 114–18, 122; writing about writing about, 115–16, 121–26; *see also* Extermination of Jews; Shoah

Austria, extermination of Jews, 70

Babylonian captivity, 26, 27

Bajazet, Racine, 87, 88

Baltic countries, extermination of Jews, 70

Barbey d'Aurevilly, Jules, *The Blue Stockings*, 55

Barbie, Klaus, trial of, x, 72–73, 146

Barney, Natalie Clifford, 43, 45, 57–58

Barthes, Roland, definition of myth, xiv

Baudelaire, Charles: *Flowers of Evil*, 53; Maurras and, 51; Vivien and, 49

Beate Klarsfeld Foundation, xi

Beaufret, Jean, 111, 112

Beauvoir, Françoise de, 105

Beauvoir, Simone de, 102–4, 161n3; *Adieux*, 104; *The Blood of Others*, de Beauvoir, 104, 112; and Cohen's *Belle du Seigneur*, 101–2; equality, and, 111; and French Left, 109; and Heidegger,

111–12; and Israel, 107–9; and language, 112–13; *Les Mandarins*, 104, 107; *On Old Age*, 104; and "other," 75; *The Second Sex*, 74, 104, 105; "Solidarité d'Israël: Un Soutien critique," 104; *The Useless Mouths*, 104, 112; *A Very Easy Death*, 101–2, 104, 105

Beckett, Samuel, 105

Being, 153; Heidegger and, 112

Belgium, extermination of Jews, 70

Belle epoque: antisemitism of, 52; Dijkstra and, 56; and feminine difference, 50; Vivien and, 45, 58

Belonging sickness, 150, 151

Ben-Chorin, S., 30

Benjamin, Walter, 18; cult of, 17

Bennington, Geoffrey, *Jacques Derrida*, 150, 151

Berkovitz, Jay R., 62

"Between the Shadow and Reality: A Study of *Les Juifves* of Robert Garnier," DiMauro, 25

Biale, David, 148

Bible, 24; Christian, Old Testament, 25, 27; French translations of, 23; *see also* Jewish Holy Scriptures

Biblical references in Racine's *Esther*, 31–33

Billig, Joseph, x

Billy, André, *L'Époque 1900*, 44

Binary categories, 77; in belle epoque, 45; Maurras and, 46; in Yourcenar's work, 94

Biological determinist theories, 56

Birnbaum, Pierre, 77

Blanchot, Maurice, 125; Mehlman and, 11–13; *Writing the Disaster*, 121

Bloch, Jean-Richard, 66

Blum, Léon, 71, 76

Blumenfeld, Kurt, 147

Bober, Robert, 115

Book of Esther (Bible), 30

Book of Malachi (Bible), 27

Books: antisemitic, 73; danger of, 90

Borges, Jorge Luis, 107

Borie, Jean, 23–24
Bosquet, Alain, 133
Bousquet, Carole, 123
Brandès, Georges, 62
Brasillach, Robert, *Je Suis Partout*, 72
Brecht, Berthold, *The Chalk Circle*, 109
Bredin, Jean-Louis, 77
Buchwald, Ephraim, Rabbi, 147
Bulgaria, extermination of Jews, 71
Byrnes, Robert, *Antisemitism in Modern France*, 160–61*n*1

Les Cahiers Bernard Lazare, 107
Capital Times, Madison, Wisconsin, 147
Caricatures of Jews, 76, 94
Cartoons, antisemitic, 78
Catholic Bible: Old Testament, 25, 27; story of Esther, 30
Catholic Church, 134–35; gestures in, 139–40; Maurras and, 48
Caylus, Madame de, *Souvenirs*, 41
Cayrol, Jean, *Night and Fog*, 5
Celan, Paul, 152
Céline, Louis-Ferdinand, 7, 76, 97; *A Fine Mess*, 99; antisemitism of, 99; *Bagatelles pour un massacre*, 72, 87; *L'Ecole des cadavres*, 99; *L'Eglise*, 77, 79, 84; Kristeva and, 9–10
Cendre(s), symbolism of, 115
Cendres juives, 117–18
Center for Contemporary Jewish Documentation, x–xi
Cercle Bernard Lazare, 107
Charles VI, King of France, 28
Children, deported from France, 72–73
Chomsky, Noam, 124; politics of, 125
Chosen people, Jews as, 26; jealousy of, Freud's idea, 9
Christian antisemitism, 7, 40, 97–98; Holocaust and, 156*n*5
Christian culture: and Jewish text of Esther, 41; Jews and, 130–31; presence of, 119–20
Christianity: and antisemitism, 160–61*n*1; decline of, 80; French culture

and, 134–35; hatred of, antisemitism as, 9; and Jewish Holy Scriptures, 24, 25–27; and Judaism, 119; Lévinas and, 120
Christianized Jews, xvii–xviii, 135
Christianocentrism, critique of, 119
Christian state, France as, 131
Christian tragedy, Racine's *Esther* as, 35
Christ killers, Jews as, 7–8, 26, 27, 40; Death of God and, 97–98
Circumcision, 39; and antisemitism, 9; Derrida and, 150–51
Civilization, threats to, in Maurras's view, 47
Cixous, Hélène, 115, 133, 141, 143, 148, 152; and portmanteau words, 149; "Sorties," 143
Classical tradition, French, Maurras and, 57
Classification, by critics, 58
Classiques Larousse edition of *Esther*, 23, 29, 35, 36
Clément, Catherine, *The Newly Born Woman*, 143
Cohen, Albert, 61, 62–69, 133, 134, 142; *Belle du Seigneur*, 67, 68, 99–101, 129–30, 135–39; de Beauvoir and, 101–2; "Déclaration," 63–65; difference of, 68; *Ezéchiel*, 158*n*1; filiation in his works, 67; "Jour de mes dix ans," 149; *Le Livre de ma mère*, 67; *Mangeclous*, 67, 68; nihilism of, 99; *O You, Brother Humans*, 67; *Solal*, Lunel and, 66–67; writings of, 67, 113
Colet, Louise, 99–100
Colette (Sidonie-Gabrielle), 153; and Vivien, 158–58*n*5
Communism, United States views, 103
Community: Jewish, 78–79, 128; Lesbian, 57, 58; social movements and, xiii
Compagnon, Antoine, *Proust: Between Two Centuries*, 24
Comte, Auguste, 47
Consciousness, Jewish, Lunel and, 66

Crayencour, Marguerite de, *see* Ysource-
  nar, Marguerite
Critics: and classification, 58; and
  women's texts, 46
Crypto-Jews, xvii, 128, 129–30, 134
Cult figure, Vivien as, 44
Cultural criticism, American, 16
Cultural studies, xiv, 74, 75; and Jew as
  other, 84
Culture, views of, 75
Cyrus, King of Persia, 26–27

Davis, Natalie Zemon, "Rabelais Among
  the Censors: (1940s, 1540s)," 22
Dawidowicz, Lucy, *The War Against the
  Jews*, 70
Death, as literary theme, xiii, 113; Cohen
  and, 100–2; de Beauvoir and, 106; in
  Derrida's works, 124
Death camps, French literature and, 85
Death of God, 7–8, 96–98; and anti-
  semitism, 97–113; identity and, 80;
  Maurras and, 47; Nazism and, 103
Decadence, Jewishness and, 64
Deconstructionism, 14–16, 77, 117; and
  denial of Holocaust, 13–14, 18–19;
  Heidegger and, 124
Deconstructionist nihilism, Hirsch
  and, 19
Deicide, 7–8, 40, 97
Delarue-Mardrus, Lucie, 46
Demonology, and Jews, 28
Denmark, extermination of Jews, 71
Deportation of Jews, 70; French litera-
  ture and, 84, 85; lists, xi
Depression, economic, 80
Derrida, Aimé, 151
Derrida, Jacques, 18, 20, 97, 115, 125, 133,
  141, 152; belonging sickness, 151; *Cin-
  ders*, 116, 122–25; *Circumfession*,
  150–51; "Curriculum vitae," 150; and
  Georgette Esther Safar, 151; *Glas*, 124;
  and Heidegger, 123; *La Carte postale*,
  124; "Like the Sound of the Sea Deep
  Within a Shell: Paul de Man's War,"

1, 11, 12–13, 124; *Of Spirit: Heidegger
  and the Question*, 123, 124; *Schibboleth: Pour Paul Celan*, 124; "Violence
  and Metaphysics," 149
Dershowitz, Alan M., *Chutzpah*, 151–52
Destouches, Louis Ferdinand, *see* Céline,
  Louis-Ferdinand
Deutscher, Isaac, "The Non-Jewish Jew,"
  xvii, 132
Difference, xiii; of Cohen, 68; de Beau-
  voir and, 111; feminism and, 107; and
  identity, 56; Jewish, 9, 61, 65; of
  women, Maurras and, 49–51
Dijkstra, Bram, *Idols of Perversity*, 43, 56
Di Mauro, Damon, xiv; comments on
  Psalm 137, 28; "Entre l'ombre et la
  réalité: Etude sur *Les Juifves* de
  Robert Garnier," 25
Discourse: antisemitic, 6, 28, 40, 71; of
  belle epoque, 45
Disorder, freedom and, 8
Displacement, antisemitism and, 10–11
Ditman, Laurent, 18
Documentation of anti-Jewish persecu-
  tions, x–xi
Double standard for women writers, 48
Doubling of Esther, in *Within a Budding
  Grove*, 38
Doubrovsky, Serge, 115
Drancy detention center, 70
Dreyfus, Alfred, 76
Dreyfus case, 81; and Jewish conscious-
  ness, 66
Drumont, Edouard, 7, 76; and anti-
  semitism, 70; *La France Juive*, 72, 77,
  78, 81, 84
Dual language of Marranos, 134, 135
Duke, David, 14
Du Maurier, Daphne, 61
Duras, Marguerite, 105; *La Douleur*, 5

Eastern European immigrant Jews, 76, 82
Egoism of women, Maurras and, 53–55
Einstein, Albert, 62; "Message," in *Revue
  Juive*, 65

Encyclopaedia Judaica, xiv
Epithets, antisemitic, 7
"Esprit juif," universality of, 66
Esther, Biblical story of, 23–24, 30–33
Esther, doubling of, in *Within a Budding Grove*, 38
Esther, Racine, xiv, 21, 23–24, 27, 28–37, 157n6; Mme de Maintenon and, 41, 42; Proust and, 37–41
Ethnocentricity, Weil and, 130
Euphemisms, Nazi, for Shoah, 112–13
Europeans, Jewish, 139
Evans, Richard J., 92
Exigency, ethics of, Lévinas's view, 119
Exiles, Jews as, 28
Existentialism, of Sartre, 106
Existentialist humanism, Heidegger and, 112
Existential other, plight of, 106–7
Experience: deconstructionist approach, 14; interpretation of, 148; Lesbian, 58
Expulsion of Jews, 81
Extermination of Jews, 70; de Beauvoir and, 105; deconstructionism and, 14–16; denial of, 2, 4–5, 8, 13–14, 93, 112, 124; fear of speaking of, 5; language and, 117; Phoenix figure and, 115–16; revisionism and, 13; writing about, 126; *see also* Auschwitz; Shoah
Ezekiel (prophet), 63–64

Faderman, Lilian, *Surpassing the Love of Men*, 58
Farias, Victor, and Heidegger, 15
Fascism, European, French thought and, 12
Faurisson, Robert, 2; *Mémoire en défense: Contre ceux qui m'accusent de falsifier l'Histoire*, 125
Faye, Jean-Pierre, 115
Felman, Shoshana, *Testimony*, 85
Feminine: Jewishness and, 10, 83; "other" as, 76; Yourcenar's *Coup de Grâce* and, 89–91, 95

Feminine difference, Maurras's theory, 50–51
Feminism: and antisemitism, 9; de Beauvoir and, 106, 111; and existential other, 107; Lesbian, Rubin and, 55–56
Feminist ideology, 74
Feminist movement, and Vivien, 44
Feminist writers, and mortality, 106
Feminists, 161n6; Lesbian, Vivien and, 58
Ferry, Luc, 19
Fiction, assimilated Jews in, 152
Fidelity, Jewish, 64
Final solution, survivors of, 6
Finkielkraut, Alain, 115, 126, 133, 142; *Remembering in Vain*, 6
Finland, extermination of Jews, 71
Flaubert, Gustave, 99–100
Fleg, Edmond, 66; *Jewish Anthology*, 61, 66, 121
Foreign influences, dangerous, in Yourcenar's *Coup de Grâce*, 90
Foreign language, teaching of, 80
Foreignness, romanticism and, 52
Foster, Jeannette H., 45
France: antisemitism in, 80–81, 94; assimilation in, 140–41; as Christian state, 131; education, teaching of Racine's *Esther*, 29; extermination of Jews, 70–71; Jewish presence in, 64; Jews and, 1, 28; punishment by God, 25; racism in, 94
La France, 1, 76; and *Le Juif*, 77–84, 119–20
Francis, Claude, 107; *The Writings of Simone de Beauvoir*, 107–8
Freedom, fear of, and antisemitism, 8
French antisemitism, 1–3, Lunel and, 67, Robbe-Grillet and, 3–5
French culture: Christian domination of, 134–35; criticisms of, 17–19; Jewish historical experience, 27
French identity, Jews and, 128–29
French Jews, 1; and Jewish identity, 128
French language, 162n1; Jewish speech

French language (*Continued*)
and, 82; Marks and, 146; Vivien
and, 48
French Left: antisemitism of, 108–9; de
Beauvoir and, 104; and Israel, 108
French literary theory, negative influence
of, 16
French literature: antisemitism in, 10–13,
87; after Auschwitz, 85; Jewish culture
and, 22; Jewish Holy Scriptures and,
xiv, 23–42; Jews in, 76; stereotypes in,
94; women writers, 46; written by
Jews, 69
—Jewish presence in, 60–61; Cohen,
135–38; Esther as, 31–37
Frenchmen, stereotypical, 76; in Proust's
work, 81, 83
Frenchness, 72; Maurras and, 48, 55
Fresco, Nadine, 114
Freud, Sigmund, 62, 133, 141; "The
Future of an Illusion," 145; Jewishness
of, 36; Marks and, xvii, 143–44, 145;
Moses and Monotheism, 9, 77, 149;
Mourning and Melancholia, 121; racial
intolerance and, 9
Frick, Grace, 87
Friedlander, Judith, *Vilna on the Seine:
Jewish Intellectuals in France Since
1968*, 115, 118, 131–32
Frisch, Max, 107

Garnier, Robert, *Les Juifves*, xiv, 23,
24–28, 148
Gates, Henry Louis, Jr., 148
Gay liberation movement, and Vivien,
44–45
Gender differences: ethnicity and,
144–45; Maurras and, 46, 50, 53
Gender identity, Maurras and, 46
Genocide: denial of, 4–5; in Yourcenar's
Coup de Grâce, 94
German-Jewish Dialogue, symposium
on, 17–18
German National Socialist revolution, 9
German philosophy, 16; and denial of

Holocaust, 13–14; and French writ-
ing, 96; Jews and, 126
Germany, 70; Jews and, 141; Maurras
and, 53
Gestures of Catholics, in church 139–40
Gide, André, 63; *L'Immoraliste*, 87; and
Jewish literature, 59–60
Gide, Charles, 62
Gilman, Sander, *Freud, Race, and Gen-
der*, 141
Giraudoux, Jean, *Racine*, 29
God: affirmation of faith in, 118; Jewish
fidelity to, 64; Maurras and, 47–48
Goitein, Denise R., xiv
Goncourt prize, de Beauvoir and, 107
Gontier, Fernande, 107; *The Writings of
Simone de Beauvoir*, 107–8
Goujon, Jean-Paul, *Tes Blessures sont plus
douces que leurs caresses*, 44
Gould, Eric, *The Sin of the Book:
Edmund Jabès*, 59
Goyim, stereotype of, 144–45
Graef, Ortwin de, 15
Le Grand Robert dictionary, 127
Greece, extermination of Jews, 70
Greek version of the story of Esther, 30
Grotesque, feminine, stereotypical Jew
and, 120
Guggenheim Foundation, project
description, xii
Guilt, and responsibility, 93
Gygès (pseud.), *Les Juifs dans la France
aujourd'hui*, 73–74

Hahn, Reynaldo, 37
Halter, Marek, 114
Haman, 30–32
Hardy, Thomas, 61
Harpham, Geoffrey Galt, 19
Hartman, Geoffrey, *Deconstruction and
Criticism*, ix
Hebrew version of the story of Esther,
29–30
Heidegger, Martin, 8, 15, 18, 105, 124;
cult of, 17; and death of God, 96;

Derrida and, 123; and extermination
of Jews, 12, 103, 125–26; Hirsch and,
16; "Letter on Humanism," 111, 112;
Nietzsche, 96, 98; silence of, 111, 112
Heine, Heinrich, 133
Heretics, Jewish, xvii, 128, 132
Hilberg, Raul, 116
Hirsch, David H., *The Deconstruction of
Literature: Criticism After Auschwitz*,
15–20
Historians, 15; of French Jewry, and
assimilation, 62
Historical analysis, and Jewish presence,
36
Historical events, deconstructionism
and, 14
Historical experience, Jewish, 27
Historicism, genealogical, 16
Historiography, French, and Shoah, 5
History, Lesbian, Rubin and, 56
Hitler, Adolf, *Mein Kampf*, 72
Holocaust, 155–56n5; denial of, 13–14; *see
also* Extermination of Jews; Shoah
Homosexuality: change in concept of,
56; Jewishness and, 83; in Proust's
work, 81, 84
Hughes, H. Stuart, *Prisoners of Hope:
Silver Age of Italian Jews, 1924-1974*,
143
Human solidarity, Rorty and, 138–39
Humor, Jewish, 144–45
Hungary, extermination of Jews, 70
Hyman, Paula, 1, 62, 77

Identification, and recognition, 151
Identification sickness, 150, 151
Identity, 57, 76, 114; ambiguities of, in
Yourcenar's *Coup de Grâce*, 89; collective, of female Jews, 152; difference
and, 56; feminine, de Beauvoir and,
111; hidden, Proust and, 38; homosexuality as, 56; Marks and, 143–53;
national-sexual, 80; otherness as, 72;
racial theories of, 56; religious, splits
in, 134–35; self, and Jewish, 128; sex-

ual, confusion of, 89; shared, of Jew-
ish writers, 62
—French, 94; and antisemitism, 2; de
Beauvoir and, 108
—Jewish, xvii, 127–29; in France,
146–47; hiding of, Esther and, 37;
of Marks, xvii
Identity politics, 97; Philipson and, 148;
refusal of, 151
Ideological differences, scripture arrange-
ments and, 27
Ideology: and antisemitism, 7, 12–13;
conservative, antisemitic, 71; progres-
sive, antisemitic, 71; of text, Yource-
nar's *Coup de Grâce*, 86
Independent women, Vivien and, 57
Inequalities, and exclusion, 75
Intentions of writer, 86, 87–89
Intertexts, 40–41; Racine's *Esther* as, 37;
for Vivien, 45
Ionesco, Eugene, 107
Israel, Jonathan I., *European Jewry in the
Age of Mercantilism*, xiv
Israel: French Left and, 108; UNESCO
and, 107, 109
Italy, extermination of Jews, 71
Izieu, France, children deported from,
72–73

Jabès, Edmond, 69, 115, 152
Jankelevitch, Vladimir, 19
Jasinski, René, "Concerning Racine's
Esther," 41–42
Jay, Karla, 45
Jean Paul II, Pope, 103
Jehouda, Josué, 61, 65–66
Jeremiah (prophet), 26–27
Jerome, Saint, 30
Jerusalem Bible, 27; story of Esther, 30
Jerusalem Prize, de Beauvoir and, 104,
107
Jewish antisemitism, 82
"Jewish colony," Proust and, 78–79
Jewish consciousness, 159n2
Jewish culture, 115, 132; active influence

Jewish culture (*Continued*)
  of, 23–42; Esther story, 30–31; and
  French literature, 22
Jewish historical experience, 27
Jewish Holy Scriptures, xiv, 25–27, 69;
  and French literature, 23–42; as Jewish literature, 60; and New Testament, 24; story of Esther, 29–30
Jewish identity, 127–29
Jewish literature, xiv, 69; Gide and,
  59–60; Lunel and, 66; Robbe-Grillet
  and, 60–61
Jewishness, xiii–xiv, 56, 94; acknowledge-
  ment of, 141–42; assimilation and,
  147; Derrida and, 150–51; and feminine, as "other," 76; fidelity to, 64; of
  Freud, 36, 145; Lunel and, 66; of
  Marks, 143–53; outward signs, 144; of
  Proust, 36; Sarraute's *Enfance* and,
  140–41; stereotypical, 136–38
Jewish presence in French writing,
  xii–xiii, 8; Cohen's *Belle du Seigneur*,
  135–38
Jewish problem, de Man and, 60
Jewish question, xii–xiii, 1–2; de Beauvoir and, 104, 111; fear of speaking of,
  5; French writing and, 117; literature
  of, x; silence about, 3
The Jewish World (*Le Monde Juif*), xi
Jewish writing, 68–69; in French litera-
  ture, 23, 62–69
Jews: and France, 77–84; literary repre-
  sentations, 76; Louis XIV and, 28;
  Madame de Sévigné and, 34–35;
  Maurras and, 48; and multiculturalism, 134; in Paris, x–xi; punishment
  by God, 25–28; stereotypes, 78–80,
  145; unassimilated, 76, 82; unconscious, 23; writing in French, after
  Auschwitz, 114–26
Jokes, Jewish, 144–45
Joyce, James: Cixous and, 149; *Ulysses*, 152
Judaic studies, 115, 118; Lévinas and, 119
Judaism: and Christianity, 119, 130–31;
  contemporary, Spinoza and, 152; Jew-

ishness and, 145, 147; Lévinas and,
  119, 120
Judeo-Christian tradition, Lévinas and,
  120
Juif, 149
Le *Juif,* and *La France,* 77–84, 119–20
Juifemme, 143, 148–50
Les *Juifves,* Garnier, xiv, 23, 24–28, 148

Kafka, Franz, *Before the Law,* 149
Kemp, Robert, 35–36
Kennedy, Margaret, 61
Kermode, Frank, 24
Klarsfeld, Beate, 72
Klarsfeld, Serge, xi, 72, 114; *Memorial to
  the Jews Deported from France 1942-
  1944,* 73, 121
Klein, Yvonne M., 45
Kofman, Sarah, 115, 121, 125, 133, 142; *The
  Enigma of Woman,* 77; *Suffocated
  words,* 114, 116, 120–22
Krell, David Farrell, 98
Kreutzer Sonata, Tolstoi, 87
Kriegel, Annie, 114
Kristeva, Julia, 8; and antisemitism, 10;
  Powers of Horror, 9–10, 77; *Strangers
  to Ourselves,* v

Lacan, Jacques: "The Mirror Stage as
  Formative of the Function of the I as
  Revealed in Psychoanalytic Experi-
  ence," 75; and "Other," 75
Lacoue-Labarthe, Philippe, 125
Language: camouflage of, 117; central
  position of, 17, 18, 112–13; Heidegger
  and, 111, 123; Jewish identity and, 128;
  primacy of, 112–13, 117; as repressed
  other, 75
Lanzmann, Claude, 115, 121, 133; de
  Beauvoir and, 110–11; *Shoah,* x, 104,
  116–17, 146
Laub, Dori, *Testimony,* 85
Left, political, de Beauvoir and, 104
Lehrmann, Chanan, *The Jewish Factor in
  French Literature,* xiv, 22–23

Le Pen, Jean-Marie, 2

Lesbian feminists, Vivien and, 58

Lesbianism: Maurras and, 46, 54–55; Rubin and, 55–56

Lesbian literature, Vivien and, 44–45, 50, 55–58

Levi, Primo, 6

Lévinas, Emmanuel, 18, 115, 118, 125–26, 19; and Christian culture, 119–20; *Difficult Freedom: Essays on Judaism*, 116, 118–20; and French culture, 134–35; "How Is Judaism Possible?" 130–31; "La Renaissance culturelle juive en Europe occidentale," 118, 120; and violence, 118

Liberation from oppression, 106

La Librairie Française, 73

La Libre Parole, 72

Lipstadt, Deborah, *Denying the Holocaust: The Growing Assault on Truth and Memory*, 13–15

Literary studies, and antisemitism, 15

Literary theory, French, and denial of Holocaust, 13–16, 20

Literature: French, antisemitism in, 10–13; and Marranism, 141; teaching of, 80

Loewenstein, Rodolphe, *Psychoanalysis of Antisemitism*, 8, 77

Lorenz, Paul, 44

Louis XIV, king of France, 28, 33–34

Loukovitch, K., 35

Lukacher, Ned, translation of Derrida, 125

Lunel, Armand, "The Jewish Renaissance in France During the Twentieth Century," 66

Lustiger, Jean-Marie Aaron, Cardinal, 133, 141

Luther, Martin, and Book of Esther, 30

Luxembourg, extermination of Jews, 71

Luxemburg, Rosa, 133, 147

Lyotard, Jean-François, 121, 124, 125, 148; "Jewish Oedipus," 150

McGarrahan, John G., "Getting Away with Murder," 93

Maimonides, and Book of Esther, 30

Maintenon, Françoise d'Aubigné Scarron, Marquise de, 28, 33–34; and Racine's *Esther*, 41, 42

Malachi (Bible), 27

Man, Paul de, 14, 62, 97, 124; Hirsch and, 16–17; "Jews in literature today," 60, 61; journalism of, 11, 15

Marks, Elaine, xvii, 76; Jewishness of, 1, 143–53; work of, ix–xiv, 76, 153

Marranism, 141

Marrano, xv, xvii–xviii, 120–30; characteristics, 134; definitions, 127; Esther as, 31, 36; as metaphor, 127–42

Marrus, Michael, 1, 77; *The Politics of Assimilation: The French Jewish Community in France at the Time of the Dreyfus Affair*, 61–62, 128–29

Marx, Karl, 133, 145

Marxist ideology, 74, 97

Masoretic text, and ideological differences, 25–27

Maternal instinct, Maurras's idea, 50, 51

Matricide, in Yourcenar's *Coup de Grâce*, 94

Mauron, Charles, 36

Maurras, Charles, 4, 45–55; Ancien régime, and, 46, 47; *Auguste Comte*, 46–47, 50; *Feminine Romanticism*, 45, 46–55; *The Future of Intelligence*, 45, 46–48; and Lesbianism of Vivien, 58; "Renée Vivien," 45–46, 48–55; and verbal materialism, 53

Medici, Marie de, and Jews, 28

Mehlman, Jeffrey, 8; *Legacies of Antisemitism in France*, 10–11

Meier, Charles S., *The Unmasterable Past: History, Holocaust, and German National Identity*, 92

Memorial to the Unknown Jewish Martyr, xi

Metaphor, marrano as, 127–42

Misogynist literature, 76

Modern Language Association of Amer-

Modern Language (*Continued*)
    ica, 16–17; conventions, papers delivered at, xi–xii
Modiano, Patrick, 115
Moisi, Dominique, 19
Le Monde, 103, 107
Mondoville, Mme de, 42
Monotheism, affirmation of, 118
Mordecai, 31–33
Mortality, as literary theme, xiii, 67; of Cohen's work, 100–2, 135–36; de Beauvoir and, 102–3, 105–7; and extermination of Jews, 8; Heidegger and, 98; Sartre and, 106
Moses, Biblical story, 33
Mosse, George, 77
Mother figure, 67, 89–92
Mourning: de Beauvoir and, 107; Derrida and, 124; Freud and, 121; narrative strategies, 117; Perec and, 122; symbolism of, 115
Multiculturalism, Jews and, 133–34
Myth: Barthes's definition, xiv; retelling of, Vivien and, 57

Naiad Press, 45
Names, Jewish, 72–74, 146–47
National Foreign Language Council Conference, 17–18
National identity, confusion of, 89
Nationalism: and antisemitism, 70; French, 80; of Maurras, 47–48, 52, 55
National Socialism, 9; Heidegger and, 111
Naturalness, Maurras's view, 51
Nazis, 161*n*6
Nazism: antisemitism and, 2; and nihilism, 103; and Shoah, 112–13
Neofascist bookstore, Paris, 73
Netherlands, extermination of Jews, 70
Newspapers, antisemitic, 72
New York Times, and responsibility, 92–93
Nietzsche, Friedrich Wilhelm, 156*n*2; and death of God, 96; and Jews, 139; Nazism and, 103; and nihilism, 96–97

Night and Fog (film), 5
Nihilism, 96–97; antisemitism and, xiii; Arendt and, 98; and atheism, 103; in Cohen's writings, 99; French, 18–19; Heidegger and, 98
Noailles, Comtesse de, 46, 51
Nonconscious presuppositions, 77, 86, 89–93
"The Non-Jewish Jew," Deutscher, xvii, 132
Nonreligious Jews, xvii, 147
Norway, extermination of Jews, 70
Nourissier, François, 68–69
Novels: of Shoah, 19; as vehicles of change, 139
Numbers of Jews, exaggeration of, 73, 81

Official doctrines, oppositions to, 134, 135
Old Testament, Bible, 25, 27; *see also* Jewish Holy Scriptures
Oppression: defiance by Jews, 9; of "other," 74, 84; social institutions and, 105–6
Orcibal, Jean, "The Genesis of *Esther* and *Athalie*," 41–42
Other: existential, 106–7; Lacan's ideas, 75; Lévinas's views of, 118, 120; woman as, 74, 75
Otherness: cultural studies and, 75; Jewishness and, 152

Palestine (journal), Lunel and, 66
Paranoia, antisemitism as, 8–9
Paris: Center for contemporary Jewish documentation, x–xi; Jewish Quarter, 82
Pascal, Blaise, *Pensées*, 153
Paxton, Robert, 77
Péguy, Charles, Lunel and, 66
Pellepoix, Darquier de, 2
Perec, Georges, 115; *W or the memory of childhood*, 116, 122
Persecutions, Jews and, 9
Peuple déicide, 7–8, 97

Phallocentrism: and Christianocentrism, 119; Cixous and, 149

Philippe, Béatrice, 28; *Etre juif dans la société française du moyen âge jusqu'à nos jours*, 28

Phoenix figure, 115–16

Physical appearance, stereotypical, 77–80

PMLA, 16–17

Poetry by women, Maurras's view, 49–55

Pogrebin, Letty Cottin, *Deborah, Golda, and Me: Being Female and Jewish in America*, 151–52

Poliakov, Leon, x

Polish Jews, extermination of, 70

Politics: and antisemitism, 12–13, 65; de Beauvoir and, 102–3, 106; and study of Shoah, 5–6

Polylogue, literary device, 124

Portmanteau words, 149–51; *Juifemme*, 143, 148–50

Poststructuralism: Hirsch and, 16; and language, 117

Prejudice, de Beauvoir and, 102

Presence: intertextual, of Jewish Holy Scriptures, 23–42; Jewish, in French literature, xii–xiii, 31

Primordial anxiety, Shoah and, 126

Prophecy, Jewish, 64

Protestant Bible, Old Testament, 25, 27

Protocols of the Elders of Zion, 72

Proust, Marcel, 66, 67, 75, 76; *Against Sainte-Beuve*, 37; *Cities of the Plain*, Proust, 39–40; Cohen and, 67; *Combray*, and Esther, 38; de Man and, 60; Gide and *Swann's Way*, 59; *The Guermantes Way*, 38–40; *Jean Santeuil*, Proust, 67; Jewishness of, 36; and Racine's *Esther*, 41; *Remembrance of Things Past*, 24, 37–40, 153; *Sodom and Gomorrah*, 83; *Swann's Way*, 38–39, 59, 152; *Within a Budding Grove*, 77, 78, 80–83; *Within a Budding Grove* and Esther, 38

Psalm 137, 157n3; Di Mauro's comments, 28

Psychoanalysis, 20, 77, 144; and antisemitism, 8–10; in France, 36; hearing and, 150; and "other," 75

Purim festival, 30

Racine, Jean: *Andromaque*, 41; *Bajazet*, 87, 88; and Jews, 28–29

—*Esther*, xiv, 21, 23–24, 27, 28–37, 157n6; Mme de Maintenon and, 41, 42; Proust and, 37–39

Rebatet, Lucien, 7; *Les Décombres*, 72, 77, 79, 84; *Je Suis Partout*, 72

Recognition, and identification, 151

Régnier, Mme de, 46, 51

Reinach, Salomon, 44

Religious identity, splits in, 134–35

Renaissance, Jewish, Lunel and, 66

Renault, Alain, 19

Representations of Jews, traditional, 68

Resnais, Alain, *Night and Fog*, 5

Revisionism, 13; denial of Holocaust, 93

Revue Juive, 61, 62–65; Lunel and, 66

Revue Juive de Genève, 61, 65–67

"Righteous" left-wing intellectual gentiles, 104

Robbe-Grillet, Alain: and antisemitism, 5, 7–8; *Le Miroir qui revient*, 3–5, 60–61

Romania, extermination of Jews, 70

Romanticism, Maurras and, 51–53

Rorty, Richard, *Contingency, Irony, and Solidarity*, 96, 138–39

Rousseau, Jean Jacques, 52; *Confessions*, 151

Rousso, Henry, 77

Rubin, Gayle, 45; and Vivien, 50, 55–58

Rubinstein, Arthur, 107

Russell, Bertrand, 107

Russia, extermination of Jews, 70

Russian Orthodox church, 140

Sadism, Jewish, 39–40, 94

Saint-Cyr, performance of Racine's *Esther*, 28, 33–34, 41

Sand, George, 52

"Sapho 1900," 44, 55, 56; critics and, 58

Sappho, Vivien and, 44, 49–50

Sarraute, Nathalie, 133, 134, 142; *Child-hood*, 129–30, 139–41

Sartre, Jean-Paul, 107; *Antisemite and Jew*, 3; *Being and Nothingness*, 106; de Beauvoir and, 104, 105; "L'Enfance d'un chef," 87; *L'Existentialisme est un humanisme*, 112; and Heidegger, 111–12

Schneerson, Isaac, x

Scholem, Gershom, 18

Schwarz-Bart, André, 107, 114; *The Last of the Just*, 116, 117–19, 121

Secularism, Jewish identity and, 128

Secular Jews, 130, 147; Marks as, 144; Marranism, 141; Yovel and, 133

Sedgwick, Eve, *Epistemology of the Closet*, 24

Semprun, Jorge, 19

Sensivity to pain of others, 138–39

Sephardic Jews, Paris, xi

Sévigné, Marie de Rabutin-Chantal, Marquise de, 33–35

Shakespeare, William, *Hamlet*, 125

Shema Israel, 118

Shoah, 1, 71, 155–56n5; and antisemitism, 74; assimilation and, in Marrus's view, 128–29; de Beauvoir and, 104, 109–12; deconstructionism and, 15–16; Derrida and, 123, 124; French historiography and, 5–6; Heidegger and, 98, 112; Marks and, 153; memories of 159n2; silence about, 6–7; as trace, in Derrida's works, 124

Shoah (film), Lanzmann, x, xiii, 116–17, 146

Significant other, 83–84; Jew as, 77, 81

Signifiers, 77; *cendre* as, 124; in portman-teau words, 149; of Yourcenar's *Coup de Grâce*, 86–87

Silence: about antisemitism, 3, 5; about Shoah, 6–7

Silone, Ignazio, 107

Slovakia, extermination of Jews, 70

Social change, de Beauvoir and, 102, 106

Social Darwinism, 57

Social harmony, *charme* of women and, 55

Socialism, 97

Social movements, xiii

Sociohistoric oppression, "other" of, 84

Solidarity, human, Rorty and, 138–39

Sollers, Philippe, *Women*, 9

Sources, Jewish, 69

Spinoza, Baruch, xvii, 133, 141

Spire, André, 66

Staël, Madame de (Anne-Louise-Ger-maine Necker), 52

Steiner, George, 133; *Martin Heidegger*, 112

Stereotypes: antisemitic, 67, 80, 81–82; fictional, 94; and Jewish identity, 127–28; non-French, 72; refusal of, 151; traditional, 68

—Jewish, 77–80, 144–45; and feminine grotesque, 120; French Jews and, 147; Pogrebin and, 152; in Yourcenar's *Coup de Grâce*, 88, 91

Sternhell, Zeev, *The Revolutionary Right: The French Origins of Fascism*, 12

Stories, humorous, Jewish, 144–45

Subjectivity, Jewish identity and, 128

Subversion, Vivien and, 55

Suffering, sensitivity to, 138–39

Symbolism, in writing about Auschwitz, 115

Talmudic studies, Lévinas and, 119

Tarn, Pauline, *see* Vivien, Renée

Texts, antisemitic, 71–72, 78

Textualization of context, 85

Themes, Jewish, 69

Theories of antisemitism, 8–20

Thinking by women, Maurras's views, 50, 55

Tikkun, 148

Todorov, Tzvetan, 112

Tolstoi, Leo: *Death of Ivan Illych*, 153; *Kreutzer Sonata*, 87

Toussenel, Alphonse, *Les Juifs rois de l'époque*, 71
Tragedy, metaphysical, de Beauvoir and, 102

Ukraine, extermination of Jews, 70
Unconscious of text, 86–87, 93–95
UNESCO, and Israel, 107, 109
United States: atheism in, 103; Jewishness in, 147; writings about "other," 74
University of Jerusalem, 63
University of Wisconsin, women's studies, ix
University politics, and study of Shoah, 6
University system, France, antisemitism in, 161*n*3
Unjust persecution, theme of, 42
Unknown Jewish Martyr, memorial to, xi

Vichy government: antisemitism of, 104; and extermination of Jews, 85
Vidal-Naquet, Pierre, 77; *Assassins of Memory*, 114, 121; *The Challenge of the Shoah to History*, 5
Villon, François, *Testament*, 153
Vivien, Renée (Pauline Tarn), 43–44; and Barney, 57–58; Colette and, 157–58*n*5; Maurras and, 46, 48–55; *A Woman Appeared to Me*, 44–45; *A Woman Appeared to Me*, Rubin and, 56, 57; *The Woman of the Wolf and Other Stories*, 45; writings of, 44–46

Wandering Jew, 152
Wardi, Charlotte, *The Jew in the French Novel, 1933-1948*, 68
Waskow, Arthur, 148
Weber, Eugen, 77
Weil, Simone, 6, 130, 133, 141, 147
Weizmann, Chaïm, 62
Wellers, Georges, 114

Wiesel, Elie, 19, 114; *Night*, 114, 116, 117–18, 121
Willis, Ellen, 148
Wilson, Edmund, *Axel's Castle*, 36
Wingspread conference, 17–18
Winock, Michel, 77; *Edouard Drumont et Cie*, 70
Women: antisemitism and, 52, 53–54, 76; independent, Vivien and, 57; and Jews, 119–20; Maurras's views of, 50, 53–54; as "other," 74, 75; representation in Yourcenar's *Coup de Grâce*, 89–91; seductiveness of, 55
Women's texts, critics and, 46
Women writers: Maurras and, 46, 48–55; placement in French literature, 46
World War II, 146, 153; roles in, 2
Writers, Jewish: Gide and, 60; literary influence, 23; Lunel and, 66
Writing: de Beauvoir and, 103–4; influences on 69

Yerushalmi, Yosef Hayim, *Freud's Moses: Judaism Terminable and Interminable*, 145
Yiddish, French language and, 146
Yiddish-speaking Jews, 80
Yourcenar, Marguerite, *Coup de Grâce*, xvi, 86–87; intentions of author, 87–89; nonconscious presuppositions, 89–93; preface to *Coup de Grâce*, 86, 87–89, 95; reviews of *Coup de Grâce*, 88; unconscious of text, 93–95
Yovel, Yirmiyahu, 141, *Spinoza and Other Heretics*, v, xiv, xvii, 132–33, 134, 152
Yugoslavia, extermination of Jews, 70

Zadoc-Kahnin, Léon, 62
Zedekiah, King, 25–27
Zermatten, Maurice, 99
Zionism: Cohen and, 65; Einstein and, 65; *Revue Juive* and, 64
Zola, Emile, 76